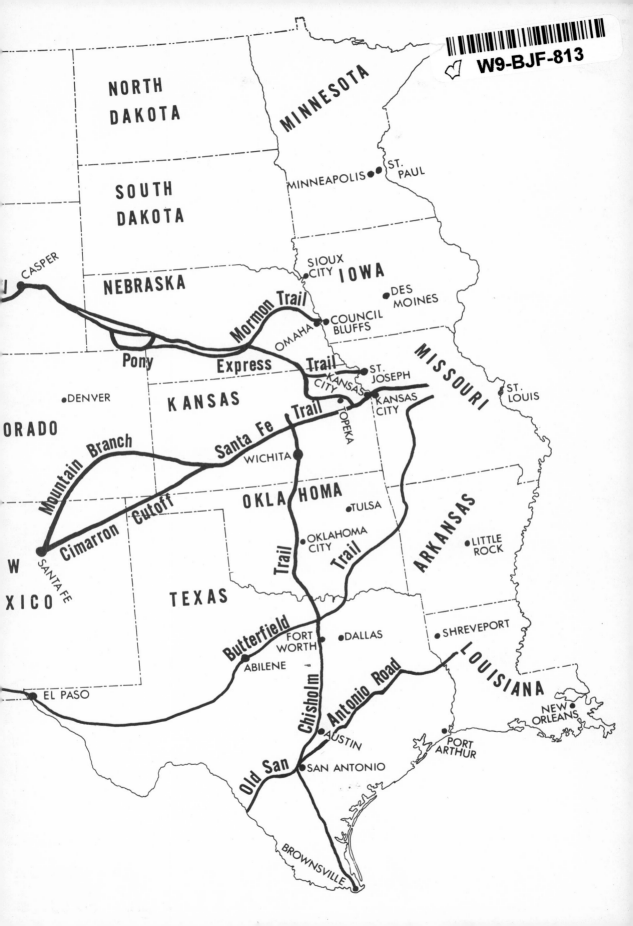

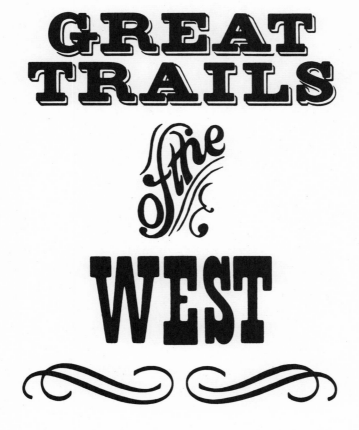

GREAT TRAILS
the
WEST

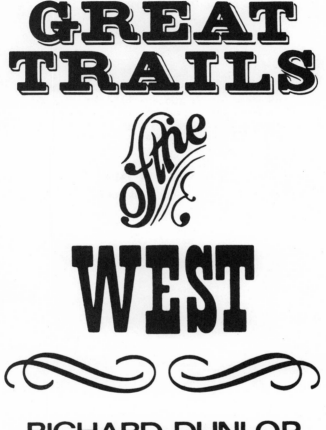

GREAT TRAILS
of the
WEST

RICHARD DUNLOP

●

ABINGDON PRESS

Nashville 🜕 New York

GREAT TRAILS OF THE WEST

Copyright © 1971 by Richard Dunlop

ISBN 0-687-15748-X

Library of Congress Catalog Card Number: 70-148065

SET UP, PRINTED, AND BOUND BY THE
PARTHENON PRESS, AT NASHVILLE,
TENNESSEE, UNITED STATES OF AMERICA

*To my mother and father
who first took me west
along the Great Trails*

CONTENTS

1

The West

●

The first snow of the season had dusted western Nebraska and brought out the age of the land. Looking down from our Chicago-to-Denver jet flight, we could see how the new snow had etched the ditches beside the road, delineated the wrinkles of the badlands between the tilled fields, and limned the old tracks and trails. Beneath us arose snow-encrusted Chimney Rock and Scotts Bluff, miniscule at 30,000 feet, but recognizable as historic landmarks for wagon trains creeping across the High Plains on the Oregon Trail.

From high in the air the West under a new snow is ancient. Close at hand beneath a sleeping bag it can be ancient, too. Harry C. James, one of the Southwest's leading conservationists and authorities on Indians, stretched out his sleeping bag on a dark night in Monument Valley. All night the rough surface beneath him dug into his ribs. In the morning he rolled his bag aside to see what manner of rocky abomination he had been lying upon. It was a fossil dinosaur track, and there close by was another and yet another, an ages-old trail leading off into the primordial morning of the West.

Just thinking of the West can send shivers up the spine of a man who has a feel for rocks, or for great canyons, or for whitewater rivers and mountain-locked lakes, for forests, for noble elk and fleet antelope, the great bears or the great cats who walk alone through life as surely as the lesser cats of a household. Think of the great trails then, of the traders' caravans to Santa Fe, of the Spanish friars trudging the road to the Cali-

9

fornia missions, of men, women, and children and covered wagons toiling along the emigrant trails, and of dashing stagecoaches and the Pony Express. Listen to the wind in the cottonwoods on the high plains, for it can bring you the scrape of a '49er's fiddle at a campfire and the soft sobbing of a child crying himself to sleep in a wagon. Your humanity will reach back through time to the fiddle and its song, to the child and his sobs. Listen in the night beneath the western stars and you may hear the hoofbeats of the Pony Express, the jingle of cowboys riding herd on the Chisholm Trail, or the shuffle of frozen feet climbing through Chilkoot Pass, for all of this was just yesterday.

It was the mountains and the rivers that told the trails where to go. The Uintatherium and the Stegosaurus first showed the way as they trampled a swath across the land in search of fresh pasturage and salt. Later the buffalo, the antelope, and the mountain sheep followed the already ancient trails, or found new paths of their own. They too took the easiest course to water or discovered a way through the lowest mountain passes to new pastures. Most of these great trails made by migrating animals have been obscured by man, but at Montgomery, Louisiana, there is a place where buffalo crossed the Red River on a rock formation. The formation is gone, blown up by Federal forces during the Civil War so that gunboats could steam up the river, but there are still deep depressions in the banks where the buffalo came down to the ford.

Then came the Indians migrating from Asia, hunting and fishing along water courses, following the trails of the animals to new homes. For at least 25,000 years the Indians lived in North America before the white men came, and they traveled and traded. Copper found in the Etowah Mounds near Cartersville, Georgia, originated on Isle Royale in Lake Superior, where the first white settlers found prehistoric copper workings. Arrowheads made of obsidian from western Wyoming have been found in Tennessee. The calumets passed around council fires by tribes all over the Great Plains were made of catlinite quarried at Pipestone in Minnesota.

The Indians blazed three great trail systems across the continent from the Missouri River to the Pacific. First there was the Big Medicine Trail, which climbed from the Great Plains through a break in the Rockies of south Wyoming that pioneers called South Pass. It followed the Platte, the North Platte, and the Sweetwater rivers across the Continental Divide, passed through the Green River Valley, looped around the mighty Wasatch Mountains, and traced the Bear and the Snake rivers to Hell's

Trails that opened the West followed prehistoric traces along watercourses. A party camps along the Gila River at the Maricopa Wells in Arizona.

Courtesy Chicago Historical Society

Forts protected the trails from Indians and furnished westering caravans with necessities. The Sutler's Store at Fort Dodge on the Santa Fe Trail in Kansas was a colorful supply point.

Courtesy Chicago Historical Society

Canyon. There it struck northwest over the plateaus and valleys to the Columbia, which it descended to the Pacific. White explorers and mountain men took the Big Medicine Trail, and it entered history as the Oregon Trail.

Then there was the waterway up the Missouri and the Yellowstone rivers and across the mountain passes to the Columbia. This was the route followed in the main by Lewis and Clark, but it never became a great pioneer trail. Last of all, there was the Southern Trail, which ran up the Kansas River from its mouth on the Missouri to the Smoky Hill River, then by portage to the upper Arkansas, which it ascended to the Rockies. The trail followed the Rio Grande to southern New Mexico, cut through the desert along the Gila, crossed the Colorado and headed due west to the Pacific Coast. Parts of this trail were used by the Santa Fe Trail and by the Butterfield Trail. Other white men's trails used other Indian trails so that white families camped where once their Indian brethren had camped.

The march of the mountains turned aside the trails. The towering summits also collected deep snows which, in melting, became the headwaters of such rivers as the Rio Grande, the Green, the Colorado, Clark's Fork, the Snake, the Columbia, the Missouri, and the Yellowstone. Flowing down from the mountains across the arid plains and the Great Basin, the rivers provided water for man and stock, and forage for the animals. The trails followed the water courses and only crossed the deserts from spring to spring when there was no alternative.

My family, some of my Boy Scouts, and I followed the trails as they are today by auto, truck camper, or four-wheel-drive, on horseback and on foot. We found that the mountains and the streams still order the lives of travelers in the West. Modern highways obey most of the imperatives obeyed by the great trails. We parked our truck camper at nights where wagon trains bivouacked on the Oregon Trail, and we set up our tents where the roadbuilders had camped along the Mullen Military Road. We stretched out our sleeping bags within a natural stone shelter atop Chilkoot Pass, where men of the Gold Rush escaped from the bitter Alaska winds, and on some occasions we managed to eat or sleep in inns which survive from the frontier past. After five years of trailing, we all share a new appreciation of the West and a determination to help conserve its beauty and heritage. We understand Josiah Gregg, who traveled over the Santa Fe Trail eight times during the years from 1831 to 1839. He wrote of his 1839 journey:

The West

This was my last trip across the Plains. Since that time I have striven in vain to reconcile myself to the even tenor of civilized life in the United States; and have sought in its amusements and its society, a substitute for those high excitements which attached me so strongly to prairie life. Yet I am almost ashamed to confess that scarcely a day passes without my experiencing a pang of regret that I am now not roving at large upon those Western Plains. Nor do I find my tastes peculiar; for I have hardly known a man who has ever become familiar with the kind of life which I have led for so many years that has not relinquished it with regret.

If America relinquishes the West and forgets the adventure of a nation westering on the great trails, then our nation will know a lasting regret.

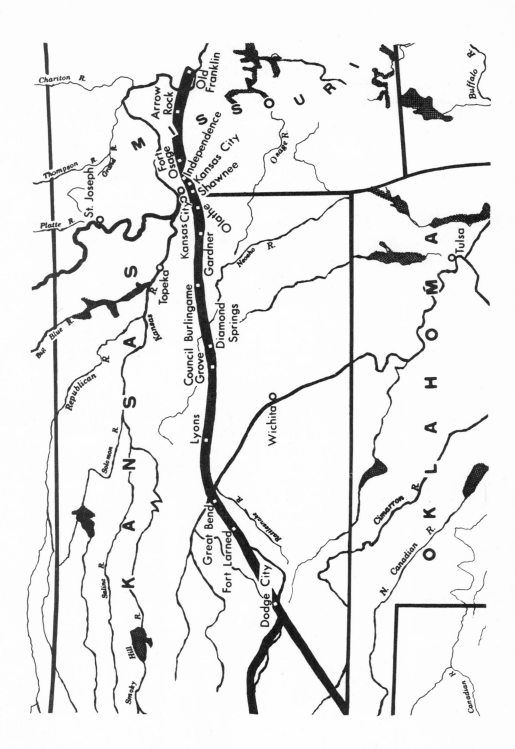

∽2∽
Santa Fe Trail:
Journey to Sundown

●

The Flint Hills of Kansas is the sort of country where, if you sit down to breakfast in a cafe with four sturdy children, an overall-clad farmer in the next booth is apt to remark, "You should have lived on a farm. Kids like that could get a lot of work done."

This happened to us in Council Grove in the Old Hays Cafe, which was built in 1857 as the Hays Tavern on the Santa Fe Trail by Seth Hays, great grandson of Daniel Boone and cousin of Kit Carson. My wife and I, our daughter and three sons were following the Santa Fe Trail. Our family station wagon was loaded with enough gear to have foundered a covered wagon, but we planned to jounce over ranch roads in search of pioneer campsites and springs and the ruins of frontier forts, and to scout out the ruts of the wagon trains themselves. We started on the main street of New Franklin, a town on the winding Missouri River about ninety miles east of Kansas City.

"From civilization to sundown, Santa Fe Trail stretches one thousand miles from Franklin to Santa Fe," reads a marker placed amid parked cars on the main street.

It was from old Franklin, crumbling on the riverbank a few miles away, that the first caravans set out over the Santa Fe Trail in 1821 to trade with the Mexicans of Santa Fe. A woman at the New Franklin post office directed us to old Franklin. We drove over a chuck-holed street, ambitiously named Broadway, down the river hill to where a few dilapidated houses mouldered in gardens tangled with old-fashioned flowers, such as early settlers planted in their dooryards. There was no sign of the warehouses and wharfs of what was once the riverport where paddle-wheeler packets landed people and goods for the journey over the Santa Fe Trail. The Big Muddy had risen in 1828 and washed everything away but the few houses that stood before us. Independence, up river to the west, had then become the jumping-off place for the trail.

A sturdy twelve-year-old boy appeared to be the only living person in the village. He walked out onto a sagging porch, and while scratching his back against a post, surveyed us with a slit-eyed stone face. He was the sort of boy who blanches at the sight of a classroom, but who can look any danger or hardship in the face without a tremor.

Kit Carson was such a boy, and he grew up here on the Missouri frontier. When he was fifteen his father was killed by a falling tree, and he was apprenticed to David Workman, the saddlemaker. He soon ran away with a freight train bound for Santa Fe.

"I will pay 1¢ for the return of the apprentice, Kit Carson, who ran away from my harness shop in Franklin, Mo. He is 16, small for his age, and has light hair," advertised Workman in an 1826 issue of the *Missouri Intelligencer*.

At last Kit was away on the plains where the August heat hung on the hillcrests. Andrew Broadus, a driver with the train Kit had joined, saw a wolf skulking along the hilltop. He pulled his gun from the tail of his wagon. The trigger caught, and the gun fired. The ball smashed the bones of his forearm. At the gunshot, the train halted, and the wagon master galloped back to Broadus' wagon. He saw the bloody arm.

"It'll hav' to come off," he said.

"No," said Broadus. He knew as well as anybody that his arm would soon start to putrefy in the heat, but he would not let the wagon master amputate. The wagons rolled on. Blood poisoning streaked up Broadus' arm. Death came nearer, and Broadus, terrified, now begged somebody to cut off his limb. He lay on the buffalo grass in the cool evening and begged that somebody take a knife and cut. No one dared until Kit spoke up.

"I kin do it," he said.

"Y're too young, Kit. Let somebody else do it," said a hunter. He had carved many a buffalo hump, and heartened by the boy's pluck he whetted his skinning knife. A teamster got out a rusty handsaw and filed a fine set of teeth on its back to cut the bone. Other men built a hot fire and heated a king bolt removed from one of the wagons. The men put the patient on his back and tied a rope around his arm as a tour-

16

niquet. A dozen men held him still. The hunter opened the arm to the bone. Then he took the saw and cut through the bone. He cauterized the raw stump with the white-hot bolt and rubbed cool axle grease over the wound and bandaged it. The stump began to heal at once, and in a few weeks Broadus was well. Nobody on the train was going to send home a runaway apprentice whose pluck could move men to resolute action. At least not for one cent.

The Missouri current boiled, murky with mud, at the foot of a clay bank where we stopped. Up this current in April, 1819, the steamboat *Independence* came from St. Louis, according to the *Intelligencer,* "with passengers and a cargo of flour, whiskey, sugar, iron castings." This was the first steamboat to reach Franklin, and the town began to grow. Even the most dull-witted merchants in their emporiums beside the muddy waters knew that, although business was good, it would be excitingly better if only a way could be found to trade with the Mexicans in Santa Fe. They knew that, as early as 1739, the French brothers, Pierre and Paul Mallet had crossed the plains to trade. Then, in the year George Washington was inaugurated, Fernando de la Concha had become governor of New Mexico. Louisiana, upper as well as lower, was then Spanish, and the new governor asked Pedro Vial "to open communication with our settlements which are located on the shores of the Missouri River."

Vial set out from Santa Fe with two companions, to whom he promised sixty pesos of silver apiece if they returned home alive. The travelers made twenty miles a day over the route that was to become famous as the Santa Fe Trail until, in what is now Kansas, an Indian tribe stopped them. The Indians shook hands cordially, but then took the Spaniards' horses and goods. They debated whether the captives should be put to death with arrows or hatchets. An Indian, tiring of the discussion, ran a dagger into the abdomen of Vicente Villanueva, "which would have proved fatal" noted Vial in his report "had he not shrunk away when the blow was delivered."

The Indians kept the Spanish naked among them for weeks, but when a passing French trapper happened along, they let them go. The Frenchman gave them clothing and helped them on their way to St. Louis, where they arrived in October, 1792. By 1805 Anglo-American frontiersmen were making the trip to Santa Fe because of the rich rewards that awaited there in bullion and specie, horses, burros, beaver skins, and buffalo robes. The Spanish proved unpredictable. Sometimes they traded amicably, although often the authorities demanded a personal share in the profits of each transaction, but sometimes they threw the hapless American traders into the calabozo and confiscated all their possessions.

Then on September 27, 1821, after three centuries of Spanish rule, Mexico proclaimed its independence. William Becknell, veteran of the War of 1812 and Missouri frontiersman, was trading with the Indians when he heard rumors of revolution in Mexico. He hurried back to Arrow Rock a few miles upstream from Franklin. He lashed trade goods onto some mules, and on September 1, weeks before Mexico proclaimed its freedom, he started out with three companions for Santa Fe. Other traders followed hard upon the hoofs of his mules, but he was the first to reach Santa Fe. He was hailed as a hero by the governor, by the soldiers, and by the population. Becknell's trading was so successful that when he returned to Franklin, his mules were burdened with jingling rawhide sacks of silver. There in the streets of the frontier town, one of Becknell's men took a sack and slashed its thongs. Silver pesos tumbled to the street and rolled into the gutter. The sight was enough to start most of Franklin rushing over the trail to Santa Fe. Nor were the profits of this first trip extraordinary. By 1824 men who put $30,000 into a journey over the prairies got back $200,000 in specie and furs.

After the first year, most of the traders gave up pack mules in favor of freight wagons. The wagons rolled upstream along an old Indian trail from Franklin to the ferry crossing at Arrow Rock. This trail along the Missouri bottomlands has long since been plowed under, but at Arrow Rock we were elated to make out the tracks of the wheels climbing up a grassy swale from the old Missouri ferry, that operated from 1817 until 1927. Santa Fe Springs, where the wagons camped, still bubbles. The trail runs along a split-rail fence from the spring to where it turns onto Main Street. During trail days the heavy wagons rumbled over a cobblestone Main Street, but we found that the cobblestones are now buried beneath several layers of smooth asphalt so that our car's wheels only made a gentle thrum as we looked for a place to park. The massive stone gutters cut and put in place by slaves still carry storm waters down the street.

Many of the houses and shops along Main Street today were standing during trail days. We joined a walking tour of the village which was being shepherded by Mrs. Omar Wetherell, a schoolteacher from nearby Pilot Grove, a redoubtable woman, who rolled minute details about the old brick and frame structures from her tongue with scant regard for the mounting heat of a Missouri noon in August. We sat on the steps of the courthouse, built of logs in 1830, and learned that George Caleb Bingham had given the two-room building immortality in his celebrated painting, "Frontier Justice." The thick walnut planks of the courthouse are as sound as ever, and its interior is neatly white-washed. Cat's-eyes wink from the hand-poured glass of the windows. Later after inspecting several pioneer churches and houses, each with twin chimneys, one for a fireplace at either end, we arrived at Bingham's house. The painter, who came to the frontier from Virginia as a child, built his house of brick in 1837 and lived in it until 1845.

If it was hot in the sun, it was an inferno inside Templeton's blacksmith shop, but there we lingered, enthralled as the smith pointed a plowshare on his anvil.

"Mostly I work on tractors nowadays," the smith said as he mopped his brow. He showed us how horseshoes were weighted to keep the animal from hitting his heels together and demonstrated how to use a dunce cap to band a wagon wheel.

"The smithy has stood here for fifty years," he said. "Before then, this was a wagon shop, building wagons for farmers and for the trail to Santa Fe."

The most interesting of all the early pioneer buildings of Arrow Rock is not the blacksmith shop, and the most interesting of all the early town citizens was not George Caleb Bingham. The most interesting building is the Arrow Rock Tavern, and the most interesting citizen was Dr. John Sappington. We found exhibits about the good frontier doctor in the tavern.

The Arrow Rock Tavern was built in 1835 by Joseph Huston, a Virginian, who put his slaves to the task of cutting primeval walnut and oak trees and sawing out timbers and boards. The slaves burned bricks, and Joseph's brother Benjamin fashioned the hardware from metal. Travelers over the Santa Fe Trail who had means stayed in the tavern. They paid a Spanish "bit" worth twelve and a half cents to spend the night. They paid another bit for dinner. The muddy boots of traders wore a path into the hardwood floor of the taproom from the door to the bar, where wine and whiskey awaited the thirsty new arrival. Today's tourists may eat lunch in the dining room at the tavern, but the tavern gave up taking overnight guests in 1952.

Where Santa Fe traders once slept, the tavern now displays pioneer furnishings and keepsakes, including a bed from the Sappington homestead and Dr. Sappington's medical chest. The doctor, in his black beaver hat, was the guardian angel of the trail, for he was the first physician on the frontier to use quinine powders to combat malaria. He sprinkled the ground-up bark into a cup of brandy and gave it to travelers who came to Arrow Rock shaking with the ague. As fame of the doctor's cures spread across the land, he compounded his Anti-Fever Pills and sold them all over America wherever malaria was prevalent. A handful of the original green pills are displayed in the old tavern. The doctor prospered, and four of his daughters married two Missouri governors. Meredith M. Marmaduke took Lavinia as his wife, while Claiborne F. Jackson wed first Jane, then Louisa, and finally Eliza. When Jackson asked the doctor for the hand of his third daughter, Sappington snapped, "Take her—but don't come back for the old woman!"

A rope hanging in the lobby of the tavern reaches through the ceiling and on up through the master bedroom on the second floor to an old steamboat bell on the roof, which is now used as a dinner bell. In the old days it served to arouse the town to fires and other alarms. Late one night a traveler arrived at the tavern and, finding nobody to receive him, rang the bell. Instead of the halting steps of a sleepy innkeeper, he heard doors slamming and men running towards the inn from all over town. The traveler met most of the town's citizens that night, but few were in a very cordial mood.

From Arrow Rock the route of the Santa Fe Trail is followed by Missouri highway 41 to Marshall and by U.S. 65 and 24 on through Malta Bend and Grand Pass to Lexington. No landmarks of the Santa Fe Trail survive until the modern traveler reaches Fort Osage, which has been restored by the County Court of Jackson to appear much as it did when its factor, George C. Sibley, set out to survey the Santa Fe Trail for the U.S. Government. The survey began at the gate of the fort in 1825.

The fort itself antedated the Santa Fe Trail. William Clark, having returned in 1806 with Meriwether Lewis from their epochal expedition to the Pacific and back, was a brigadier of the Missouri Militia. In 1808 he led a company of 81 men of the 1st U.S. Infantry and eighty volunteer St. Charles' Dragoons mounted militia to a point on the Missouri three hundred river miles from the nearest white settlement. The men arrived at a high promontory overlooking the river about twenty miles east of today's Kansas City on September 4, and began construction of block-houses and a palisade of hewn white-oak logs. In eleven days they had completed so much that Clark and the militia started back to St. Louis, leaving the infantry to finish and garrison the fort.

From the start Fort Osage was a successful Indian trading post and a strategic base for American penetration of the vast Louisiana Territory. Ironically, in 1822, only a year after William Becknell stopped there on his pioneering journey over the Santa Fe Trail, the government shut the post down. By 1827 it was abandoned, and its timbers removed by settlers to build their homes.

When the Missouri River washed away old Franklin and Fort Osage was abandoned, Independence became the jumping-off place for the Santa Fe Trail. Here, in late April, traders rendezvoused and bought their provisions and trade stuff. They packed a minimum of fifty pounds of flour and bacon, twenty pounds of coffee and sugar, and a few pounds of salt for each man to go with the buffalo they were certain to shoot as meat. For luxury men added dried fruit, potatoes, and eggs packed in corn meal, which could be used up after the eggs were eaten. For weapons they carried long rifles, pistols, knives, and a double-barreled fowling piece good for Indian night attacks. Some traders had small cannons. They loaded their wagons with freight.

The bulk of the goods were cotton fabrics, cutlery, hardware, and odds and ends such as rings, bracelets, beads, hairpins, brushes, razors, mirrors, needles, and scissors. A trader could buy a dozen bottles of whiskey for four dollars apiece, drink the contents on the way and trade the empty bottles in Santa Fe for produce worth six dollars apiece.

First there were the Conestoga wagons, but later much larger Murphy wagons took their place. That the Murphy wagon took the place of the familiar Conestoga wagon is due to the rapacity of New Mexico's Governor Pedro Armijo. Don Pedro imposed a heavy tax of about $500 on each wagon entering Santa Fe. The traders complained. Don Pedro would not listen, but Joseph Murphy, a St. Louis wagonsmith, would.

"We'll give the furrin' bandit a run for his money," he said, and he

21

Travelers with means paid a Spanish "bit" worth twelve-and-a-half cents to stay overnight at the Arrow Rock Tavern. Visitors to the historic trail village in Missouri still
may eat meals at the tavern.

Ozark Frontier Trail Photo

Fort Osage, near Kansas City, has been rebuilt of logs to appear much as it did
when its factor, George C. Sibley, set out to survey the Santa Fe Trail.

Ozark Frontier Trail Photo

set about building the enormous wagons which would carry a load of better than five thousand pounds, enabling the traders to spread the wagon tax out over a much larger quantity of goods. Wagons were painted light blue with bright red wheels. Canvas stretched over hickory bows protected cargoes from rain and sun. Not only freight but the wagons themselves were brought by steamboat to the Blue Mills landing at Independence, where a cement plant now stands.

In the fall of 1832 Washington Irving visited Independence and found it "the utmost verge of civilization." At the corner of what is now Kansas and Liberty streets, traders stopped at the famous Weston blacksmith shop to repair their wagons or to buy new wagons, which were made right on the spot. This was the house of wagon tires, kingbolts and linchpins, guns and spurs, axes and bridles, where iron rang on iron in the long low brick building. With hundreds of wagons waiting their turn for repairs, the traders had plenty of time to swap stories and warnings of hardships to come and sample the liquid refreshment of neighboring taverns, a mixture of whiskey and molasses affectionately called "skull varnish."

Independence, queen city of the trails, is now Independence, the home of Harry Truman. There is a Santa Fe Trail marker on the grounds of a junior high school close to the former President's big Victorian frame house at Delaware Avenue and Truman Road, and it is no wonder that Mr. Truman, growing up as he did in Independence, became a trail buff. His grandfather, Solomon Young, was a wagon master, and on the desk in his office at the Truman Library and Museum the former President keeps a small model of the pioneer woman and child monument that has been set up at important points along the trail.

We visited the Truman Museum to see the Thomas Hart Benton mural "Independence and the Winning of the West" at the entrance and then went to the Old Jackson County Jail, which once imprisoned Frank James. The red-brick building contains twelve cells of two-foot-thick blocks of limestone and quarters for the jailer and his family. Truman's press secretary at the White House, Charles Ross, was born in the jail, for his father was a marshal.

Despite its historic importance the old jail was scheduled for demolition in 1959. When the wreckers arrived, they found amateurs of history staging a sit-down in the building while others were trying to raise money to save it. The phones of well-to-do citizens began to ring.

"This is Harry Truman," said an unmistakable voice. "I'm calling about the old jail."

Truman's first call won a thousand dollars to save the jail. The campaign he sparked raised sufficient funds, and today the jail stands as one of the most interesting landmarks in the queen city of the trails. There is little else left from the past. The pioneer spring still flows east of Noland Road, but it is imprisoned in a concrete basin and littered with trash. Some old wagon ruts at 110th Street and the Red Bridge Road are pointed out to visitors as being those of the Santa Fe Trail.

Close to where the Red Bridge now spans the Blue River, the huge prairie schooners forded the stream. Sometimes floods kept the traders back for weeks, and this, together with the existence of a safe landing ledge of Bethany limestone near the small town of Westport, eighteen miles west of the Blue Mills landing, inexorably turned more and more traders away from Independence. In 1844 the Missouri washed away the landing at Independence, and it was Westport's day to be queen city of the trail. Francis Parkman described the Westport of 1846:

Westport was full of Indians, whose little, shaggy ponies were tied by dozens along the houses and fences. Sacs and Foxes, with shaved heads and painted faces; Shawnees and Delawares fluttering in calico frocks and turbans; Wyandots dressed like white men, and a few wretched Kansas wrapped in old blankets, were strolling about the streets, or lounging in and out of the shops and houses. Whiskey, by the way, circulates more freely in Westport than is altogether safe in a place where every man carries a loaded pistol in his pocket.

Westport in turn found a new rival in what was first called the Town of Kansas and then Kansas City. The new city in time absorbed Westport so that today Westport is Kansas City's Fourth Ward. The past has left its landmark in the bustling metropolis of the present, and in the Fourth Ward, visitors can find the store of A. G. Boone at the corner of Westport Road and Pennsylvania Avenue. Built in 1836 by a prominent trail outfitter, this is the oldest building in the city. There are old houses left from pioneer Westport, too, and wagon tracks still can be made out at Twenty-seventh and Topping Streets.

Across the state line in Kansas, Interstate 35 swings through burgeoning suburbs where covered wagons camped on their first night out from Westport during trail days. Here, where ranch houses and split levels stretch, wagon trains were made up and captains elected for the long trip west. Men from the East grew poetic at their first glimpse of the great plains. In his journal of 1839 Thomas Farnham described the "treeless plains of green, as they had been since the flood, beautiful, unbroken

24

by bush or rock; unsoiled by plow or spade; sweetly scented with the first blossomings of the spring."

In historic Shawnee, now also a suburb, wagon masters made their homes. When a new market was built in 1962, the home of wagon master Dick Williams, a Shawnee Indian, was dismantled and moved to the Shawnee Mission Park, four miles west of town, where it is to be used as a museum. Three large brick buildings of the old Shawnee Mission stand in the park, too. The original Wells Fargo Office is now a part of the Calkins Electric Company, a block north of the first territorial jail in Kansas on Neiman Road.

Interstate 35 is called the modern Santa Fe Trail. We sped over it at 75 m.p.h. to the intersection with U.S. 56 in Lenexa, where an old stone building remains as staunch today as it was when it sheltered pioneer families from Indian raids. From this point westward across Kansas, U.S 56 follows the Santa Fe Trail.

When in 1846 the first stagecoaches of the Independence-Santa Fe Mail started over the Santa Fe Trail, the Mahaffie depot, still standing in Olathe, was the first stop out of Westport. Coaches with water-tight bodies so that they could ferry streams without wetting the passengers, rattled over the prairies behind six-mule teams. Passengers paid $150 for the trip. Their fare included the right to bring along forty-five pounds of baggage and to eat and sleep on the ground. One passenger quoted in Carl Coke Rister's "The Southern Frontier" complained:

Twenty-four days and nights—twenty-five being scheduled time—must be spent in that ambulance; passengers becoming crazy with whiskey, mixed with want of sleep, are often obliged to be strapped to their seats; their meals, dispatched during their ten-minute halts, are simply abominable, the heats are excessive, the climate malarious; lamps may not be used at night for fear of non-existent Indians.

If passengers got too obstreperous, the driver hollered, "Indians!" That was a sure-fire way to quiet them down. If a man cursed too much or otherwise showed disrespect to a lady passenger, he was set afoot. But all of this was still ahead of the passengers who disembarked at the Mahaffie depot to stretch their legs and draw in big drafts of the bracing prairie air.

We drove over the ribbon of concrete to the spot west of Gardner where a rough board once directed immigrants over the Oregon Trail. Today what was one of the most important road forks in the nation is in

25

a small roadside park, where tourists picnic. There another sign pointed the way southwest to Santa Fe, still 750 miles away.

For two decades after the end of the Mexican War the army supplied its southwestern forts on the Santa Fe Trail from Fort Leavenworth. Fort Leavenworth, still an active military post, maintains a museum of military transportation in the old cavalry stables. Visitors find many interesting exhibits relating to the Santa Fe Trail, which is appropriate since the fort was command headquarters not only for the protection of the trail from the Indians, but from Red Legs and bushwhackers sympathizing with the South during the Civil War. Military trains came over Government Lane from Fort Leavenworth to its junction with the Santa Fe Trail close to the place where the Oregon and Santa Fe trails separated.

As we drove west, the Santa Fe Trail was sometimes to our right, sometimes to the left, and sometimes buried beneath the pavement of U.S. 56. Only in rare places can the ruts still be seen. One hundred feet south of Black Jack roadside park near Baldwin is such a place. Here, where a skirmish was fought in a grove of blackjack oak during the "bleeding Kansas" struggle on the eve of the Civil War, the trail forded Captain's Creek.

Baldwin itself is a daughter of the trail. Citizens of Palmyra, later to be called Baldwin, counted 4,472 wagons, 1,267 horses, 6,542 mules, 32,281 oxen, and an estimated 13,056 tons of freight passing their settlement in a six months' period in the 1850's, and were certain that their town would prosper beside such a busy channel of trade. John Baldwin thought so, too. He hauled the equipment for a steam sawmill over the trail by wagon, and established the first sawmill in the area. He gave his name to the town where God-fearing Methodists soom established Baker University and built the "Old Castle" in 1858. Wagon trains stopped to see the glorious structure of sandstone, all of three stories high with plastered walls and ceilings. We stopped to see the Old Castle too, for it is now a museum housing such things as ox bells, which once came jingling down the trail. Next to the building is the old U.S. post office at Palmyra, which stood beside the trail until it was moved to its present location on the campus to make way for a gas station on U.S. 56. We refused to buy gas at the station, which had taken the rightful place of a historic trailside structure.

West of Baldwin is the Hole in the Rock where travelers on the trail used to shelter beside a spring. In Burlingame the trail ran down what is now the main street and then continued west on Buttermilk Lane. A thunderstorm broke with all the violence for which the Kansas prairie

Council Grove, Kansas, began as the last chance to buy bacon, beans, and whiskey. The trail ran right down the main street.
Courtesy Santa Fe Railway

is known as we passed through Burlingame, but we continued on to Council Grove to spend the night. This town has been famous on the trail since the day in 1827 when Kit Carson cut its name on a buffalo hide and nailed it to the Council Oak. It was beneath this oak that Sibley and the other U.S Government commissioners had parleyed with the Osage Indians to open up the trail through their lands. Today the Council Oak is only a stump.

The nearby Post Office Oak in which wagon train men left messages for friends following on the trail has fared better, although it is crowded by an apartment building. One of Harry Truman's Madonna of the Trail statues is in Council Grove. When we were there, somebody had rubbed lipstick around the pioneer mother's mouth, but she was still striding purposefully ahead, carrying one child while a small boy clutched her skirt. At her feet is the old wagon camp site.

Here, 145 miles from Independence, wagon trains lay over for a while. Susan Shelby Magoffin kept a diary of her travels over the trail with her husband Samuel, a successful Santa Fe trader in 1846. She wrote of Council Grove:

It is a thick cluster of trees some miles in length through which runs a small creek called Council Grove Creek. There is a quantity of fine timber consisting of oaks, hickory, walnut, etc. Each company coming out generally stops here a

27

day or so to repair their wagons, rest the stock, get timbers for the remainder of the journey; these are lashed under the wagons. They also mould bullets and prepare their fire arms for now they are coming into the region of game. Another thing is the washing of cloth(e)s; there is a great borrowing of soap and slopping of water now.

To the West stretched the prairie dotted with a few clumps of cotton-woods. Up to this point the Indians were friendly, but beyond Council Grove they were hostile. Traders banded together for protection and elected a captain, whose duty it was to direct the course of the march and pick the campgrounds.

"There may be some honor in it, but not much profit," said one veteran captain.

The newly organized companies varied in size. Major Wetmore described his company of 1824 as follows: "We this evening ascertained the whole strength of our company to be 81 persons and 2 servants; we also had 2 road wagons, 20 dearborns, 2 carts, and 1 small piece of cannon. The amount of goods taken with us is supposed to be about $30,000. We have with us about 200 horses and mules."

Josiah Gregg's company of 1831 had nearly 100 wagons, merchandise worth $200,000, and two cannons mounted upon carriages.

Much of Old Council Grove remains. The Last Chance Store was, according to a sign, "Last Chance for bacon, beans, and whiskey." The wide-plank floors are intact, and the stone walls have been tuck-pointed. The city calaboose, built in 1849, was long the only jail between Independence and Santa Fe. It appears as it did in 1859 when during an Indian raid a mob dragged two Indian captives from a cell and hanged them. The Kaw Mission, built in the winter of 1850-51 as an Indian school, still stands, too. VIP travelers over the trail stayed at the mission. Out in front is a double horse trough. One pump simultaneously filled two troughs so that two horses could drink at once. A dipper was kept handy for people, hot and thirsty from the trail. Inside the mission we found many relics of the trail ranging from an ox yoke to men's shoes shipped to Santa Fe with a caravan. They failed to sell in a Santa Fe store. When in recent years the store was taking inventory, checkers found them, decided that nobody was going to buy them after more than a century, and sent them to Council Grove to the museum.

The morning of departure from Council Grove came for every caravan. The wagons were divided into two to four divisions for the march with a lieutenant heading each division.

"Stretch out! Stretch out!" cried the captain.

28

The drivers cracked their "Missouri pistols," long saplings with a lash ending in a buckskin thong, and the wagons moved into places in the line. They began to roll. Outriders galloped ahead to dig out stream banks so that the heavy wagons could cross more easily and to prepare the next campsite. We breakfasted in the Old Hays Cafe, once a stopping place on the trail, and started out over the rolling shortgrass prairies in the wake of the caravans.

The trail led southwest to Diamond Spring, which is on a road running south from U.S. 56 just west of Wilsey. Discovered by old Ben Jones, a hunter for Sibley's party in 1825, the spring gushes out of the head of a hollow in the prairie on Diamond Spring Ranch, and was so named because Sibley believed it must be superior to a fountain in Arabia called "Diamond of the Desert." Therefore it should be called the "Diamond of the Plain." From 1849 until 1863 there was a stage station there, but in May of that year Dick Yeager and a parcel of Quantrill's raiders destroyed it.

One of the tasks of the outriders was to shoot buffalo for meat. Once the plains over which we were now driving were thick with the "big-humped cattle," as Coronado, who in 1541 ventured this far in Kansas, called them, but today they are gone except for small herds in reserves. Between Hillsboro and McPherson we found the largest of the state's herds in the Maxwell State Game Refuge. The shaggy beasts snorted and pawed the earth, and we were pleased that a barbed wire fence separated us from them.

"The bulls aren't as dangerous as they look," said a rancher who was standing nearby. "But just come between a cow and her calf, and you'll learn how fast a buffalo can move."

There are artifacts from the Santa Fe Trail in the County Courthouse farther down the road at Lyons, but they are not nearly so interesting as the fragments of chain mail and the sword of Toledo steel that can also be seen there. Lyons is in the middle of what was Quivera, a half mythical kingdom of "trees hung with golden bells and people whose pots and pans were gold" sought by the adventurous captain of Spain, Francisco De Coronado. One of his men lost the sword, and another died in the chain of mail. West of Lyons there is a thirty-foot granite cross erected to the memory of Father Juan De Padilla of Coronado's expedition, whom the Indians killed in the vicinity when he returned alone the next year. Coronado found no gold, but he did observe that the country was "the best I have ever seen for producing all the products of Spain." The land of agricultural plenty through which our family drove proved him right.

A mile south of the cross is a well opened up by Buffalo Bill Mathewson at the old Santa Fe Trail crossing of Cow Creek. The trail reached the Arkansas River, a lifeline of precious water, flowing from the mountains in the west, close to modern-day Ellinwood. Josiah Gregg was impressed with the river's "imposing and majestic appearance. Beneath a ledge of wave-like yellow sandy ridges and hillocks spreading far beyond descends the majestic river," he wrote, "bespeckled with verdant islets, thickly set with cottonwood timber."

The Arkansas River may have appeared majestic at first, but as the caravans toiled along the valley, the monotony of high sandy hills, flat, grassy islands in the river, and groves of stunted cottonwoods oppressed the traders. They cooked their buffalo steaks over buffalo-chip fires, and took potshots at rattlesnakes.

The Great Bend of the Arkansas River was a landmark on the Santa Fe Trail which ran past Fort Zarah, established in 1864 where the trail crossed Walnut Creek. The sandstone buildings of the fort are all gone, but a state park two miles east of today's city of Great Bend preserves the site. The trail continues on into Great Bend to pass where the courthouse now stands. U.S. 56 follows Tenth Street, called the Oil Artery of Kansas, through the city which is rich with a black gold which would have ensorceled Coronado, once he understood the worth of it.

Pawnee Rock was an even more important landmark. The sandstone cliff on the north rim of the Arkansas Valley was quarried for stone to build the railroad and Kansas homes so that it no longer commands the plains. It can still be easily made out where the highway passes through the town of the same name. Although hostile Indians used it as a lookout, freighters and emigrants camped at its foot and even carved their names on its stony sides. When Kit Carson was sixteen that first summer on the trail, he stood guard there one night. Hearing a stealthy rustling sound in the dark, he fired at what he was certain was an Indian. He was chagrined to learn he had shot his own mule. A state park protects what is left of Pawnee Rock. We drove to the top on a park road and looked out over the plains, now a vast sweep of wheat.

There were so many Indian ambushes and attacks on wagon trains near Pawnee Rock that Fort Larned was established in 1859 a few miles farther west at Pawnee Forks to safeguard the trail. The soldiers called the original post of sod and adobe buildings Camp Alert because of the incessant Indian raids. In 1864 sandstone was quarried from nearby Jenkins Hill and white pine was brought from Michigan to rebuild the fort in such an imposing fashion that the Indians would not dare attack. This failed to intimidate the Kiowa chieftain Santanta, who struck with a small party in the night, killed a sentry, and escaped with the horse herd. He then sent a message to the post quartermaster.

"The horses are inferior. Would the army provide better stock in the future?"

The fort was abandoned and its land returned to the public domain in 1882 by a bill signed by President Chester Arthur. Unlike many other frontier forts, it was bought intact by a rancher, who did not tear the old buildings down for their materials. Today the old fort is a National Historic Site. Nine stone buildings still surround the parade ground. One of the officers' quarters is furnished with original and antique furniture, and the quartermaster depot contains a museum of horse-drawn vehicles. The commissary is now a harness shop. On a wall of the officers' quarters an officer, trying to preserve his privacy amid military life on the frontier, scribbled, "Hands off my wardrobe." His scrawl is still there. As we strolled about the quarters, a tantalizing smell of cooking was wafted in the door. We followed our noses to the old bakery and central mess hall. There we found a Boy Scout troop preparing its dinner. Complete overnight equipment is kept in the hall for visiting scout troops.

Five miles east of Dodge City on U.S. 164 Fort Dodge was built in 1864 where wagons camped. A few old fort buildings that remain today are part of the Kansas Soldiers Home. Not many tourists visit the fort, for they are far more fascinated by Dodge City, self-styled "Cowboy Capital of the World," which sprang to life as the brawling son of the Santa Fe Railroad. When the rails following the Santa Fe Trail reached the vicinity of Fort Dodge in 1872, the town was established close by where it would

In 1931 the ruts of the Santa Fe Trail still cut deep into the prairie beyond Dodge City. Even today, the trail can be seen for two miles climbing a knoll and swinging through the Arkansas River bottomlands.
Courtesy Santa Fe Railway

be safe from marauding Comanches and Kiowas, who only four years before had attacked the fort and killed four soldiers and wounded seventeen. The same year the Cheyennes and Arapahoes, not to be outdone, overwhelmed a Mexican wagon train near the fort and killed and scalped sixteen traders.

Overnight Dodge City became the end of the trail for herds of longhorns driven up the Western Trail from Texas. Luke Short, Bat Masterson, and Wyatt Earp still seem to haunt the rebuilt Front Street. Up on Boot Hill at least forty cowboys and badmen who died "with their boots on" lie buried as proof that Dodge City's reputation for settling arguments with a six-shooter is justified. We strolled along the board walk to such places as the Long Branch Saloon, the Tonsorial Palace, and the Beeson Museum, which exhibits keepsakes of the town's best-known gunfighters. That night after dinner the sound of gunfire brought us into the street.

"It's a real shootout!" shouted a small boy in the milling crowd.

It was a shootout all right, with a man toppling to the pavement and all, except that when we tourists were no longer looking, the victim got up, dusted himself off and sauntered into the Long Branch Saloon for a restoring libation.

West of Dodge City some three and a half miles, bulldozers obliterated the site of the Caches, which was up a hill one thousand feet northwest of the marker on U.S. 50. In the fall of 1822 James Baird and Samuel Chambers and fifty men set out over the Santa Fe Trail with a pack train of heavily laden mules. Late fall blizzards caught them just short of the Cimarron Crossing of the Arkansas, and they could go no farther. During the winter the mules died one by one until none were left to carry the packs to New Mexico. When the spring at last came, the traders buried their goods in deep holes and hurried to Taos, where they bought more mules. They returned and dug up their cached goods and resumed the trail to the West. After that travelers over the trail told all manner of horrendous tales around their campfires to explain the origin of the mysterious jug-shaped holes.

Only another three and a half miles west on U.S. 50 we found one of the best preserved of all the remaining stretches of the Santa Fe Trail in Kansas. For two miles the trail swings in an arc around the Arkansas bottomlands. It climbs a knoll north of U.S. 50 and then skirts the north side of a bluff overlooking the valley. It snakes through shallow ravines and then finally cuts southwest down a draw and breaks out onto the bottomlands, where each wagon seemed to find its own way over the eight-hundred-foot-wide trail that leads on towards the Cimarron Crossing and still distant Santa Fe.

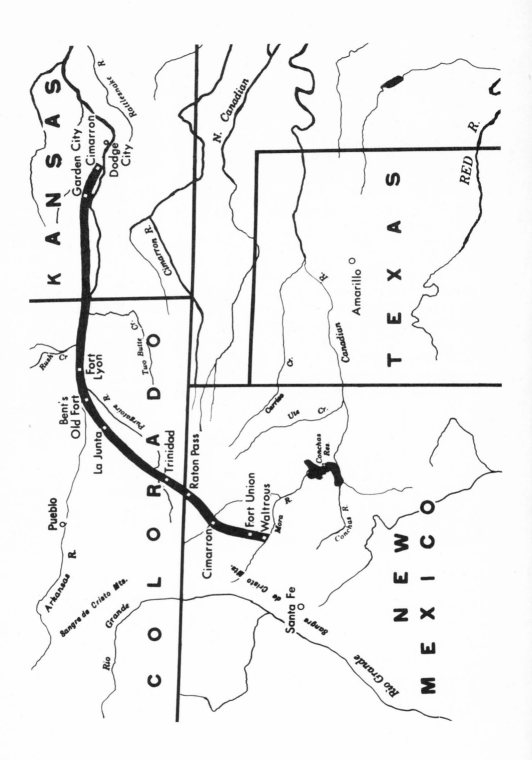

3

Santa Fe Trail: Mountain Branch

●

They say that the Barlow and Sanderson Stage drivers on the Mountain Branch of the Santa Fe Trail were a breed apart. They observed the finest of niceties. A passenger might sit with impunity on the rear seat on top only if invited by the driver. Otherwise, he was liable to be toppled backwards from his place, for this seat was reserved for the guard. In a hold-up, the driver was duty-bound to protect the passengers' lives, but he need not be concerned about their valuables. That was their business. Greenhorns riding the stage were told that if a coach tongue broke, the driver would get down and seize hold of the first rattlesnake that ventured up to see what the commotion was. He would tease the snake until it coiled tightly around the broken tongue. The snake could be counted on to hold it tight until repairs could be made.

Traders traveling to Santa Fe over the Mountain Branch were a breed apart too, for the trail climbed at Raton Pass to a mere ten feet short of 8,000 feet in altitude. The branch was 100 miles longer too, but they preferred it because it was less parched than the Cimarron Cutoff, and because the hair on a man's head rested easier than down on the plains where the Comanche and Kiowa avoided forts and military escorts to pillage and murder when they could, which was much of the time. In 1847 plains Indians killed 47 travelers, destroyed 330 wagons, and stole 6,500 animals. They all but closed the Cimarron Cutoff, and even made the Mountain Branch dangerous.

The Mountain Branch separated from the Cimarron Cutoff at the

Cimarron Crossing of the Arkansas River just west of today's Cimarron, Kansas. It ran up the north bank of the river, as does U.S. 50 today. Wagon trains labored along a sandy road close to the riverbank, which was so poorly timbered that men often had to wade into the river to cut wood on one of the low islands to build the evening's cook fire. In some places to this day the country is covered with large stones, but for the most part it is a level plain. Now rich fields of wheat and sugar beets grow where then buffalo fed and prairie dogs mounded their villages.

Usually the caravans stopped at Chouteau's Island, a rendezvous of the fur-trading Chouteaus from St. Louis, that was west of modern-day Garden City, one hundred miles upriver from the Cimarron Crossing. In 1828 a caravan captained by John Means took the Cimarron Cutoff on its way back to Independence with thirty to forty thousand dollars in silver, and was attacked by Comanches. Means was shot and scalped, and several others lost their lives. Fighting a running battle with the Indians, the caravan pressed on. One night the Comanches stampeded all the mules and horses and sped off to the east to lay still a new trap on the trail. Loading their supplies and the silver on their backs, the men struck north to escape the Indians and came out on the Mountain Branch close to Chouteau's Island. They buried the silver on the island and made their way down the trail toward civilization. Hardships and terror broke the party. The strongest hurried ahead to get help. When rescue parties came back out the trail they found one man, blinded by starvation, lying on his back, flailing at a rapacious pack of wolves with a stick.

Later in the year some of the men returned with a westering party headed by Charles Bent of Bent's Fort and found their silver where they had buried it. The river had flooded the island and washed away the sand covering the packs. Indians had waded out to the island to dig white clay for painting their buffalo robes, but they had not discovered the treasure exposed by the current.

In western Kansas there are no important remains of the trail, although four miles east of Syracuse and a mile south of U.S. 50 we could make out traces of rifle pits and trenches dug at Fort Aubrey. From this temporary post, troopers tried to protect travelers on the trail during the Indian War of 1865. Zebulon Pike and his expedition came this way in 1806 on their exploration of the upper Arkansas, and it was in eastern Colorado, near what is now Las Animas, that he first got a shadowy glimpse of the mighty peak on the horizon, that geographers named James' Peak after Dr. Edwin James of Long's Expedition. James was first to climb the peak on July 13-14, 1820. Mountain men, trappers, and

36

traders to Santa Fe would have none of this and called the great mountain overlooking the high plains, Pike's Peak. The geographers were finally bested, and James' Peak yielded on maps to Pike's Peak. The nation was spared the expression "James' Peak or Bust." Pike's Peak became a celebrated landmark of the Mountain Branch.

William Becknell on his first trip to Santa Fe thought it best to follow the route of Zebulon Pike and came this way. As he neared the towering Rockies, the high plains grew broken. He happened upon wild horses.

"We now had some cliffs to ascend," he wrote in his journal, "which presented difficulties almost insurmountable, and we were laboriously engaged nearly two days in rolling away large rocks before we attempted to get our horses up, and even then one fell and was bruised to death."

Lack of wood, water, food, and winds that blew flurries of snow down from the slopes of the mountains made Becknell's journey trying. It was late fall, and he still had to climb over the summit of Raton Pass.

Later travelers found shelter from the storms and a haven from Indians at Fort Lyon, which stood just west of the present-day John Martin Reservoir on the Arkansas River in eastern Colorado. In 1867, Kit Carson, now grown old and sick, himself found shelter at Fort Lyon. While on a hunting trip a few years before, he had been thrown and dragged by his horse. He had been internally injured, and now he lay dying on a bed of buffalo robes. Army surgeon Tilton ordered a light diet and no tobacco. On May 23 Kit cocked an eye at the cook.

"Cook me some first-rate doin's—a buffalo steak and a bowl of coffee and a pipe are what I need," he said.

Surgeon Tilton objected, but Kit blistered the cook's ears with some of the most colorful oaths he had learned since the day he ran away from saddlemaker Workman's shop in Franklin. The frightened cook prepared a real trailman's meal, buffalo steak and all the fixings. Kit ate with an appetite and called for his pipe. No fancy store pipe would do but the pipe given to him by an Indian in the days when he was young and the Santa Fe Trail was a glorious adventure. He smoked and yarned about the high mountains in the old times. He coughed and spat blood. Then a violent aneurism ruptured into his trachea.

"I'm gone! Doctor, compadre, adios!" he cried.

Kit Carson died on the trail that he loved.

Not far above Fort Lyon was Bent's Fort, heart of the great trading empire of the Bent Brothers, William and Charles, and their in-laws, the St. Vrains. From the fort, trappers ranged the mountains. The Arapahoes, Cheyennes, Kiowas, and Comanches brought their skins and buffalo robes to the fort where they could deal in peace with men they came to trust. The Bents had brought skilled Mexicans to the upper Arkansas to build their fort of adobe bricks. Lacking straw to mix with the adobe mud, they used buffalo wool, and constructed great walls, four feet thick with two circular bastions, ample storerooms, living apartments, and a huge open courtyard.

Susan Magoffin describes the fort in her diary:

Well, the outside exactly fills my idea of an ancient castle. It is built of adobes, unburnt brick, and Mexican style so far. The walls are very high and very thick with rounding corners. There is but one entrance, this is to the East rather.

Inside is a large space some 90 or an hundred feet square, all around this and next to the wall are rooms, some 25 in number. They have dirt floors—which are sprinkled with water several times during the day to prevent dust. Standing in the center of some of them is a large wooden post as a firmer prop to the ceiling which is made of logs. Some of these rooms are occupied by boarders as bedchambers. One is a dining-room—another a kitchen—a little store, a black-smith's shop, a barber's do., an ice house, which receives perhaps more customers than any other.

Susan was astounded that there was a billiard room, and that she was given a private room with such furniture as bed, chairs, washbasin, and table, and that guests of the Bents were offered iced mint juleps. Susan might also have been as amazed as the Indians were at the goat which St. Vrain had brought over the trail from Missouri, and the peacocks, which the redskins called "thunder birds." Here, at Bent's Fort, black-smiths and carpenters repaired wagons and shod mules and oxen.

When New Mexico fell to General Stephen W. Kearny in 1846, Charles Bent became the interim governor. He was murdered at Taos during an uprising in 1847. His brother could not stand the ghosts that now haunted his great fort on the Arkansas. He ordered his men to strip the place. They loaded twenty wagons with belongings, and William Bent led the train to a creek five miles down the river and told them to camp. Then he rode back to the fort. He rolled powder kegs into the storage and trading rooms. He went from room to room, brandishing a flaming torch to set the ceilings afire. As he galloped eastward along the Mountain Branch to where his men were camped, he heard the booms of the shattering explosions which tore apart his past life. Later he built a new fort of stone a few miles farther east on the trail.

Once again Bent's Fort was one of the key posts on the Mountain

Branch, but times were changing. The great trading empire of the Bents passed into history as the Indians fought furiously back against the rising tide of white settlement. William Bent, friend of the Indians, could no longer prosper in a world where the death agony of a people poisoned life.

By 1859 the old fort's adobe walls were partly rebuilt to shelter a Barlow and Sanderson stage station. There were repair shops. Surviving buildings became cattle corrals. By the time Kit Carson died at Fort Lyon, the upper Arkansas was getting to be a tame place for the men who had lived as free as any man has ever lived on this earth. Today the last vestiges of Bent's Old Fort are preserved in a National Historic Site situated eight miles northeast of La Junta on Colorado 194.

At Bent's Fort caravans following the Mountain Branch left the Arkansas and headed southwest towards treacherous Raton Pass. The trail crossed a dusty plain broken with sandhills where mirages danced. There were only a few potholes of brackish water. When a caravan reached a pool, the men fought with the animals for the first drink. If the animals won, they often excreted in the pool as they drank, and this made the water objectionable to even the thirstiest men. Still the men drank the water.

"Shut both eyes and hold your breath until the nauseating dose is swallowed," advised one veteran of the Mountain Branch.

U.S. 350 follows the route of the trail from La Junta along Timpas Creek to Trinidad. In 1837 twenty-two-year-old Marcellin St. Vrain and a party with twelve pack mules started up the trail along Timpas Creek. The Pawnees attacked, killed one trader, and wounded three. They also captured three saddle horses and nine mules and their packs. In the packs were such things as two illuminated Latin missals and ten reams of printing paper and twenty-five pounds of printer's ink intended for the small press brought over the trail to publish a newspaper in New Mexico. The attack put the newspaper out of business, and furnished the Indians with black ink with which they daubed their faces in preparation for the next raid. The Bents reasoned that since the Pawnees, who were U.S. Indians, had raided the caravan, the U.S. Government was responsible. They put in a claim to Washington for $3,273 in damages. Washington took a different view of the matter. Beyond the Arkansas was then Mexican soil; the affair on Timpas Creek was the responsibility of the Mexican government.

At last the wagons wound among stony foothills toward the mountains. The wagons camped among the cedar-crowned rocks at the Hole in the Rock and at the river the French named Purgatoire, "river of the souls in

39

purgatory," and which the traders corrupted into the "Picket-wire" River. Then the wagons were rolling among the great rocks which marked the approach to Raton Pass.

Trinidad grew up around a trading post on the Mountain Branch. The Baca House, an eight-room adobe built in 1869, still stands opposite the post office on Main Street, and it contains old wagons and relics of the trail. We drove down Main Street and followed U.S. 85 south of town in the direction of Raton Pass. To a motorist the road through Raton Pass is a marvel of highway engineering, which affords spectacular views of mountains and a sweep of New Mexico beyond, but to the bullwhacker and muleskinner it was a different matter.

"It takes a dozen men to steady a wagon with all its wheels locked," wrote Susan Magoffin, "and for one who is some distance off to hear the crash it makes over the stones is truly alarming. Till I rode ahead and understood the business, I supposed that every wagon had fallen over a precipice. We came to camp about half an hour after dusk, having accomplished the great travel of six or eight hundred yards during the day."

The trail ascended Raton Creek Canyon to the pass summit directly over the present Santa Fe Railroad tunnel, then turned west and bore a little north on the ridge for about a quarter mile. Then it descended the course of Willow Creek southward to the town of Raton, some six miles south of the pass. In 1865 Uncle Dick Wooton, scout and trader, decided to settle down in Raton Pass. He had driven 8,900 sheep from Taos to the Sacramento Valley of California and sold them for $50,000 in gold. He hired a crew of men and set to work with explosives and picks to transform the trail through the pass into a toll road. The crew blasted and cut their way until at last Uncle Dick could open his road. Traders, miners, the Barlow and Sanderson stages, and herdsmen paid their tolls to use the new roads. Not so Ute Indians, who saw no reason to pay to cross their mountains. Posses chasing after horse thieves also were waved through free of charge, because Uncle Dick rightly surmised they wouldn't slow down enough to pay a toll anyway.

Today there is a marker to show where the tollgate stood. Wooton House, an inn established by Uncle Dick, is still in the pass, although it has been rebuilt. Once it was a nooning stop for stages and the haunt of freighters and of youngsters from Trinidad and El Moro, who danced until the floors shook. One night a couple of strangers came into the hotel to see Uncle Dick. They were Santa Fe Railroad men. When they told Uncle Dick that they wanted to buy his tollroad as a right of way

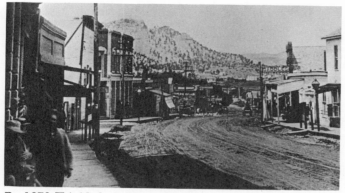

By 1878 Trinidad, Colorado, had grown up around a trading post on the Mountain Branch. The Baca House still stands on the town's main street. *Courtesy Santa Fe Railway*

Bullwhackers and muleskinners drove their teams over the precipitous trail that led ever higher to the summit of Raton Pass. *Courtesy Santa Fe Railway*

From the earliest days of the trail, pack mules plodded on their weary way to Santa Fe. A mule train made from twelve to fifteen miles in a day. *Courtesy Santa Fe Railway*

for a new railroad through the pass, he gave them a long hard look.

"Well," he said, "I guess I'll have to get out of the way of the loco-motive."

Later he refused $50,000 from the railroad for the right of way.

"No," he said, "I don't want that much money in a lump. I'll tell you—you give me and my family a lifetime pass and $25 a month in groceries, and we'll call it square."

Uncle Dick died in 1893, but his widow drew the cash until her death and their invalid daughter after her. Another route of the Santa Fe Railroad had already paralleled the ruts of the Cimarron Cutoff and taken away all but local traffic from that old road. Now the Santa Fe Railroad cut, graded, and tunneled in the pass, and when the high rails were laid it meant that the Mountain Branch of the Santa Fe Trail was also a part of history.

Traces of the trail still may be seen at the summit of Raton Pass, but construction of the railroad and of old U.S. 85 destroyed most of the wagon tracks in the celebrated pass through which the traders once struggled. A few miles south of Raton a rancher, Tom Stockton, built a stage stop in 1866-70 that he called Clifton House. Although Clifton House was built of adobe, it was encircled by promenade balconies and was crowned with a shingle roof. Barlow and Sanderson agents added barns, outbuildings, and a blacksmith shop. Stages stopped at Clifton House for thirty minutes. The meals and lodgings were judged to be the best in northern New Mexico. Today only a chimney, a few broken walls, and foundation stones remain on a ranch off U.S. 64, five miles from Raton.

The Mountain Branch ran southwest across the Canadian River, named for its canadas or canyons and not for any person from Canada. It is still a limpid stream purling down from the mountains on its way to join the Arkansas. The trail entered the domain of Lucien Maxwell, friend of the Bents and of Kit Carson. The Mexican government had awarded Charles Beaubien and Guadalupe Miranda a tremendous land grant. In March 1842, Lucien Maxwell wedded Beaubien's lissome daughter Luz, although she was scarcely fourteen. In time Lucien's marriage brought him owner-ship of the grant, which staked out at more than 1,714,000 acres. At Cimarron he built a mansion in which he entertained travelers on the trail and a stone flour mill. His mansion burned in 1885, but the flour mill looks today much as it did a century ago when travelers replenished their flour supplies and Jicarilla Apaches and Utes drew government flour rations at its door.

We found other buildings surviving at Cimarron from the days of Pittsburgh wagons. What was first a pioneer brewery built in 1854 became Swink's Saloon, among the most notorious gambling halls in the territory. A plaque on the building, which is now a gas station, advises tourists: "Taos lightning, powder smoke and bullets caused many to bite the dust and caused many to be carried out feet first." The old courthouse and the old jail remain too, although a wall of the jail had to be replaced after it was dynamited by a lynching party.

The Don Diego Hotel dates from the last days of the trail. Built in the 1870's by Henry Lambert, once chef to Presidents Lincoln and Grant, the hotel opened as the St. James. It too has its notoriety, for twenty-six men are supposed to have been killed within its walls.

The Mountain Branch ran south of town, where New Mexico 21 runs toward the crossing of the Rayado River. It cuts into a 138,000-acre remnant of Maxwell's grant, which is now the Philmont Scout Ranch, where teen-age Explorer Scouts from all over the nation, as well as scouts from abroad, learn to live in the open. More experienced scouts often take newcomers to a place two miles south of Philmont's camping headquarters. There the ruts of the Mountain Branch are etched deep into the turf. Few boys can look at them without the goose-pimply sense of the past drawing near. Then the wagons are rolling again, the great 300-pound wheels almost as high as a man are turning, and the whips are cracking as the weary oxen plod onward to Santa Fe.

It is only a short distance to the Rayado, where Kit Carson and Lucien Maxwell established a trading post in 1847. Two wings from Lucien's home still stand. Their yellow adobe walls and porches are poignant with a vanished life. Kit's simpler two-room adobe was destroyed long ago, which was not to the liking of the Explorer Scouts. They rebuilt it and in so doing brought their hero back to life. Enter within the walls of adobe mixed by the scouts and look at the furnishings, reverently collected for

Kit Carson spent much of his adventurous life on the Santa Fe Trail. He died at Fort Lyon on the trail that he loved.
Courtesy Chicago Historical Society

43

authenticity's sake. Years after Kit's death, his body was taken from Fort Lyon to Taos, but certainly his spirit has chosen to go to the house on the Rayado rebuilt by youths who are among the few Americans of this day that he would understand and enjoy knowing. His ramrod rifle hangs on the wall and the big double bed he shared with his black-eyed wife awaits his return from a long journey into the mountains.

From the Rayado the trail headed south across modern route 120, climbed through a saddle between mesas and swept southward past the Turkey Mountains. For miles the tracks still are plain to the hiker or rider who chooses to follow them. They come at last to Fort Union, once greatest of all the southwestern forts.

Established in 1852 as the headquarters and supply base for the forts of the Southwest, Fort Union was strategically located close to where the Mountain Branch and the Cimarron Cutoff came together. Troops from the fort galloped out on punitive expeditions against the Indians harassing both trails and escorted wagon trains and the stages carrying the U.S. mail.

The original thirty or so buildings of the fort were jerry-built by soldiers who knew little of building. Only four years later in 1856, assistant Surgeon Jonathan Letterman took a dim view of the results:

The entire garrison covers a space of about eighty or more acres, and the buildings, being of necessity widely separated, cause the post to present more the appearance of a village, whose houses have been built with little regard to order, than a military post. Unseasoned, unhewn, and unbarked pine logs, placed upright in some and horizontally in other houses, have been used in the erection of the buildings, and as a necessary consequence are rapidly decaying. In many of the logs of the house I occupy, an ordinary-sized nail will not hold, to such an extent has the timber decayed, although several feet above the ground. One set of the so-called barracks have lately been torn down to prevent any untoward accidents that were liable at any moment to happen from the falling of the building.

The unbarked logs provided hiding places for bedbugs, who drove the men out of the buildings to sleep except in the most bitter weather. It wasn't until late in 1862 that the Army got around to building a stauncher fort, and by that time some of the first buildings had collapsed. To save the taxpayers' money, the soldiers were required to grow crops for subsistence, too, and it is a wonder that they found time to go galloping off to the rescue of beleaguered wagon trains and stagecoaches. Somehow they fought several Indian campaigns and helped to protect the Santa Fe Trail.

The new fort was built of adobe bricks and stone, and as its importance swelled with the intensified Indian fighting after the Civil War, it grew until it was the most massive of all the forts in the Southwest. Men who served there took a fierce pride in the fort and in its importance to the Santa Fe Trail. Then the railroad came, and the trail itself no longer was important. Captain William Rawle Shoemaker, who served at the fort for thirty years, never forgave the railroad for bringing an end to the adventurous days of the trail.

"That very courtly old gentleman," wrote the chaplain's daughter about the captain, now grown old, "could not be persuaded to ride on the Santa Fe R. R., and had not been in Las Vegas for many years. He preferred his seclusive life within a certain radius of the Arsenal and the garrison, and was constantly in the saddle, a wonderful horseman, even though in his eighties." When he retired in 1882, Captain Shoemaker built a house near the fort where he died four years later. In 1891 the fort itself was abandoned. The garrison marched down the road to Watrous, where they boarded the railroad cars hated so fervently by Captain Shoemaker for shipment to their new post.

The fort's building materials were taken by people living nearby, roofs fell in, and the rains and snows melted away the adobe. The huge walls of adobe dug from the earth inexorably returned to the earth. We visited the fort, now a national monument, at dusk when the ranges of brick chimneys rose against the dying light of the western sky like sentinels watching over the deserted fifteen-hundred-foot parade grounds. Rabbits sprinted about in the roofless commissary storehouse. The wind rustled the prairie grass growing over the deep ruts of the Mountain Branch which ran close to the fallen walls. It chanted among the ruins.

We drove in silence down the road to Watrous where the Mountain Branch and the Cimarron Cutoff became one again to run together to Santa Fe.

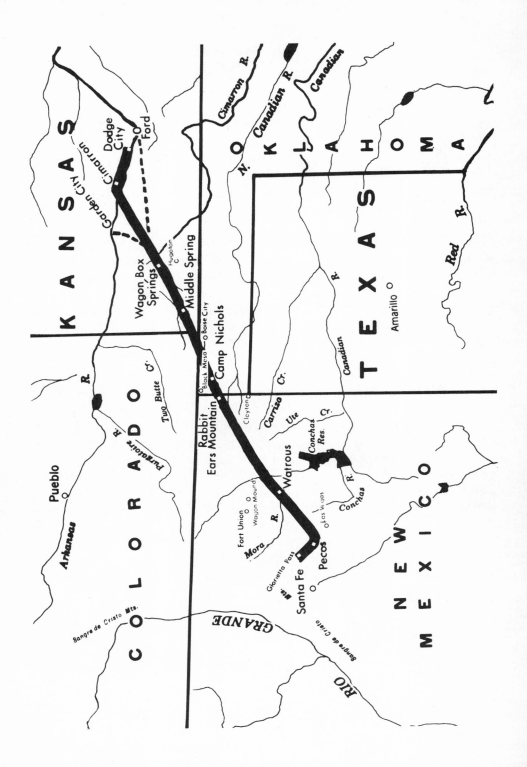

4

Santa Fe Trail:
Cimarron Cutoff

●

"Even the jackrabbits carried three days' rations and a canteen of water," a wheat farmer told us outside a grocery store in Cimarron, Kansas. He was telling about pioneer days in the country between the Arkansas River and the Cimarron River traversed by the Cimarron Cutoff of the Santa Fe Trail. Today the land through which we drove to Hugoton is prosperous, but in the 1930's it was the Kansas Dust Bowl, and long before that it was the dreaded Jornada where wind and sandstorms and Indians tormented the wagon trains.

Josiah Gregg caught the immensity of the Jornada, which fills the mind as it fills the eye. To Gregg the Jornada was "the grand prairie ocean; for not a single landmark is to be seen . . . scarcely a visible eminence by which to direct one's course. All is as level as the sea, and the compass was our surest as well as principal guide."

There were three major crossings of the Arkansas. The Lower Crossing was in the vicinity of Ford, some twenty miles east of Dodge City on U.S. 154; the Upper Crossing was at Chouteau's Island west of Garden City on U.S. 50; and the Middle or Cimarron Crossing was just west of present-day Cimarron. The river and agriculture have wiped out all traces of the crossings.

Most of the trains used the Cimarron Crossing, although the sinkholes and quicksand made it dangerous. The water was shallow, but the river was broad and the current swift. Wagons tipped over in the holes and, if a team paused but for a moment, wheels sank into the sand up to the

47

hubs. It often took a train an entire day to make the crossing, and usually there would be trade fabrics laid out on the sandhills on the south bank to dry.

In the first decades of the trail, the Arkansas was the border with Mexico, and here at the crossing U.S. escort troops halted. Sometimes there were waiting Mexican troops to protect the caravans on the remainder of the journey to the frontier Mexican settlements. Usually there were Indians, watching from afar for weak and undefended trains that would be suitable targets for a raid. After the Mexican War, U.S. troops were responsible for fending off the Indians all the way.

Filling their kegs with Arkansas River water, caravans moved out on the trail to the Cimarron River, fifty miles away. There was no water until the Cimarron, which usually was dry. Caravans had to come out of the Jornada at Wagon Box Springs or risk disaster. William Becknell on his second trip to Santa Fe in 1822 took the Cimarron Cutoff. He had traveled over the Mountain Branch the year before and was looking for a shorter way to Santa Fe. With twenty companions, and three wagons stocked with $3,000 worth of trade goods, he moved off onto the plains. The wagons were the first to go over the Santa Fe Trail.

In the Jornada the caravan suffered horribly. Canteens were dry, and the sun burned down. Men ran short of food, killed their dogs, and dined on their scrawny carcasses. They tipped their mules' ears and sucked the blood. A buffalo blundered into their camp. Gregg wrote about the incident in his *Commerce of the Prairies*: "The hapless intruder was immediately dispatched and an invigorating draught procured from its stomach. I have since heard one of the parties to that expedition declare that nothing ever passed his lips which gave him such exquisite delight as his first draught of that filthy beverage." Reasoning that the buffalo couldn't possibly have so much water in its stomach if there were no spring handy, the men reconnoitered the countryside and found a spring.

The wheat fields through which we drove on U.S. 56 are heavy with grain made possible by irrigation water pumped from four hundred feet deep in the earth where we were assured there was a limitless supply. Yet only ten miles north of us, caravans over the Cimarron Cutoff suffered in what was then the "Cimarron Desert." As the wagon trains searched for water, Comanches and Kiowas searched the plains for them.

In late May, 1831, Jedediah Smith, perhaps the greatest mountain man of them all, came along the Cutoff with William and Thomas Sublette and Broken Hand Fitzpatrick. He was making one more journey with a trading caravan before going east to write his memoirs. Water ran short

48

as the company crossed the Jornada. Telling Fitzpatrick to hold the caravan in a sheltering hollow, Diah rode ahead in search of a spring. On the banks of the dry Cimarron he came upon a Comanche hunting party. He made signs of peace, but the Indians waved blankets to frighten his horse. As it wheeled in terror, they shot Diah in the back. Falling to the ground, he still killed the chief with a straight shot before the warriors rode him down with lances. We turned north from Hugoton on U.S. 270 where after an eighteen-mile drive we came to the place where the Santa Fe Trail reached the Lower or Wagon Box Springs in the dry bed of the Cimarron. Close to where he is thought to have died, there is a monument to Jedediah Smith, a man who knew the Bible and Shakespeare's poetry as he knew the wilderness.

The Lower Spring which meant life to the caravans crossing the Jornada is now a dry cistern. Then it formed a narrow pool in the river bed several hundred feet long around which grass grew. In 1914 the dry Cimarron became not only wet but rose in flood. Tree seeds were swept into the area around the spring, and since then they have grown up so that we found a small tangle of woods where caravans found only a grassy marsh. In the later days of the trail a trader put an old wagon box into the spring to provide a trough from which to drink. A rancher named James found the wagon box there long after the last caravan had passed into history, but there is no sign of it today. We could make out the trail coming from the northeast and running off to the southwest from the springs.

From Wagon Box Springs the trail ran along the tortuous Cimarron. Although the riverbed was usually dry, men sometimes could find water by digging into the sands. Otherwise they had to reach the Middle Springs before they could slake their thirst.

Kansas State Highway 27 leads north of Elkhart into the Cimarron National Grasslands. About nine miles from town it crosses the Cimarron River. Just beyond the bridge a ranch road runs to the Middle Spring. The dust storms of the 1930's buried the spring, but it has been dug out again and now is tapped by pipes hidden in the tall grass. The old trail can easily be made out through this wild country. It runs north of the springs and across the face of the Point of Rocks, which travelers over the trail fondly likened to the prow of a ship. Today a dirt road climbs to the top of Point of Rocks, which is three miles to the west.

Kit Carson first earned frontier fame here at Point of Rocks. In 1841 Kit and five other trappers were attacked by two hundred Comanches. Caught in the open without cover, the party killed their mules and hid behind the bodies. The trappers defeated the Indians in a three-day battle.

Cimarron Cutoff touches the southeast tip of Colorado and cuts into Oklahoma where wagon trains crossed the Cimarron just south of the border. Here, where cottonwoods shade pools of water, Albert Speyer and his caravan of mules were marooned in September, 1844, by an unseasonal snowstorm. Most of the mules died of starvation and the bitter cold that followed the snow. For years to come travelers on the trail arranged and rearranged the hapless animals' bones in macabre patterns so as to perplex and entertain the men in the next caravan to pass.

The trail slices through the Oklahoma Panhandle's range country to Cold Springs and Upper Spring, now called Flag Springs by people in the vicinity, both northwest of Boise City. Swinging southwest around the massive Black Mesa, towering cliffs of volcanic lava that rise seven hundred feet above the high plains, the trail reaches Cedar Bluff Springs, from where it can easily be traced for a score of miles.

A quarter mile east of the campgrounds at the Cedar Bluffs Spring and three miles northeast of the ranch town of Wheless, Kit Carson and his New Mexico and California Volunteers established Camp Nichols in May, 1865. The post was intended to protect wagon trains using the Cimarron Cutoff, halfway on the three-hundred-mile stretch between Fort Union and the Cimarron Crossing of the Arkansas. By June the men had built six officers' quarters and a quartermaster building. The men were housed in tents that at least had the luxury of stone walls. Breastworks of stone and banked earth protected the camp from Indian attack. During the summer of 1865 trains bound east from New Mexico assembled at Camp Nichols and then set out with an escort of fifty men for the Arkansas. The camp was abandoned that September, and today broken stone walls and foundations are all that are left. The breastwork still looks as if it would be hard to assault. In the center of the enclosure is an area twenty feet wide by one hundred feet long that is paved in flagstone. The tie rack for the horse herd was here.

Clayton, New Mexico, lies close to double-peaked Rabbit Ear Mountain, an outcropping of the Rockies, which to the traders was the very symbol of the Cimarron Cutoff. Trains kept it in view for four days as they plodded west from the upper springs. In the area near Clayton are several campsites and springs that are all protected in the National Registered Historic Landmark called the Clayton Complex. Just across the New Mexico border east of Clayton, we turned off U.S. 56 and drove north on New Mexico 18 to McNees Crossing. The owners of the land have never broken the soil out of respect for the historic trail. The ruts of the wagons descend the ridge to the east and lead to the banks of Corrumpa Creek.

In 1828 two young traders, McNees and Monroe, galloped ahead of the slow-moving caravan with which they were returning home to Franklin from Santa Fe. At Corrumpa Creek they drank their fill of the cool water, washed, and fell asleep. No sooner had they fallen asleep than a party of Indians emerged from cover and, taking their guns, shot them. When the caravan came up, the traders found McNees dead and Monroe dying. McNees was the first trader to be killed by Indians on the Santa Fe Trail.

The traders buried McNees on the creek bank, and the crossing soon took his name. They carried Monroe forty miles to the Cimarron before he died. As they were burying the murdered youth, a half-dozen Comanches appeared on the opposite bank of the river. The Indians made signs of peace, but the grieving traders, not caring whether these were the guilty men or not, opened fire. All but one Indian pitched from his horse. The survivor rode away to tell his tribe what had happened.

From that point on the Comanches harried the caravan clear to the Arkansas. Attacking and attacking again, the Comanches stole a thousand mules and horses. Then they fell back to strike at the next caravan on the trail. The bloodshed commenced at McNees Crossing and on the banks of the Cimarron continued for decades.

The camp sites and springs north of Clayton are unspoiled. Only names have changed. What traders called Turkey Creek is now Alamos Creek, and Rabbit Ears Creek is now Cieniguilla Creek. The ruts of the wagons are weathered but plain to see, and the campsites on these streams are as attractive to today's campers as they must have been to the traders. From the Rabbit Ears traders sent a messenger riding ahead to Santa Fe to let the people know that they were coming.

The trail runs on today much as it did one hundred years ago to Round Mound or Pilot Mountain and Point of Rocks. At Point of Rocks in October, 1849, Santa Fe merchant J. M. White, his family, servants, and two other travelers were attacked by the Jicarilla Apaches. The Indians killed all the men and rode away with Mrs. White and her daughter. They had not gone far when Kit Carson and his scouts caught up with them. The Indians killed Mrs. White rather than surrender her to the scouts. The little girl vanished, even though the thirty-first Congress of the United States in 1850 voted a $1,500 reward for her return. U.S. 56 passes close to the place where the White family and their party were attacked.

Point of Rocks is the southeasternmost spur of the Raton Mountains. It is only a short journey from their tumbled slopes to Wagon Mound, last great landmark of the Cimarron Cutoff. Traders camped in a natural bowl at Santa Clara Springs two miles northwest of the mountain. The bowl proved an ideal shelter from the wind that blew across the plains, but it also was a natural trap. Indians ambushed dozens of trains camped at the springs.

The first Mexican settlements were at La Junta at the junction of the Mora and Sapello rivers where outlying ranchos of Mexican sheepherders and later a fort and stores were built. At La Junta, now called Watrous, the Mountain Branch and the Cimarron Cutoff came together. The trails became one again near the Sapello Crossing where later the Sapello stage station and the corral for Fort Union were established.

The Santa Fe Trail leads on through New Mexico to Las Vegas. The plaza of the old town in west Las Vegas looks much as it did when the caravans rolled into it. Townspeople ran to the wagons peddling eggs, cheese, and fiery aguardiente. Traders got their first glimpse of the dark-eyed Mexican girls. In the plaza Kearny's soldiers paraded while the general stood on the balcony of a building that still stands today to read his proclamation that the United States had come to New Mexico to stay. Here also in Old Town was the Imperial Saloon on Moreno Street, which was the lair of Vicente Silva. Not all Mexicans accepted American rule. Among these were Vicente Silva and his forty bandits. They probably wouldn't have accepted Mexican rule either. They enlivened the last days of the trail by robbing stagecoaches and waylaying pack trains. They terrorized the Las Vegas area for twenty years and managed to keep their roster secret. This isn't too surprising when the fate of two defectors is learned. One was hanged from a bridge in town. The other was stuffed down a privy just off the plaza.

San Miguel, a rude collection of adobe huts on the banks of the Pecos River, was the next settlement on the trail. The adobe houses, dirt streets, and central plaza of the town are still dominated by the church. The trail rounded the southern prow of the Sangre de Cristos Mountains and came to the crumbling ruins of Pecos Pueblo. U.S. 85 follows the Santa Fe Trail as it swings in from the southeast towards Santa Fe. The ruins of Pecos are just off the highway three miles south of the town of Pecos.

The well-fortified pueblo, which was old when Coronado stopped there in 1540, and its mission which was founded in 1617, withstood the attacks of marauding Indians until the nineteenth century. Then it was stricken by smallpox in 1838, which left it so weak that the survivors moved away to Jemez rather than face annihilation from the threatening Comanches. The immense deserted pueblo fascinated the traders, who were convinced that the great Aztec emperor Montezuma must have lived there. Excavations at the pueblo, now in a state park, have revealed the ancient kiva, the foundations of the terraced four-story houses and the great stone wall which once kept out enemies.

Only a few miles from the ruins the trail enters Glorieta Pass, described by James Josiah Webb in 1844:

We enter the big canyon, where the road winds and turns, crossing steep pitches and ravines, over rocks, and around boulders, making short and difficult turns, with double teams to make an ascent. At other places the turns are so short that only two or three yoke of cattle can be allowed to pull a load, from danger of turning over into the ravine. One of these difficult passes we called the "S," which required all the skill of the best drivers to get around. And often wagons would be turned over with all the precautions we could use. Six or eight miles a day was considered good traveling.

Here in the pass Governor Manuel Armijo made a show of defending Santa Fe against General Kearny's American invaders, and here on March 26 and 27, 1862, Union forces defeated Confederates striking east from Santa Fe. The "Gettysburg of the West" ended significant Southern military action in New Mexico.

At last the laboring caravans reached Arroyo Hondo, where they camped in preparation for tomorrow's entry into Santa Fe.

"Los Americanos! Los Carros!" cried the people as the freight wagons rolled down what is now College Street to the Plaza. Each wagon swung once around the plaza, setting up a cloud of dust, and then came to a halt at the end of the Santa Fe Trail. Josiah Gregg described the scene:

Crowds of women and boys flocked around to see the newcomers, while crowds of "leperos" hung about, as usual, to see what they could pilfer. The wagoners were by no means free from excitement on this occasion. Informed of the "ordeal" they had to pass, they had spent the previous night in "rubbing up;" and now they were prepared with clean faces, sleek-combed hair and their choicest Sunday suit to meet the "fair eyes" of glistening black that were sure to stare at them as they passed. There was yet another preparation made to show off to advantage. Each wagoner must tie a brand new cracker to the lash of his whip, for on driving through the streets and the "plaza publica" everyone strives to outvie his comrades in the dexterity with which he flourishes this favorite badge of his authority.

We drove down College Street, too. Santa Fe's La Fonda is still the hotel at the end of the trail, and there we stayed.

We walked through the Plaza where artists were painting the Palace of the Governors, which has stood there since 1610. Indian women from the nearby pueblos were selling pottery, jewelry, and blankets to tourists beneath the shady arcades. Black-eyed shoeshine boys flashed ready grins to solicit trade, and when the bell in the cathedral chimed, they all set up a melodious chorus of imitated bells in response. As it began to grow dark, gas lights were lit and the city took on a festive air. There was the sound of singing from the cantinas, and the aroma of peppery food cooking. We had come from Franklin to sundown at the end of the Santa Fe Trail.

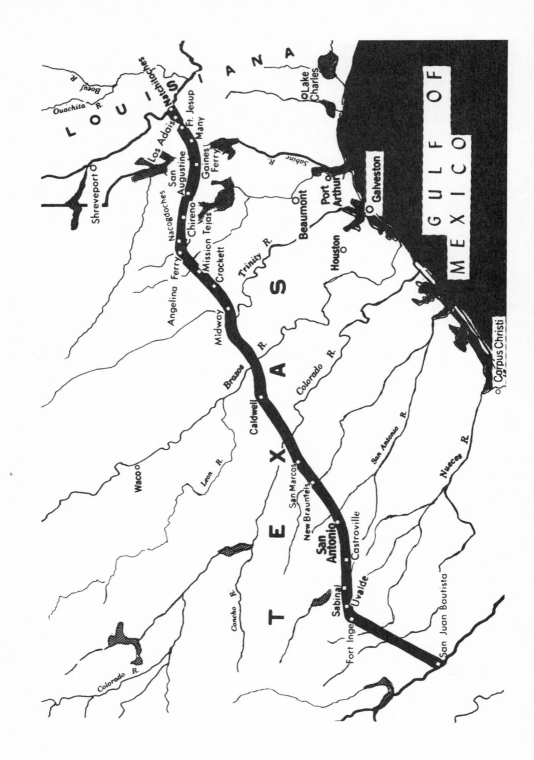

5

El Camino Real:
The Old San Antonio Road

●

LaSalle and his men followed the Indian trail, later known to the Spanish as El Camino Real, and found it "as well beaten a road as that from Paris to Orleans." This was in 1685, and yet 168 years later, in 1854, when Frederick Law Olmsted took the trail, by then known as the Old San Antonio Road, from Natchitoches, Louisiana, across Texas to San Antonio and on to the Mexican border, he reported that "the road could hardly be called a road. It was only a way where people had passed along before. Each man had taken such a path as suited him, turning aside to avoid on high ground the sand, on low ground the mud. We chose generally the untrodden elastic pavement of pine leaves at a little distance from the main track."

Louisiana State Highway 6 runs southwest of Natchitoches along the route of the trail to the Texas border where Texas State Highway 21 traces the route except for one long stretch west of Midway, where a road marked on maps simply "OSR" for Old San Antonio Road follows it.

"We paved the Old San Antonio Road to make it a modern highway," a Texan explained to me. "It is a road tied up in our history with the Alamo and the settling of the country, and we're not about to lose track of just where it ran."

When seen from across the expanse of Cane River Lake, once a channel of the Red River, Natchitoches has the unmistakable Creole roof lines which distinguish the Vieux Carré of New Orleans. The city, founded by the French in 1714, is older than New Orleans, and above the plate-glass store fronts downtown hang old galleries edged with iron lace. Walk the residential streets where shady oaks shelter old houses built of adobe with hand-hewn cypress sills and rafters joined by wooden pegs. Many of the houses have outside stairways winding up to the second floor. Roistering young bachelors returning home from late-hour revels used an outside stairway to enter the house without disturbing mama and papa who were snoring in the massive canopied bed in the master bedroom.

In Natchitoches people laze in the sun on wrought-iron benches along Front Street or fish in the lake for catfish with shrimp and minnow bait. The city is a sleepy college town, but once it was the great entrepôt at the headwaters of navigation on the Red River. Just above the town the river was choked by a hundred-mile long tangle of logs known as the Great Raft, and boats could go no higher. At first flat and keel boats heaped with merchandise were poled or cordeled upstream from New Orleans. Then after 1820 steamboats carried ever greater cargoes to the city wharves along Front Street, where trade goods were packed onto mules or loaded into freight wagons for the long haul over El Camino Real to Texas and Mexico.

Timothy Flint, a missionary who traveled widely along the early nineteenth century frontier, visited Natchitoches, noted its strategic position between Mexico and the Mississippi River system, and wrote, "It will one day become the largest town in this country, except New Orleans." Flint could scarcely have known that not many years after his visit the Red River would burst into a new channel and leave Natchitoches stranded five miles away on a shallow backwater. By the time Olmsted arrived, he had to go ashore at Grand Ecore and follow the old dry channel to Natchitoches.

From the start Natchitoches was linked with Mexico. The gallant French trader Louis Juchereau de St. Denis and twenty-four French voyageurs and six Indian guides built the first two cabins on the west bank of the Red River in November of 1714. The next year they began erecting a comfortable and staunch fort. Fort St. Jean Baptiste de Natchitoches became a bastion of the French king on the border of the domains of the King of Spain. The earthworks of the fort still stand in the American Cemetery in Natchitoches.

Even as the fort was being built, St. Denis hastened over the trail to the Presidio of San Juan Bautista on the Rio Grande, where he tried to persuade the Spanish to trade with him. He argued that the Spanish had much silver and gold, and the French had merchandise. His arguments ran counter to the edicts of the Spanish king, who wished to channel all Spanish colonial trade to Spain, and St. Denis was arrested and taken to Mexico City where he was thrown into prison.

Such was the young Frenchman's charm that he soon talked his way out of prison, married Manuella, the beautiful granddaughter of Don Diego Escalante de Ramon, Commandant of the Presidio of San Juan Bautista, and was engaged to guide a group of Spanish priests and soldiers along the trail to east Texas to establish a chain of missions. He was delighted to do this, for he astutely reasoned that if he could get the Spanish to settle in east Texas close to his new post on the Red River, they would have little choice except to trade with him.

Seventy-five soldiers, settlers, artisans and herdsmen set out to found the new missions. They were afoot, on muleback, on horseback and riding in big-wheeled oxcarts loaded with blue and red woolen cloth, tobacco, butcher knives, beads, medals, and ribbons to charm the Indians. In the carts there were also hardtack and flour and chocolate to eat on the way, and hoes, axes and cook pots, brass candlesticks, copper fonts and bells for the missions. To add to their diet on the trail the party hunted for game, fished, and traded for corn and beans in Indian villages.

One Spanish governor once remarked that if it were in his power he would even stop the birds from flying over the border into Texas, but as a practical matter most of the governors ruling Texas from Los Adais, founded in what is now Louisiana close to Natchitoches, winked at the trade between the Spanish and French. The pattern was set for trade between first Spanish and French, then Spanish and Americans, and finally Mexicans and Americans. Even Spanish padres were dependent upon the French for a source of wine to celebrate mass, and El Camino Real became a pathway of commerce. Of course, a smuggler's detour took traders around each Spanish post along the road so that Spanish law could officially be upheld while everybody except perhaps the King in Madrid knew that trade was flourishing across the frontier.

The Bayou Amulet in Natchitoches, now choked with vegetation, was originally called "Bayou à Mule" because of the traders' mules tied to the trees along its banks. Pack trains of as many as four hundred mules and horses came over the trail from San Antonio and even distant Mexico City, carrying bars of silver, dried buffalo tongues and skins. They took home French silks, woolen and cotton goods, groceries, spirits, and tobacco. Spanish soldiers stationed at the Presidio of Los Adais spent their silver and gold coins for French goods, and the wives of Spanish settlers looked to the French for household necessities. The French had no priest, and they regularly attended church services at the Spanish mission. After mass, the Spanish women told the visiting French women what they needed, and next Sunday the French women brought small articles concealed in their voluminous garments from the eyes of the Spanish officials, who knew exactly what was going on but knew better than to interfere with the pretty smugglers.

I rented a car to drive from Natchitoches along the Old San Antonio Road. Lunching in a restaurant at the edge of town, I gazed out over a junior high school playing field where youngsters, looking at a distance like hyperactive puppets, were exercising to where the Old San Antonio Road climbed out of the Red River bottoms into the hills.

"How do we find the Old Stone Fort?" a tourist asked the cashier.

"That's in Nacogdoches," the cashier replied.

"Isn't that where we are?"

"No, this is Natchitoches, Louisiana, and the Old Stone Fort is in Nacogdoches, Texas."

Motorists following the Old San Antonio Road have good reason to resent a Caddo Indian chief of long ago. One day as the tribe camped on the banks of the Sabine River, which now divides Louisiana from Texas, he called his two sons to him. One, he said, should take several families with him and travel for three days to the east and found a new village. The other should take several families and travel three days to the west and also found a new village.

The sons did as they were asked. Fifty miles east of the Sabine, one founded a village which is now Natchitoches; fifty miles west of the Sabine, the other founded a village which is now Nacogdoches. In so doing they mixed up early French and Spanish travelers over the road, the U.S. Post Office, which regularly sends mail to the wrong town, a troop of actors who mistakenly opened their play in Nacogdoches when they were expected in Natchitoches, and novelist Erskine Caldwell, who lectured at the college in one town when he had promised to lecture at the college of the other.

It is only a four-mile drive through rolling hills and creek bottoms to the Arroyo Hondo, a small stream which once separated French from Spanish territory and later delineated the eastern border of the Neutral Strip between Spain and the United States. A few miles farther down the road I turned off at McCoo's Grocery Store to visit a hilltop, which for fifty years, until 1773, was the capital of Spanish Texas. The wind moaned through the pines, and fallen needles were springy underfoot. In a clearing, picnickers were playing baseball, for the site is now a state park. I half expected a boy sliding into third base to turn up a rusting Spanish halberd, because the game was taking place where in 1721 the Spanish under the Marquis de Agauyo built the Presidio de Nuestra Señora Del Pilar de Los Adais, just fifteen miles from French Natchitoches. Somewhere in the now vanished fort, Spanish governors penned angry reports about their French neighbors for the benefit of the viceroy in Mexico City, while in reality they were attending parties and dinners with their presumed enemies. When in 1744 St. Denis, grown old and tired, died, Spanish Governor Morales wrote to Mexico City, "St. Denis is dead, thank God, now we can breathe easier." He then put on mourning to go to the Frenchman's funeral, where he shed tears for the loss of a dear friend.

From atop the hill I could look across another hill where cattle grazed. There in 1717 the Spanish established the Mission of San Miguel de Los Adais, the only Spanish mission built in what is now Louisiana. The presidio and mission of Los Adais were abandoned by the Spanish when Louisiana became a possession of Spain. Their inhabitants were forcibly removed to San Antonio because they were no longer needed to protect the border.

Between the Arroyo Hondo and the Sabine River the Old San Antonio Road crossed the Neutral Strip, a no man's land which was set up by General James Wilkinson representing the United States and General Herrera representing Spain. This forty-mile wide strip of territory was involved in the Burr-Wilkinson plot to detach part of the American Southwest and combine it with part of the Spanish realm to create a new nation. When the intrigue was exploded and Burr brought to trial, the Free State of Sabine instead of becoming a portion of a new nation became the domain of bandits and filibusters, together with a few honest trappers and settlers. A traveler on the Old San Antonio Road carried his own security in the form of a rifle or a pistol.

Bandit gangs in the Neutral Strip fought among themselves until the son of a Methodist minister brought quarreling gangs together. John Murrell had learned to quote scriptures from his father and learned nefarious ways from his mother, who kept a tavern near her husband's church. Posing as a Methodist circuit rider by day, he led the bandit gangs by night. He organized the outlaw factions into seven clans, each responsible to him. A clansman riding along the Old San Antonio Road knew when he was passing the home of a friend, because the homesteaders in the Strip who sympathized with the clans set out a white locust tree between two Spanish dagger plants. The "Reverend Devil," as he was known to his followers, reportedly buried several treasures, and today men with metal detectors go prospecting for them on weekends.

On the east side of the Old San Antonio Road and a mile northeast of the remains of Fort Jesup is the site of Halfway House, where smiling Peter Parker and his gang played innkeeper to unwary travelers. People who stopped at the tavern were robbed of their belongings.

Parker, who had the manner of a gentleman, advised his guests, "Pull your latch string inside your door when you retire at night, or someone may slip into your room when you are asleep and rob you and may even steal your clothing."

He refrained from mentioning that there was a small crack in every door through which a thin bladed knife would be inserted when the guest had fallen asleep. The cross bar was then easily lifted, and the guest robbed. In case a sleeper awoke and found a Parker henchman in the room, the man explained that he had been trying the doors and having found this one unlocked was checking to see that the guest had not been disturbed. The Parkers were always courteous to women traveling with their husbands, because they reasoned that women whom they treated hospitably would tell other people about the fine, honest Parkers and this would counteract any ill reports that men robbed at the inn might spread. A man appropriately named John Doe was among the criminals who frequented the Halfway House. He created bogus dollars in a mint in the cellar.

The kitchen is all that is left of Fort Jesup, once command headquarters for all U.S. troops west of a line drawn from west Florida to Lake Superior.
Hodges Gardens Staff Photo

James Gaines, brother of the commander at Fort Jesup, built the Gaines House at his ferry across the Sabine River. It was dismantled to make way for the Toledo Bend Reservoir, but it is to be rebuilt on higher ground.   *Hodges Gardens Staff Photo*

The Halfway House at Chereno, Texas, appears huge and gray, a massive structure from the days of stagecoaches rattling along the Old San Antonio Road.
Hodges Gardens Staff Photo

Gil Y Barbo built the Old Stone Fort in Nacogdoches, Texas, as a trading post. It stood on the Old San Antonio Road until it was twice moved. Today it can be found on the Stephen F. Austin State College campus. *Hodges Gardens Staff Photo*

In 1822 Zachary Taylor marched into the Neutral Strip with U.S. troops to found Cantonment Jesup on a hill overlooking the Old San Antonio Road to protect the U.S. border and to subdue the bandits preying upon travelers. Stone was quarried in the neighboring hills for some forty buildings, and by the 1830's Fort Jesup had become one of the most important posts in the West. Only the original kitchen still stands, but a restored officers' quarters contains a museum. Where once regimental bands played, belles and their beaux strolled arm in arm, and horse races and gander pullings were held is now a grassy meadow.

Soldiers patroled the countryside in vain, for the bandits slipped away on back trails known only to themselves. The criminal element paid the soldiers back for their attention by establishing Shawnee Town close to the fort to afford entertainment for the men languishing in the wilderness. The Rev. R. M. Maure says that Shawnee Town was established "to supply the evils which in those days were believed to be necessary to every frontier garrison. Here flourished the saloon, the gambling house, and the other auxiliaries of disorder."

A game of cards called Bragg often lasted for six days with a new soldier taking the place of each player as he quit in exhaustion or bankruptcy. Fort Jesup had the largest payroll in Louisiana, and the bandits of Shawnee Town found that they soon were taking far more money from the military than they ever had from the travelers that the soldiers had come to protect.

Fort Jesup became command headquarters for all United States troops west of a line drawn from West Florida to Lake Superior, and it was the staging point in 1845 for Zachary Taylor's invasion of Mexico. After the Mexican War the frontier was advanced to the Rio Grande, and Fort Jesup was abandoned as a military post. In 1850 the government offered the site to the new Louisiana State University, but it was declined. The land was broken up into lots and sold. Buildings facing on the San Antonio Road became stores and inns. Drunken loafers moved into other old buildings and set fire to them or carted away the lumber. Only the kitchen remained, and it was used as a schoolhouse, a church, and finally for roller-skating and gambling. Now it has been furnished as it was in army days so that travelers along today's Old San Antonio Road can see how the army lived on the now vanished southwestern frontier. The site is a prime source for old cannonballs and uniform buttons. Lieutenant Donald E. Taber brought an army radio mine detector to the site from Camp Leroy Johnson at New Orleans, and he found all kinds of things in the topsoil ranging from old pieces of farming equipment to triggers and knife blades.

It is an easy drive down a modern highway to Many today, but it was different for the pioneers that Frederick Olmsted passed on the road. He wrote:

Before you come upon them you hear ringing through the woods the fierce cries and blows with which they urge on their jaded cattle. Then the stragglers appear, lean dogs or fainting negroes, ragged and spiritless. An old granny hauling on by the hand a weak boy—too old to ride and too young to keep up. An old man, heavily loaded with a rifle. Then the white covers of the wagons jerking up and down as they mount over a root or plunge into a rut, disappearing one after another where the road descends. Then the active and cheery prime negroes, not yet exhausted, with a joke and a suggestion about tobacco. Then the black pickaninnies staring in a confused heap out at the back of the wagon, more and more of their eyes to be made out among the table legs and bedding as you get near; behind them, further in, the old people and young mothers whose turn it is to ride. As you get by, the white mother and babies and the tall, frequently ill-humored master on horseback or walking with his gun, urging up the black driver and his oxen. As a scout ahead is a brother, or an intelligent slave, with the best gun, on the lookout for a deer or turkey.

After 1803 Moses Austin and thousands of colonists entered Texas over the Old San Antonio Road. Wagon trains traveled ten to fifteen miles a day, and it usually took two days to go from the settlement of Many to the Texas border. Often the pioneers stopped in the vicinity of the old Camp Sabine blockhouse. Now a blacktop and dirt road leads off the Old San Antonio Road to the Beulah Baptist Church, which is the site of the old blockhouse. What looks like any other country church with a graveyard was once a strategic outpost of Fort Jesup. Here in 1806 General Wilkinson met with Burr's representative to plan for a private southwest empire. After the outpost was deserted, the blockhouse became a famed Baptist meetinghouse, which was torn down for the present church. The spring used by the soldiers remains about one hundred yards south of the church.

The Old San Antonio Road today sweeps over the hills and down to the banks of the Toledo Bend Reservoir formed by the dammed waters of the Sabine River. Sitting at dinner in a motel in San Augustine, Texas, I was approached by a rangy superintendent of the Deep East Texas Electric Co-op named Ray Wells.

"You the fellow who's following the Old San Antonio Road?" he asked. "Do you want to fly over it?"

After storms Ray flies a Champion Citaborca, which is Acrobatic spelled backwards, along the power lines to spot breaks. Since he was born on a Sabine River bottoms farm, he knows the old road well. Early in the morning we took off from a grassy runway and flew back to the Toledo Bend Reservoir on the Texas-Louisiana border. Air currents buffeted us as we came in low. Below us drowned trees thrust out of the water like reeds sticking from a pond. We could make out the old river channel swirling down through the desolation of the forest.

Until a few years ago the oldest house with glass windows in Texas stood on the west bank of the Sabine where the road crossed the river. Roses rambled up the leading chimney of the house built by James Gaines, a Virginian who established a ferry at the point in 1806. Later a man named Strather took over the ferry. He was the best shot in the county and delighted in shooting his old Kentucky rifle at a miniscule target 120 yards away, a feat that kept Neutral Strip bandits from ever trying to rob the ferry. From the air we could make out the old well from the Gaines house on a little island on the Texas side of the river channel. Water flows over the old road. We flew over a graveyard.

"Davy Crockett had a fight down there on the way to the Alamo," shouted Ray over the roar of the motor as we banked in low. "He came out the winner. The other fellow started the graveyard."

It was easy to make out the old road snaking among the hills. West of San Augustine we saw upright old houses, gaunt and proud along the route of the abandoned road. The Halfway Inn at Chireno appeared huge and gray from the air, a massive structure stranded in time. As we flew over Egg Nog Creek, a dry wrinkle in the woods, Ray explained its history:

It was named by some Texans. A bunch of Texan rebels had holed up in the Old Stone Fort in Nacogdoches. They rode off to the east when the Mexican army approached down the road from the west. They camped on the creek down there and waited for reinforcements. To while away the evening, they made egg nogs. Powered by egg nogs they galloped back towards Nacogdoches. The Mexicans, seeing a big cloud of dust coming, decided that a whole regiment must be charging to the attack. They fled the town. A little later an old Indian woman came into town as a spy. She hurried back and told the Mexicans that the same small bunch that ran away before had made all the commotion. The Mexican army returned and got ready to attack. By now the Texans were sobered up, and they once again rode off to the east to camp on Egg Nog Creek.

San Augustine was settled by Anglo-American settlers in the early nineteenth century close to where the Spanish had built the Mission

Nuestra Señora de Los Dolores in 1717 on the banks of Ayish Bayou. It became the gathering place for adventurers and filibusters bent on over-throwing Spanish and Mexican rule in Texas, and today it is proud to call itself the "Cradle of Texas Independence." Where the Old San Antonio Road runs through the town there are many houses out of the colorful past of the city. Old women wearing sunbonnets bend over the blooms in their gardens and are proud that Sam Houston walked the town's streets and that Davy Crockett stopped here on his way to the Alamo. To pioneers San Augustine meant that they were finished with the pine forests. Olmsted found San Augustine to be a straggle of houses and shops around a muddy square.

"As to the people," he reported, "a resident told us there was but one man in the town that was not in the constant habit of getting drunk, and that this gentleman relaxed his Puritanic severity during our stay in view of the fact that Christmas came but once a year."

Olmsted arrived in San Augustine in time for the Christmas celebration in 1853. A band of men and boys blowing horns and beating on tin pans marched around the square. They went from house to house, kicking open the doors and pulling out all the male citizens to join them in the merry hullabaloo. If the householder would not join them, they tore down his fence to show their disapproval of his lack of Christmas spirit.

In the 1840's both the Methodists and the Presbyterians established colleges in San Augustine. There were few students to be enrolled on the frontier, and Wesleyan College quarreled with the University of San Augustine over boys and girls who came to town for an education. One day the president of the Presbyterian college was shot dead in the street by a supporter of the Methodist college. The murder led to a frontier ecumenical movement in which both colleges were combined in the University of East Texas under the supervision of the Masons. Boys stayed in one building, and girls in the other. The University of East Texas shortly expired, and the San Augustine Elementary School now occupies its site.

Stripling's Drugstore on Columbia Street close to the square has a pioneer well at the soda fountain. An early-day saloonkeeper on the spot kept his beer cool by lowering it into the well. In 1917 the First National Bank of San Augustine bought the frame saloon building and tore it down. The bank bricked over the well. In 1951 the bank built a new building and sold its old one, including its bricked-over liquid assets, to R. N. Stripling, who cleaned out the well. Soda jerks crank a windlass to pull up an old oaken bucket. Coffee made with the water is served to travelers along the modern Old San Antonio Road.

Highway engineers have straightened out some of the old road's swoops and loops so that west of San Augustine you have to quit State Highway 21 to see pioneer Chereno, which grew up along the road. A mile west of Chereno I came to Halfway House, which was built of lumber brought over the Old San Antonio Road by ox team. A woman with sagging stockings showed me around the inn.

"We've got an old-timey bathtub," she announced, and indeed there it was, sitting next to a modern tub in a bathroom. In the winter the woman closes up the pioneer fireplaces and heats with electricity. Years ago the tavern's owners papered the interior walls to keep out the drafts, but the driving rains have seeped through and the wallpaper has cracked. I was able to look outside through holes large enough to stick a finger in. No wonder Olmsted reported that he could see the stars through holes in walls of inns where he stopped.

The inn looks rude to modern eyes, but to pioneers it must have seemed a palace. Most early-day travelers stayed in cabins where supper was almost invariably fresh or salt pork, cold cornbread, and boiled sweet potatoes eaten in a lean-to behind the house. Breakfast was the same, with the addition of coffee. During a norther it was so chilly at night that travelers slept in overcoats, hats and boots, covered by blankets. They used their saddlebags as pillows.

Main Street, Nacogdoches, was once the Old San Antonio Road. An Andalusian, Gil Y Barbo, moved the Spanish settlement at Bucareli in 1779 because it was exposed to floods and Indian attacks and located it where Nacogdoches now stands. All the picturesque old buildings have disappeared from Main Street. Even the Old Stone Fort, erected by Gil Y Barbo as a trading post, was torn down in 1902 to make way for a drugstore. Considering that Davy Crockett, Jim Bowie, Thomas Rusk, and Sam Houston had taken their oath of allegiance to Mexico in the building and that it had been the "capitol" of the abortive Republic of Fredonia, this seemed a sorry fate for the Old Stone Fort. It was rebuilt in 1907 on the corner of the Nacogdoches High School grounds and then torn down again and rebuilt of the original stones on the campus of Stephen F. Austin State College. It is now a museum crammed with such things as fading dresses, arrowheads, and a pouch which once belonged to Sitting Bull.

West of Nacogdoches the road winds down into the Angelina Bottoms where in the 1850's the traveler rode among fields of cotton. Today the land is covered with scrub forest broken by brushy meadows in which cattle graze. Then a rude causeway led for two to three miles to the Angelina ferry. A bridge now crosses the Angelina River, which is a narrow stream flowing between clay banks.

The road leads southwest through Davy Crockett National Forest past Indian mounds and old Spanish mission sites. Springs gush from which Davy Crockett and Jim Bowie stopped to refresh themselves, but they are posted, "water unsafe for drinking." Vacationers were camping at Pine Springs Camp Grounds where pioneers also camped, and a short hike down a path leads to one of the historic springs.

San Francisco de Los Tejas Mission State Park contains a replica of the first mission founded in east Texas by Franciscan friars in 1690. When the friars arrived, the Hosinai Indians kept repeating "Tejas." This was their word for "friend," but the Spanish took it to be the name of their tribe. Soon the whole region and ultimately the state of Texas were named "friend" because of the Franciscans' linguistic error. At first the Spanish mission prospered, but then smallpox spread among the Indians. Three thousand died, and the fathers scurried about baptizing the sick before they could die unchristened. Their zeal failed to please the Indians, who came to believe that the holy water and chants brought death. Mounting Indian anger and the failure of crops caused by a drought led the Franciscans to abandon their mission. In 1693 they buried the bell because it was to heavy to carry, burned the wooden chapel, and started back along El Camino Real to the west.

Crockett is twenty miles west of the site of the mission. Five miles east of the town I stopped to see an old stagecoach inn built as a home by Joseph D. Rice in 1828. The local historical society intends to restore the old inn, but meanwhile a visitor can look right through its broken walls to see an old saddle decaying on one wall and a box of nails sitting on the floor. Crockett is a quiet place with a big concrete and stone courthouse in the square. During pioneer days, settlers fled into its predecessor —a log courthouse—when Indians threatened. Olmsted found that the citizens were indifferent Christians, who kept their stores open on Sunday and let anybody preach in their church who happened to come along the road. He also commented that crackers in Crockett cost 20 cents a pound, poor raisins 30 cents a pound, and Manila rope 30 cents a pound. I enjoyed a basket of crackers and a meaty chili at the Hotel Crockett for 65 cents. I also did not have Olmsted's troubles with the local pigs. He had to buy a dog to keep off the hungry hogs, one of which ran right through a traveler's campfire, seizing the chicken from the spit.

Olmsted found the Trinity River flowing between canebrake broken by huge oaks draped with Spanish moss. There is still Spanish moss draping the trees on the west bank, but grassy swales have replaced the cane. I found a U.S. Geological Survey stream gauger, Leonard Lamar, standing on the Trinity River bridge, checking the river's flow. He counted each click caused by the currents. It was here where the wind sweeps the Trinity bottoms that the Spanish built Bucareli, only to remove the settlement to Nacogdoches in a few years. During the Anglo-American emigration into Texas over the Old San Antonio Road, a ferry crossed the Trinity at this spot. First Joel Leakey in 1821 and then Nathaniel Robbins and finally the Elisha Clapp family operated the ferry, which was abandoned in 1930 when the old bridge was built. Lamar pointed out the remains of the old bridge.

"The 1930 trestle bridge was dynamited," he said. "They just let the wreckage stay where it fell because it helps to control erosion."

At Midway I followed the road marked OSR through towns where the aroma of woodsmoke hangs over the houses and country stores flourish. Bluebonnets bloomed along the highway. The Brazos River slid smoothly beneath the highway bridge. When St. Denis and his party of Spanish friars and their military escort reached the river, they crossed on a raft. An alligator nosed near, and Spanish Captain Domingo Ramon shot it through the eye.

Caldwell is now a comfortable town. Olmsted spent the night in Caldwell at the Caldwell Hotel which stood on the north side of the Public Square. His room had the luxury of glass windows, but some were broken. His door could not be closed from the outside, and once it was closed it could only be pried open with a pocketknife. He ate his dinner quickly so that it would not freeze on the table and went to bed in a room with four other travelers. One of them spit on the candle before jumping into his bed, explaining that he always did so. Before the candle guttered out, he was able to get safely beneath the blankets.

During pioneer days the Colorado River was considered the real beginning of west Texas.

"Its still limpid, blue-green surface appeared very charming as the ferryman slowly pulled us over," wrote Olmsted.

Dams on the river have made it lose its character; it is about as limpid as dishwater. After San Marcos, I had little choice but to follow Interstate 35, for the old road has vanished through this part of Texas. It came as a happy surprise to turn off the expressway into New Braunfels and discover that the old German town has retained its charm. German bands still play the old songs, and there is an annual wurst festival. Since it was founded in 1845 by Prince Carl of Soms-Braunfels, commissioner-general for the Society for the Protection of German Immigrants in Texas, the town has been a Teutonic island. The half-timbered buildings, with brick and stone between the posts, remain. In pioneer days New Braunfels' Germans were famous for their wagons, which were large and rugged. Pulled by three to four pairs of mules or five to six yokes of oxen, they were a jingling commonplace on the Old San Antonio Road. The house of the first wagonmaker still stands on Mill Street.

The Germans of New Braunfels have much to be proud of, not least being the introduction of the outhouse into Texas. Germans built the first outhouses at a time when most settlers believed it was far more sanitary to step out into the woods. A mob gathered at the construction of the first outhouse and accused the offending German of indecency. They dragged his outhouse away. The Germans are a tenacious people, and by the end of the first year there were better than a dozen Teutonic outhouses. Even the anti-privy people had to admit that the outhouse had come to Texas to stay. When Olmsted was in New Braunfels he discovered to his amusement that, as a Christmas day prank, boys and young men lined up all the town's outhouses in the public square.

Once the Old San Antonio Road ran into San Antonio through fields edged by chaparral past the creamy-white limestone houses of the German settlers. Today the old road has been superseded by an expressway, which hurried me into the heart of this cosmopolitan city which keeps the Alamo at its heart. Almost any schoolchild can recite the litany of heroes who fell at the Alamo. Many of the heroes came over the Old San Antonio Road to stand and die in this now peaceful structure in the center of the city. Texans feel so strongly about the Alamo that the late historian J. Frank Dobie once said that Texas would never split into five states because no one could decide who would get the Alamo. I always go to the Alamo when I am in San Antonio, because its very stones speak of bravery and dedication to freedom.

Much of Spanish San Antonio still lives. Walk through La Villita, once a suburb. Mexican craftsmen work in small shops, and strolling musicians sing south-of-the-border songs. In preparation for an approaching fiesta, pink and yellow banners and paper roses festoon the houses. Bouquets and love charms are on sale in lantern-lit shops, and tacos and tamales are served piping hot from charcoal braziers. Then also there is the Haymarket, lined with open-air stands where Mexican farmers offer their produce and craftsmen their wares. There is San Fernando Cathedral, from which Santa Anna aimed his cannons at the Alamo, and the Spanish Governor's Palace, where visitors enter beneath the imperial double-headed eagles of the Hapsburg rulers of eighteenth-century Spain.

Olmsted found San Antonio a lively jumble of Germans, Americans, and Mexicans, a city with a stuccoed stone cathedral and a cracked bell. The Alamo was being used as an arsenal by the U.S. Quartermaster, and Mexicans herded cattle and sheep in the old cells and courts of the now prized missions. Gun battles are rare in San Antonio today, but not during Olmsted's visit.

"The parties meet upon the plaza by chance," he noted, "and each, on catching sight of his enemy, draws a revolver and fires away. As the actors are under more or less excitement, their aim is not apt to be of the most careful and sure; consequently, it is not seldom the passers-by who suffer."

Through San Antonio the Old San Antonio Road followed the irrigation canals or acequias that served the missions. Mission Concepcion, Mission San Juan, Mission Espada, and Mission San Jose are as compelling in their crumbling beauty as the missions of California. West of San Antonio U.S. 90 follows the route of El Camino Real. Travelers once forded the Medina River at a place where emerald water flowed knee-deep over white limestone rocks.

On September 1, 1844, seven hundred emigrants from Alsace assembled in San Antonio and started over El Camino Real for the banks of the Medina. They hauled a board building stuffed with provisions on a cart. In a fortnight they built huts of boughs and leaves and a few adobe houses, planted a common garden, erected a church and elected officers. They named their town Castroville for their leader, Henry Castro. I drove into Castroville late on a Sunday afternoon and found the old Alsatian houses basking in the sun. The Landmark Inn built by a Frenchman, Caesar Monad, about 1844 as a one-story home and store still takes guests. By the 1860's a second floor and a lead-lined bathhouse had been added to make an inn. All went well with the inn, except that during the Civil War the bathhouse was stripped of its lead to make bullets.

"Old-fashioned prices," advises a sign outside the landmark. This turns out to be singles $5. and doubles $8.50 for the night. There were no vacancies, so apparently the price was right.

U.S. 90 climbs the hills overlooking the town and heads on west. To follow the old road I turned to the right at Dunlay and drove among the

German settlements on Quihi Creek and the Seco River. Here thatched limestone houses similar to those to be seen along the Rhine still stand. Farm Road 2676 winds west along the old road past the Bethlehem Lutheran Church built in 1852 and stone houses to the ford at Hondo Creek. The German town of D'Hanis is on U.S. 90, which runs on west past the old stage stop town of Sabinal to Uvalde, noted as the home of the late Cactus Jack Garner, Vice-President of the United States.

The Garner home, now a museum dedicated to the memory of the first Texan to be elected Vice-President, contains some interesting relics of the Old San Antonio Road. Square nails, horseshoes, spurs, an ox yoke, and the great iron rims from oxcarts used before 1836 are testimonials dug from the earth that Uvalde started as a trail town. To find the trail itself it is necessary to drive south of town to where Fort Inge once stood.

The Old San Antonio Road entered the fort past the guardhouse. Olmsted found Fort Inge surrounded with a stockade of mesquite trunks. Thatched sheds served as stables, officers' quarters, barracks, bakery, hospital and guardroom. Blackberries and elms shaded the parade ground where sentinels mounted guard, and officers chatted in the evenings. I picked my way over this historic site among broken glass and discarded tin cans.

Some travelers sheltered at Fort Inge while others stayed in Uvalde, where the F. A. Piper Company allowed wagon families to camp in its wagonyard free of charge. Horner's Store marks the spot where families cooked, where young men played practical jokes, where guitars strummed, and where goods and horses were swapped.

From Fort Inge, El Camino Real headed southwest through the brush to San Juan Bautista on the south bank of the Rio Grande, thirty miles downriver from Eagle Pass. There among the ancient trees stand the ruined but still forbidding walls, the roofless nave and decaying dome of San Juan Bautista, where a young Frenchman named St. Denis came to talk of goods and trade, and talked also of love. From this citadel and mission on the Rio Grande, El Camino Real, the Old San Antonio Road, crossed Texas to the distant outposts of Spain in Louisiana.

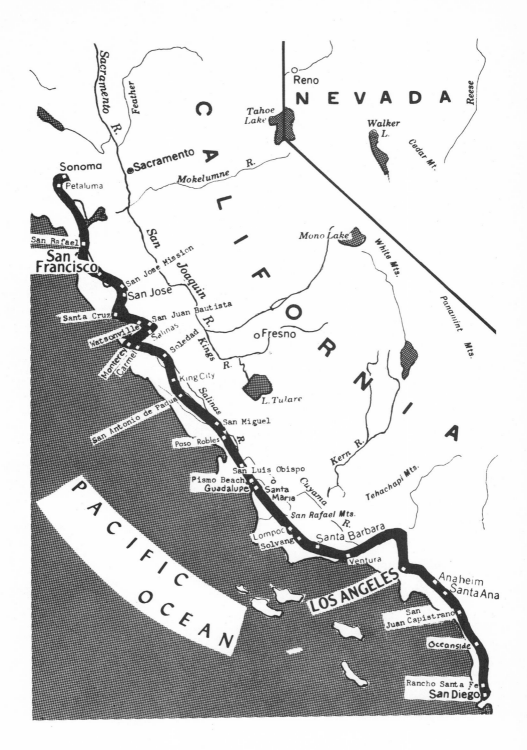

6

Royal Road to the California Missions

●

Governor Don Gaspar de Portolá and Father Juan Crespi returned to San Diego smelling of mules. It was January 24, 1770, and they had traveled as far as San Francisco Bay, roughly along the way which was later to be known as El Camino Real, the Royal Road. They and their Sacred Expedition had been reduced to five tortillas a day. They had found that devouring mussels picked up on the beach gave them cramps, deer were hard to shoot, sea gulls were tough eating, and mules were equally tough eating and were needed to carry supplies. They had undergone many hardships and failed to find Monterey Bay, which they had set out to find. Padre Presidente Serra in San Diego could scarcely believe that the expedition had failed to find the bay.

"Don't fret," he said. "You have merely been to Rome without seeing the Pope."

"I've been to hell and have shaken hands with the devil!" replied Portolá.

The Royal Road of the future was to follow their route only in part, for it often changed its course until it linked together the twenty-one missions that the Spanish were to establish in California, as well as the big ranchos and the royal pueblos. The road was to survive long after the Spaniards had gone as the backbone of the golden state.

The starting place of the Royal Road was Mission San Diego, from where it stretched seven hundred miles to San Francisco Solano at Sonoma. Padre Junipero Serra, fifty-six years old and lame from a spider bite, founded the "mother mission" of San Diego de Alcala in 1769. Indians and gray-robed Franciscans planted olive, orange, and palm trees and grape vines to make wine. At first the mission stood on Presidio Hill in San Diego's Old Town, but then it was moved six miles east to Mission Valley to be closer to a good water supply. Indian uprisings in 1775 drove the mission back to the Presidio, but in 1813, it was returned to the valley, where it first prospered and then decayed after the secularization of the California missions in the 1830's. Early in this century it was in ruin. San Diegoans shot doves among the crumbling adobe walls, and the palms and olive trees grew scrubbier by the year. Today the once desolate mission has been restored, and the chapel is used for church services.

Motels and a huge shopping center along Interstate 8 have obliterated all traces of the Royal Road which ran west down the valley to Presidio Hill. Old Town, San Diego, is an enclave of the Spanish past in the metropolis. We parked our car near the plaza and strolled about among the adobe houses, which today serve as a candle shop, restaurants, and even as a motel. In Presidio Park, site of the Spanish fort, we visited the Junipero Serra Historical Museum. Padre Serra, father of the California missions, was also father of the Royal Road, which the chain of missions made necessary, and the museum encompasses much of his life and spirit.

The Royal Road skirted Mission Bay and ran up Rose Canyon north of San Diego. Close to where the freeway tunnels through the rock, Lewis Rose operated the coast's only tannery in 1856 and planted his farm. Stagecoaches rattling over the old road came to the Torrey Pines Grade just beyond this point. It was so steep that many passengers begged to get out and walk rather than risk their necks in the hurtling vehicle.

The old road turned inland at Torrey Pines, but it has long been destroyed by the press of population in what is now the nation's most populous state. It looped through the hills behind Del Mar past the adobe McKellar Stage Station where travelers stopped on their first night out of San Diego. It passed through the San Dieguito Valley and came to Rancho Santa Fe, which was the vast Rancho San Dieguito of Spanish days.

We drove up Via de la Valle along the dry bed of the San Dieguito River. The road winds among the drooping eucalyptus and oversized ranch houses set amid private golf greens and orange groves. The countryside has a manicured charm. Even the filling station where we stopped possessed a Spanish-tiled roof. Things have changed a lot since the 1830's when Juan Maria Osuna held the ranch. He was a redoubtable Spaniard who lassoed grizzly bears for sport. Bing Crosby bought his crumbling hacienda and restored it. Other wealthy and famous people

76

bought parts of the old ranch and settled down to a life of guarded anonymity. They masked their identity behind their wives' maiden names or other pseudonyms and frowned upon telephones. We stopped at the Rancho Santa Fe Inn, where two matching gardeners, dressed alike and with identical equipment, were cultivating the two sides of the entrance.

Old U.S. 101 was labeled El Camino Real, but through this part of the California coast the actual road ran farther inland, changing from year to year to tie together new settlements and to take advantage of easier grades, shade trees, and watering places. It kept to the hills behind Encinitas and emerged at Mission San Luis Rey east of Oceanside.

California 76 takes modern travelers east from Oceanside to what was the largest and richest of all the California missions. Franciscan monks guided us through Mission San Luis Rey, which once possessed 30,000 cattle, sheep, and horses and produced thousands of barrels of wine every year. Its fields yielded 400,000 bushels of grain in a harvest. The buildings, courts and gardens covered more than six acres. This great mission fell into ruin too. Now it is restored, and once again religious services are held in its chapel. On Sunday mornings the Padre choristers raise their voices in song where once the beloved Father Antonio Peyri taught Indian boys to sing mass. Father Peyri stayed at the mission even after secularization made its ruin certain. When his Indian converts learned that he was at last to go away, five hundred mounted their horses and galloped to San Diego to implore him to stay.

There is no sign of the old road along the San Luis Rey River, nor any along the coast toward San Juan Capistrano. The road passed through what was first the Asistencia of San Pedro, then the Rancho Santa Margarita y Las Flores, and now the Camp Pendleton Marine Base. Once travelers over the Royal Road came up to San Juan Capistrano village from the sea and found it among the most charming of all California towns. Today the same approach is cluttered by mushrooming villas. Outside the mission itself souvenir stands hawk cheap curios and snacks, but once inside the mission the distractions of modern California fade away and it only seems yesterday that the earth shook in 1812 and brought the great tower, the seven domes, and the arched roof crashing down, killing forty neophytes praying in the sanctuary. We found no swallows at Capistrano, only pigeons, which is scarcely surprising since it was not St. Joseph's Day, when the birds celebrated in song and story make their blessed return.

North of Capistrano the Royal Road ran close to Interstate 5 through what is now El Toro and along Trabuco Road past the enormous Irvine

Ranch. It was from the Santiago Hills to the east of today's Tustin that Portolá and Crespi first looked out over the spreading plain that was to become Los Angeles and its suburbs. The Royal Road ran through what is now Anaheim, Fullerton, and La Habra into Whittier, but the Portolá expedition kept to the eastern hills, where they were more certain to find water. They were resting at an Indian village on the Santa Ana River in the middle of July, 1769, when Miguel Costanso, the cartographer, noted in his journal:

> *At this place we experienced a terrible earthquake, which was repeated four times during the day. The first vibration or shock occurred at one o'clock in the afternoon and was the most violent; the last took place at about half-past four. One of the natives, who, no doubt, held the office of priest among them, was at that time in the camp. Bewildered no less than we by the event, he began, with horrible cries and great manifestations of terror, to entreat the heavens, turning in all directions, and acting like one conjuring the elements. To this place we gave the name of Rio de Los Tremblores.*

U.S. 101 has been proclaimed the Royal Road through Los Angeles, but actually the original road turned at the Rio Hondo to run north to Mission San Gabriel, not on Mission Drive in San Gabriel. Father Serra founded the mission in 1771, but it was destroyed by an earthquake. The doughty padres rebuilt the church of stone between 1791 and 1803, and to show their disdain for the violent earth, they adapted a "T" for *tremblores* as their cattle brand.

San Gabriel also boasted of the oldest winery in California. On stone floors which still survive, well-scrubbed Indians trod the grapes for the wine. At one time the winery was supervised by a young Belgian, Victor Eugene Auguste Janssens, who, after he had fed the stills, would retire to his room. The Indians left to tend the fires lifted the covers of the stills and helped themselves to the wine. Janssens soon discovered the sub rosa imbibing and put padlocks on the covers. For a while the Indians were wineless, but then a copper man of inventive disposition solved their problem. As two men carried an open barrel to the cellars for aging, another followed behind, supporting the barrelhead on a pole. Since the barrel was heavy, the carriers sat down to rest.

"Oh, if this stick were only hollow!" sighed one Indian.

"A hollow cane would do," answered another, "and we could then take our turn carrying the barrelhead." It was just as easy as sipping soda through a straw, and the Indians working in the winery of San Gabriel were noted for their jollity. San Gabriel Mission is still regal, and its

78

companario, or bell wall, is unsurpassed among all the missions of the New World.

From San Gabriel Mission to Nuestra Señora la Reina de Los Angeles it is a short nine-mile drive through the tangle of Los Angeles streets. On September 4, 1781, Spanish soldiers, Franciscan friars and eleven families marched with Governor Felipe de Neve from San Gabriel to found the Pueblo, which still is centered about the plaza. By 1800 there were thirty adobes within the pueblo walls. The mission stood on the plaza and was the heart of the town's life and the first place that a traveler over the Royal Road stopped. James Ohio Pattie, a trader from Kentucky, came to Los Angeles over the Royal Road in 1829. He described the town of the angels:

The houses have flat roofs covered with bituminous pitch brought from a place within four miles of the town where this article boils up from the earth. As the liquid rises, hollow bubbles like a shell of large size are formed. The material is obtained by breaking off portions that have become hard, with an axe or something of the kind. The large pieces thus separated are laid on the roof, previously covered with earth, through which the pitch cannot penetrate when it is rendered liquid by the heat of the sun.

Pattie already knew something about the hospitality of Los Angeles at this time, for in the previous year the Angelenos had thrown him into the calabozo. Governor Echeandra, suspicious of their intentions in coming to California, jailed both Pattie and his father. There the senior Pattie died. A smallpox epidemic was raging, and Pattie had smallpox vaccine in his packs. He agreed to vaccinate the Angelenos if the governor would release him from prison. Governor Echeandra agreed, and Pattie vaccinated men, women, and children. He traveled up and down the Royal Road and vaccinated 22,000 people before he ran out of serum. The appreciative Mexican authorities offered him five hundred mules and five hundred cattle with land if he would stay in California, but he refused and returned to the States.

The flat-roofed adobes of Los Angeles mainly have given way before the modern city, but in the state historical monument surrounding the original plaza, enough of them remain to preserve the flavor of the sleepy town found by James Ohio Pattie. The Avila Adobe still stands on Olvera Street, once called the "Walk of Angels," and to this day a picturesque Mexican market spills from the old buildings into the street as it did in the days when the Royal Road was the only means of travel.

Father Crespi and Governor Portolá led their party approximately along present-day Wilshire Boulevard, past the La Brea tar pits from which came the pitch for the roofs of the Angelenos, and along the coastline until they had passed the Santa Barbara Channel. Earthquakes shook the Los Angeles basin as they crossed it, and Costanso wrote that some of the Spaniards were convinced that "there were large volcanoes in the mountain range that lay in front of us extending towards the west." Scouts, reported Costanso, came across "about forty springs of tar, or pitch, boiling up out of the ground molten, and the water runs to one side and the pitch to another; they saw great swamps of this pitch, enough they said to caulk many vessels." They found the coast way around the Santa Monica Mountains blocked by a vast cliff against which the Pacific surf was crashing and finally made their way through the mountains in what was probably Sepulveda Canyon. From the summit of the pass they looked down on the beautiful San Fernando Valley, where a large Indian village was set among copses of live oaks and walnut trees.

In 1823 the California missions were at their height, and the Royal Road linking them had become a busy route traversed not only by priests trudging the weary miles on foot but also by horsemen, traders' wagons, and mule trains. After the American conquest, stagecoaches also rolled over the road. The Royal Road left Los Angeles on what is now Sunset Boulevard. We drove out Sunset and turned onto Cahuenga Boulevard. As recently as 1938 a writer–hiker named John Harrington found ruts of the old road near Lankershim and Cahuenga boulevards, but the Los Angeles urban sprawl has since obliterated them.

Cahuenga Pass is now choked with overpasses, underpasses, ramps and lane after lane of hurtling express traffic, and it is difficult to conceive of it as the site of an encounter between two Mexican forces that might have delighted Cervantes. It was December 5, 1831, and Governor Manuel Victoria, having come from Monterey along the Royal Road with a small army to put down a rebellion in Southern California, found the rebels encamped just beyond the pass at about Hollywood and Vine. Victoria, who had made himself unpopular by his pettifoggery in the face of the American threat and the mounting misery caused by the secularization of the missions, was opposed by a small army under Captain Jose Maria Avila. The governor demanded that the rebels surrender. Avila refused. He ordered a volley fired. The volley was returned, but nobody was hurt, since both armies fired over the heads of the other.

Captain Pacheco, mounted on a black charger, rode forth for the governor. Brandishing a lance six feet long, he galloped out and wheeled his horse to a stop. Captain Avila, brandishing a lance equally long, charged out and spurring his mount, bore down on Pacheco. The two men jousted while the armies watched. It was tacitly understood by both armies that the battle would be won by one of the two champions. The soldiers climbed up trees to see better. Both riders were great horsemen, and the men cheered each maneuver.

At last Pacheco caused Avila to lose his lance. Then the game ended. Avila pulled a pistol from his belt and shot Pacheco dead. With a cry of rage, Governor Victoria galloped his horse forward and in turn shot Avila. With a cry of rage of his own, Captain Portilla of the rebels charged forward and ran his lance into Victoria's face. The governor fell in agony. Both sides gave up the battle. The rebels returned to Los Angeles, and the governor and his men went to Mission San Gabriel, where he could get medical treatment from the padres.

There is no way to locate the Royal Road among the burgeoning subdivisions of the San Fernando Valley, but Mission San Fernando Rey still remains. The mission was noted the length of the Royal Road for its hospitality to travelers. The padres' brandy was particularly renowned for its flavor and its strength. The great heavy doors swung open to admit the hungry and tired regardless of the hour. Cats had it even better, for the Indian neophytes cut holes in the door so that they could slip through at their convenience in pursuit of rats.

There are no signs of the old road which ran north from the mission to cross over Fremont Pass to Newhall and then descended the Santa Clara River to Ventura. Some historians of the trail maintain that the road took still another route, northwest through the San Fernando Valley and across the Santa Susana Mountains and then through Camarillo to Ventura, but there are no signs of this route either.

Ventura is a bustling city of oil derricks and lemon and orange groves. Father Serra founded the Mission San Buenaventura in 1782, and the mission church is on Main Street. The fields and canals for which the mission was famous are gone. In the museum we saw two-foot-high bells carved of oak.

"They were rung during Lent," explained a Ventura woman, "when it was wrong to ring metal bells because they were too cheerful."

"Yeh!" agreed her son. "These old wooden bells just went 'clunk clunk.'"

Actually, there never were any metal bells at San Buenaventura.

From Ventura U.S. 101 follows the coast route of Portolá's expedition, but the Royal Road turned north along the Ventura River. Recently archaeologists have discovered the site of the Asistencia of Santa Gertrudis where Coyote Creek flows into the Ventura, but the Rancho Casistas has largely been flooded by Casitas Reservoir. The old road cuts through Casitas Pass to rejoin U.S. 101 at Rincon Point near Carpinteria.

At Rincon Point travelers on the Royal Road often had to ride their horses into the surf at high tide because the mountains dropped so sharply down to the sea. Stagecoaches careened through the waves to the dismay of lady passengers. In the early 1900's the road was paved with planks, which were often washed away, and even today the surf sometimes is driven by storms to crash against the modern highway.

Santa Barbara is called the "Queen of the Missions" because of its serene beauty. It is the only California mission that has never passed out of the hands of the Franciscans, and has been given the care that most of the California missions deserve. The city around it, although pre-dominantly Anglo, works hard at keeping alive Spanish charm. It treasures its old adobes and builds its new buildings to be compatible with the Spanish and Moorish architecture of the twin-towered mission. The city of Santa Barbara is patently well-bred today, but in the nineteenth century it was a garish collection of saloons, gambling halls and billiard parlors, waiting for the stagecoaches to come speeding down the Royal Road.

In Santa Barbara we stayed in a comfortable motel. We found others like it every night on the road. It was different during the early days on the Royal Road. Then travelers stopped at missions or ranchos. Ranchers greeted them with "Mi casa es suya," "My house is yours." A visitor was both a newspaper and entertainment, so was made welcome. Missions were perhaps less comfortable than ranchos. In a mission a traveler's room was damp and unheated, with no glass in the windows. There was no plumbing, and fleas invaded the bed of cowhide fastened to a frame mounted on four legs. In the morning rancher or padre sent a traveler on his way with bread, cheese, hardboiled eggs, a whole broiled chicken, and most likely a bottle of wine or brandy.

North of Santa Barbara on Refugio Bay the Rancho El Refugio of the Ortega family once spread its hospitable ranges. Here in 1816 Thomas Doak waded ashore on the beach after jumping overboard from the ship *Albatross*, which had sailed from Boston to smuggle goods into California. He had had enough of the nautical life and sought refuge at El Refugio. Doak was baptized a Catholic, was married to the daughter of Don José de Castro, a rich rancher, and became the first American to live in California.

At Goleta the old road turned inland through San Marcos Pass. California Highway 154 leads directly from Santa Barbara through the pass today. It follows the Santa Ynez River close by the old road to the white adobe Santa Ynez Mission on its hillock overlooking the Danish town of Solvang. Costanso described the Santa Ynez Valley as the Portolá party found it: "This river flows through a very beautiful valley containing many willows, and much land capable of producing all kinds of grain. We saw bears of great size, and many of their tracks."

The Royal Road ran on down the Santa Ynez River's north bank to Mission la Purisima Concepcion. Preserved in a state park and restored during the 1930's by the CCC under the supervision of the National Park Service, the mission appears as it did in the days before secularization. The old road can be made out close to its sturdy walls. Overgrown by shrubs and sage, it runs across the mesa toward the noble buildings where travelers once found shelter for the night.

From the Mission la Purisima Concepcion, not U.S. 101 but California 1 closely follows the Royal Road into the lush truck gardens of the Santa Maria Valley. The old road went by way of Casmalia and Guadalupe to Arroyo Grande, where it crossed the modern U.S. 101. This is peaceful country today where the worst that can happen to a traveler is that he might be sprinkled with insecticide from a crop-dusting plane, but once it was the haunt of bandit Dolores Pico. Robbed of his Sierra gold claim in 1849 and beaten for protesting the robbery, Pico declared war on Anglos. He hid in the mountains below Santa Maria, where his father had once been the Mexican *comandante*, and killed and robbed Anglo travelers on the road. He always slashed off his victim's ears.

"But why does he cut off ears?" a traveler asked a smiling Mexican.

"Pico wants to make a rosary of Gringo ears for every girl he loves," replied the Mexican, "and he loves many girls."

During his ten years of banditry Pico was able to make innumerable rosaries to please the fancy of his many loves.

From Arroyo Grande the Royal Road ran up Carpenter Canyon, the route of old U.S. 101 before it was rerouted to Pismo Beach. The old road avoided the marshes and sand dunes of the coast south of Pismo Beach. It reached San Luis Obispo Creek where the mission of the name was built in 1772.

It was west of San Luis Obispo that Portolá's men discovered that California grizzlies were no ordinary bears. Working their way through the coastal hills they came upon scores of the shaggy animals. Hungry for meat the soldiers rode to the chase and succeeded in shooting one. "They, however, experienced the fierceness and anger of these animals," wrote Constanso.

When they feel themselves to be wounded, headlong they charge the hunter, who can only escape by the swiftness of his horse, for the first burst of speed is more rapid than one might expect from the bulk and awkwardness of such brutes.

Their endurance and strength are not easily overcome, and only the sure aim of the hunter, or the good fortune of hitting them in the head or heart, can lay them low at the first shot. The one they succeeded in killing received nine bullet wounds before it fell, and this did not happen until they hit him in the head.

Other soldiers mounted on mules had the boldness to fight one of these animals. They fired at him seven or eight times, and doubtless, he died from the wounds, but he maimed two of the mules, and, by good fortune, the men who were mounted upon them extricated themselves.

The Indians of the region were not as friendly and tractable as those farther south, and in 1776 they shot flaming arrows into the thatched roof of San Luis Obispo Mission and burned it. The padres replaced the roof with the first tile roof on a California mission. This not only frustrated the Indians but proved so attractive that other California missions were given tile roofs.

The Mission of San Luis Obispo also was proud of the fertility of its fields and of its hospitality. It provided one facility that pleased travelers enormously. Travelers soaked their tired legs in a nearby mineral springs, as did both the Indians and the grizzly bears.

U.S. 101 and the Royal Road alike climb through Cuesta Pass toward Santa Margarita, where an *asistencia* stood during mission days. At Paso Robles the old road emerged into the rich Salinas Valley. For miles it is buried beneath the pavement of the modern road. Mission San Miguel Arcangel beside the road in San Miguel delighted us. Its walls are frescoed in bold contrasting colors. The painters were Indians who painted under the direction of Esteban Munras, an artist from Spain.

The Royal Road turned northwest from U.S. 101 at Bradley. We drove on highway G14 up the San Antonio River valley past adobe ranch houses and quiet villages that were on El Camino Real. We entered the Hunter Liggett Military Reservation, once part of a William Randolph Hearst ranch. Then the serenity of the valley was exploded in an instant by a fleet of army tanks that came bursting over a hill. A jeepload of officers sputtered past us on the road. Then there was instant quiet again. In only a few moments we came upon a fawn and its mother standing beside the road as if stertorous mechanical monsters had not just raged past.

Except for a few soldiers touring the Mission San Antonio de Padua, it was hard to believe that the military reservation was so close. San Antonio stands beneath the oaks that were there when Juan Bautista de Anza first came to the valley and called it the Valley of the Oaks. One of de Anza's soldiers, Juan Palamino, left a mare here too, and the mission became noted for a race of golden horses descended from her.

It was a hot and dusty day, and we were reluctant to leave the cool colonnade of the mission for the sun. It was easy to drowse beneath the live oaks and think of the day in July, 1771, when Father Serra read Mass beneath the great trees. Ten friars stood with bowed heads. When an Indian slipped out of the brush to see what the ceremony was about, the fathers hung a string of glass beads around his neck. Soon other Indians came for beads and ended up building the mission. The mission, its gristmill, winepress, and even the reservoir and its undershot water-wheel have been rebuilt.

San Antonio de Padua Mission is on a spur of the Royal Road that branches off at Jolon. We returned to Jolon, only a few miles southeast, to take highway G14 over the route of the old road to King City. U.S. 101 follows the Royal Road from King City to Soledad. Just south of the town we came to a two-story adobe and wood building in a wayside park which was once a stage stop. Costanso described the Salinas Valley as the Sacred Expedition found it: "The whole plain that it [the Salinas River] waters is luxuriant of foliage. The soil seems to be of good quality, and produces a variety of fragrant plants, among others the rosemary, which abounded, the sage, and rosebushes loaded with blossoms."

José Maria Soberanes, at sixteen one of the youngest members of the expedition, must have thought the valley beautiful, too, for he dreamed of living the life of a ranchero there. When he was mustered out of service in 1795, he was given a grant in the vicinity of Mission Soledad. The Soberanes family prospered. In 1839 a tailor from Baltimore, Maryland, named William Richardson came to the valley and married Maria Josefa Soberanes. He built a home for his bride close by the Royal Road, and this was the home we now were visiting. Richardson planted locust seeds from his native Maryland about the house, and the trees have grown tall. They were young when stages running over the Royal Road from San Francisco to Los Angeles stopped at the house for refreshment and to drop off the mail.

Soledad Mission is a short way west of U.S. 101, and so is the Royal Road. There is nothing to be seen of the ancient road, and we drove to Monterey by way of Salinas. California 68 follows close to where a branch of the Royal Road ran on its way to Monterey, the capital city of Spanish and Mexican California.

Robert Louis Stevenson called the Monterey coast "the most magnificent meeting place of land and water in existence." Looking at the peninsula's seagirt cliffs and chapparal-clad mountains, we were inclined to agree with him. There are rocks where sea lions and sea otters bask, and rocks where brown pelicans, cormorants, sandpipers, gulls, and tattlers nest. Above all, Monterey is the heart of old Spanish California where white stucco adobe houses, the Presidio and Carmel Mission recall the romantic days when, according to Governor Victoria, "any citizen was supposed to be able to leave his purse in the plaza for a week without molestation."

Sebastian Vizcaino, Spanish explorer, sailed into the half-moon bay in 1602 and named it Monterey for the Count of Monte-Rey, Viceroy of Mexico. He described the bay with such superlatives that 167 years later Gaspar de Portolá set out to reach it overland. He twice camped nearby without recognizing the bay. In the next year Father Crespi and Father Serra rediscovered the bay and established the Carmel Mission.

We strolled into the town's past when we visited some of the over forty early-day structures, including the Royal Presidio Chapel, the Old Pacific Building, the Custom House, California's first theater where nineteenth century drama is still enacted, Colton Hall, and the Larkin House. Thomas Larkin was the United States Consul in Mexican Monterey, and his house, a pink-plaster adobe banked in bougainvillea, is open to the public.

One evening at dusk we came upon the Carmel Mission, erected of sandstone blocks in 1771 by Father Junipero Sera. The year before the good father had built the mission near the Presidio at Monterey, but he moved it down the coast to the Carmel River to put five miles between the mission and the garrison. Five miles might keep the soldiers from seducing the Indian girls. We mounted on worn sandstone steps to the balcony lit by a star-shaped window. On a Sunday morning we returned to see the faithful hurrying to services within the chapel decorated so long ago by primitive Indian converts.

It was to Carmel that Father Serra returned after a last trip to the Mission Dolores now in San Francisco.

"I have come home to die," he told Padre Francisco Palou.

On August 28, 1784, he died, was wrapped in his brown robe tied at the waist, and buried before the altar at Carmel. Priests chanted a litany, the bells tolled, and offshore ships fired a last salute.

Life in the little Spanish town of Monterey was not uneventful. Grizzlies menaced outlying settlements. In 1805 they killed four hundred livestock. Tio Armenta had a tavern by the Royal Road. One night two traders who had been drinking late and gambling with Armenta started home down the road. A huge bear emerged out of the shadows and started toward them. Both men fell into a ravine in their haste to get away. The bear turned out to be Victor Arroyo, a practical joker, who had dressed himself in a bearskin to scare belated travelers.

The Royal Road continued on from Salinas to San Juan Bautista, now in a state historical park. At San Juan the old Plaza still is surrounded by the buildings of its past. We found the Plaza Hotel filled with reminders of the day when San Juan Bautista was a stopping place for seven stagelines. Caballeros rode up to the bar at the hotel and sipped their amontillado in the saddle. With his deerskin shoes, gold and silver embroidery and black broadcloth trousers and a sash of red satin around the waist, his waistcoat of blue, black or gray, his velvet gold and silver braid broad-brimmed hat and chin strap, a caballero made quite a picture, with or without a glass of amontillado in his hand.

Next to the hotel is the Castro Adobe, built in 1841 to provide quarters and offices for General José Castro's secretary. Castro sold the adobe in December, 1848, to Patrick Breen, one of the survivors of the Donner Party. The old livery stable holds horse-drawn vehicles. Next to the stable is the Zanetta House, made of brick from a mission adobe which housed unmarried Indian girls. Finally there is the mission itself, founded in 1797. Father Estevan Tapis is buried in the sanctuary where he once taught Indians music from colored notes. Outside the mission in the churchyard are the graves of five thousand Indian converts, and next to the cemetery is the roadbed of the Royal Road. It is one of the few places left in all of California where the great road of the state's past can still be seen.

California Highway 129 took us along the Royal Road to Watsonville, Aptos, and Santa Cruz, where a half-scale replica of brick stands close to where Mission Santa Cruz stood. Over the road which we followed, "knights of the rein" once guided their four to six horses at breakneck speed, chewed tobacco, and jawed with coach passengers. Among the drivers was Charley Parkhurst, who wore a black patch over his bad eye, and was therefore known up and down the road as Cockeyed Charley.

Charley put down his reins for the last time and opened a halfway house on the road. All of his friends gloomily told one another that Charlie would never make a go of his new business. He enjoyed whiskey too much and surely would drink up all his profits. Charlie proved them wrong and when he died in 1879 he was a respected citizen of Santa Cruz. Then an amazing thing was discovered. Charlie was really Charlotte, and she had been born in New Hampshire. Remembering that Charlie had voted in the Santa Cruz election of 1866, folks claimed that she was the first to practice women's suffrage in California.

California Highway 17 is the route of the Royal Road through Los Gatos to San Jose, first city in California to be established by the Spanish crown as a town. At San Jose in early days a branch of the road led to San Jose Mission, but the main road continued on to Santa Clara Mission, now on the University of Santa Clara campus. The Royal Road ran on into San Francisco along U.S. 101, San Jose Avenue, and Valencia Street to where Mission San Francisco de Asis, more commonly known as the Mission Dolores, stands on Dolores Street at Sixteenth. All around the old mission spreads the exciting city that has grown from its seed.

The Royal Road crossed the Golden Gate on a ferry from the foot of Hyde Street to Richardson's Bay, but we drove across the famed bridge. There is nothing left of the Mission San Rafael. The last portion of the road ran to Petaluma and on to Mission San Francisco Solano at Sonoma, last and northernmost of the missions.

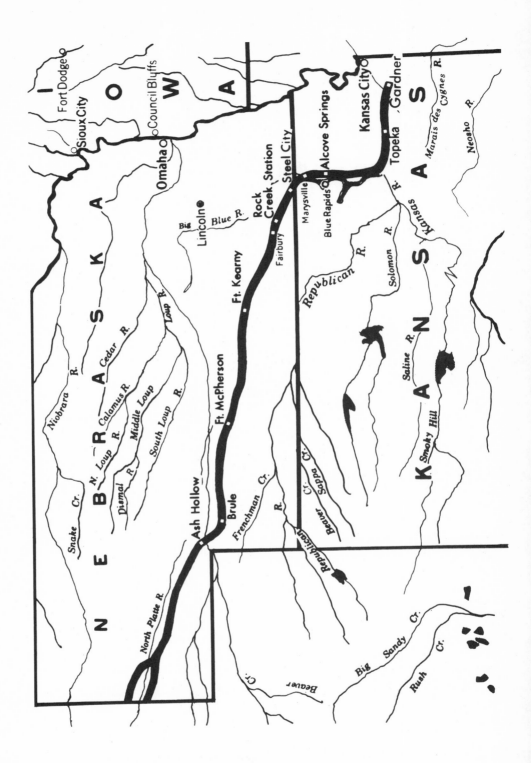

7

Oregon Trail:
Across the Plains

●

The oxen of Enoch Conyers, Oregon Trail pioneer of 1852, were lame. Their feet had been splintered by the stony and sandy ground. Conyers noted in his journal:

We cut a piece of hide from a dead ox by the roadside making small holes in the border of this piece of hide. Through these holes we run a string or a narrow strip of hide for a drawstring. We then put this piece of hide on the lame oxen's feet, flesh side out, drawing the string tight enough to hold it on the foot, and then tie it fast. This completes the job. Two days' wear is sufficient for a cure.

The American nation moved westward along the Oregon Trail on the feet of oxen, often wrapped in the hide of their fellows fallen by the way of exhaustion and disease. Men and sturdy boys rode horseback or walked, but women, the sick, and small children rode in wagons or at least they rode in wagons as far as the wagons held together. In the dry air of the high plains, spokes, hubs, and felloes shrank. Iron tires fell off and had to be put back in place with wedges because there were no blacksmiths to shorten them. Sometimes when a wagon train camped by a stream, men took off the wheels and left them in the water overnight to swell. Wagon boxes jolted apart, and cloth covers were frayed by the wind.

Still, wagons meant transportation and shelter against Indians, the storms and the gloom of night; and if a wagon train court found a man must be hanged, two wagons could be brought together and their tongues raised and joined to form a gallows. So many westering Americans went over the Oregon Trail in wagons that the Indians called it "the white-topped wagon road."

My son Rick, thirteen years of age with his arm typically cradling a guitar, Val Schaffner, a fifteen-year-old New York lad with a camera dangling about his neck, and I set out one early August morning in a truck camper to follow the white-topped wagon road from Kansas to The Dalles, two thousand miles away on the Columbia River in Oregon. We wanted to locate places where things we had read about in pioneer diaries and journals had happened. I am a scoutmaster and enjoy tent camping, but we were using a truck camper because it was self-contained. We wanted to camp as close as we could to where the wagon trains camped, and people will let a truck camper stay overnight in spots where tent campers are not welcome.

"Our truck camper's a lot like a covered wagon," said Rick. "We've got all we need on wheels." This might be questioned by true covered wagon standards. Joel Palmer, who took the trail in 1845, listed in his journal that these things were needed: 200 pounds of flour, 30 pounds of pilot bread, 75 pounds of bacon, 10 pounds of rice, 5 pounds of coffee, 2 pounds of tea, 25 pounds of sugar, a half-bushel of dried beans, 1 bushel of dried fruit, 10 pounds of salt, a half-bushel of cornmeal, and a small keg of vinegar. An emigrant should travel light, said Palmer, but he should bring along a sheet-iron stove, a Dutch oven, a cast-metal skillet, tin plates, cups and saucers, two churns, one for sweet and one for sour milk, a keg for water, and tools such as a handsaw, plow molds, an ax, shovel, rope, and a rifle and shotgun.

"Every man ought to carry a Bible and other religious books," suggested the captain of a wagon train starting from Bloomington, Iowa, in 1843, "as we hope not to degenerate into a state of barbarism."

Of course, a covered wagon had to carry enough spiritual and physical supplies to last for six months, while we planned to shop in small town stores along the way.

Today even where the Oregon Trail has not been plowed under or flooded by reservoirs, it is only an eroded wrinkle in the earth's crust, which leads sometimes past bustling towns but more often across lonely back country. Once it was the great highway into the Northwest. Two hundred and fifty thousand travelers took it in the 25 years after 1841 when the first 20 wagons and 69 adventurous pioneers of the Bidwell-Bartleson Party passed over most of the route. The high tide of emigration was reached in 1850 when by August 14, army officers at Fort Laramie counted 39,506 men, 2,421 women, 2,609 children, and 9,927 wagons on the trail. A Blandinsville, Illinois, boy, Henry Gilfry, went with his parents over the Oregon Trail two years later. Judging from what the Gilfrys saw when they camped by the trail near Fort Laramie, 1852 was another record year.

"During that 24 hours spent not far from old Fort Laramie in washing and mending clothes and sewing buttons," Henry Gilfry later wrote, "fully 900 wagons passed, going on and on and on into the Western wilderness."

During our trip as we crossed the back country of Wyoming and Idaho, it was hard for the boys and me to visualize an almost unbroken procession of wagons where herds of antelope scattered before our jouncing truck, and we only met a few sheepherders and an occasional ranch hand. It is wilder along some stretches of the Oregon Trail today than it was one hundred years ago.

The previous summer I had driven a short distance west on U.S. 56 from Gardner, Kansas, to a roadside picnic area which belongs among the most historic places on the plains. Where today motoring families spill out of their cars, bolt down their picnic lunches and rush away down the highway to their evening's destinations, a rough board once directed travelers on the "Road to Oregon." Another sign pointed southwest to Santa Fe, which was 750 miles away. This is where the Oregon Trail separated from the trail to Santa Fe. To get to the benches, picnickers walk across planks stretched over a shallow ditch, which in wet weather becomes muddy. Few of them glance at the marker at the far end of the park which identifies the ditch as the ruts of the Santa Fe and Oregon trails.

Between the place where the trails separated and Alcove Springs, some 110 miles northwest as a jet from Gardner Air Force Base might fly, there are no vestiges of the Oregon Trail, as far as I know. We decided to drive west from St. Joseph, Missouri, to the old wagon camp at the springs. U.S. 77 took us south from Marysville to where gravel roads twist to Alcove Springs. During pioneer days wagon trains forded the Big Blue River at nearby Independence Crossing. Oxen and wagons plunged down precipitous banks to what the English adventurer, Sir Richard Burton, called "a pretty little stream, brisk and clear as a crystal."

The crossing is gone, but Alcove Springs remain. We could easily make out the ruts cut by wagons laboring up a ridge from where U.S. 77 now runs. The emigrants stopped to bury their dead in a meadow where there are still known to be over two hundred graves. The hardships and the diseases of the trail struck first at old people and the very young, and for many families what had begun so hopefully only a few weeks before had already brought tragedy by the time they reached the springs.

In 1849 William G. Johnston went with the train led by the Scottish trapper, Jim Stewart. The Stewart train camped on May 9 near the graves by the Big Blue River. Johnston wrote:

Graves sometimes marked with boards, rudely inscribed, sometimes by the skull of a buffalo on which with red chalk, or other transitory substance, is made a simple inscription; often a mere stick performs a similar service, but more frequently only the turf elevated slightly above the vast surrounding plain is the evidence that there, taking its final rest, is the body of one like ourselves.

After burying their dead, the trains creaked and lurched down to the campsite while oxen bellowed in anticipation of water and men shouted. We drove our truck into a small park maintained by citizens of Blue Rapids, a town a few miles down the Big Blue River, and followed a path to the spring where pioneers found grass for their beasts and timber to repair their wagons. As the oxen rested, pioneers hunted and fished to supplement their usual meager diet which, for the Stewart party at least, consisted as a rule of two meals a day of "oatmeal mush, bacon sides with pilot bread fried in the fat and coffee."

In their idle moments the emigrants carved their names on the rock ledges. The Donner Party camped here from May 26 to May 31, 1846, and we read the name and date, "J F Reed, 26 May, 1846," that this member of the ill-fated group cut deep into the rock. Reed was one of the leaders of the expedition that was first known as the Reed and Donner Party. He was of Polish blood, for his ancestors had fled Russian oppression in Poland to settle in County Armagh, Ireland, and his true name was Reednoski. As a youth he worked in the lead mines of Galena and campaigned with Abraham Lincoln in the Blackhawk War before settling down in Springfield, Illinois, as a cabinetmaker. Resting by the trail at Alcove Springs, he scarcely could have known that in the West for which he hankered he would be reduced to eating rancid tallow found in a tar bucket beneath an abandoned wagon and that he would kill young John Snyder in a quarrel over tangled oxen harnesses. At least he was to escape the cannibalism to which many in the party would be reduced by starvation in the High Sierra snows.

While the party was camped at Alcove Springs, Reed's mother-in-law, Sarah Keyes, a redoubtable old lady of seventy, died. The Reeds made a coffin from the trunk of a cottonwood tree and buried her on a knoll overlooking the little valley. A stately oak watches over her now as on that day when the oldest of the Donner Party was laid to rest at the outset of a grim adventure from which the good Lord had saved her.

During the spring rains, water flows over a ledge and tumbles to the floor of the valley. The small waterfall was named by the Donner Party for three-year-old Naomi Pike, who played at its foot. Close by the waterfall we were able to make out wagon ruts. A little north of the springs we could see where the wagons fanned out into a meadow. Cattle were grazing among the overgrown ruts just as had the oxen of the pioneers. Today a pair of outhouses taken from an abandoned country school have been set up at the old camping area. The small park surrounding the springs is neat and well kept.

"It ought to be clean," E. B. Weller of Blue Rapids, who was showing the springs to a group of out-of-town visitors, told us. "When boys around town get into trouble—petty vandalism and that sort of thing— our judge sentences them to work here in the park. He figures that a boy who helps to preserve his country's past will quit tearing up his town."

We parked our camper for the night where wagon-train families had camped. The fireflies danced for us while we ate our dinner as they must have danced for the pioneers. We spoke in soft voices for we half expected that ghosts would rise out of the graves in the meadow to tell us of the hardships of the trail, of death by Indian arrows or much more likely by cholera. Instead, as we strolled just before bedtime along the old trail beneath the crinkling stars, a man-launched satellite sped across the sky.

In the morning we drove along the county roads which crisscross the cornfields between the Big Blue and its tributary, the Little Blue. Richard Burton, traveling along the Oregon Trail through Kansas in a stagecoach in 1860, remarked that "in the rare spots where water lay, the herbage was still green, forming oases in the withering waste, and showing that irrigation is its principal, if not only, want." We found that even without irrigation the August fields were lush with corn. The Oregon Trail crossed into Nebraska at Cottonwood Creek and continued northwest toward the Platte River. We followed a farm road into Nebraska where at Steele City, a slumbering crossroads town, we stopped to ask of Joe Payne, the postmaster, how to get to the old Rock Creek station. Rock Creek station was established as a post office on the Oregon Trail in 1859, and we imagined that a modern-day postmaster would know where it was. We were right.

"The house is burnt down, but the old rock post office is still there," he said from behind the counter in the frame post office. "Take the hill road even if it is as crooked as a bowl of snakes."

The hill road took us over rocky hills and grassy knolls. The land is still virgin prairie because it is too rough for farming. We pulled off the road onto a weedy shoulder where a sign announced the "Echoes of the Oregon Trail Pageant." The pageant itself has become history, and the grounds were deserted. We walked through pastures to the site of the old station. Cattle were drinking from a hollowed-out log, and bob-whites called from the banks of Rock Creek, so-called because pioneers found rock salt along it. Goldfinches flitted around the stone post office, which is a restoration of the original structure built in 1859.

It was in that year that David C. McCanles, a dark buffalo of a man, quit as sheriff of Watauga County, North Carolina, and headed west to the Pike's Peak gold strike. He left behind his wife and children but took with him Sarah Shull, aged twenty-six, blue-eyed, jet-haired, and a striking beauty. The former sheriff and his fair companion were traveling over the Oregon Trail when they met disappointed goldseekers returning to the East. Men who only a few months before had hastened to Colorado under the banner of "Pike's Peak or bust" were coming home busted. McCanles and Sarah decided to forego the gold strike and settle beside the trail in southern Nebraska.

McCanles built a station. He supplied emigrants, freight wagon companies, and stagecoach drivers with water, feed, and fresh horses. He repaired wagons and built a tollbridge over Rock Creek. He erected a ranch house on either side of the creek and added a barn, stables, and a corral. Surprisingly, he sent for his wife and children as well as his brother, J. L. McCanles, and his family. He moved into one ranch house with his family and installed Sarah in the other so that when he had a mind to he could follow a well-worn path to her door. Both ranch houses are gone today, but not Richard Burton's description of what he saw when he arrived at the McCanles family ranch by stage.

Upon the bedded floor of the foul "doggery" lay, in a seemingly promiscuous heap, men, women, children, lambs, and puppies, all fast in the arms of Morpheus, and many under the influence of a much jollier god. The employees, when aroused pretty roughly, blinked their eyes in the atmosphere of smoke and mosquitoes, and declared that it had been "merry in hall" that night—the effects of which merriment had not passed off. After half an hour's dispute about who should do the work, they produced cold scraps of mutton and a kind of bread which deserves a totally distinct generic name. The strongest stomachs of the party made tea, and found some milk which was not more than one quarter flies.

We ate a much more savory lunch from cans that the boys, who did most of the cooking on our trip, heated up while I determined where the ranch houses had stood. Within six months after Burton described his station, McCanles sold it to Russell, Majors and Waddell, owners of the stagecoach line. He moved to a ranch on the nearby Little Blue, but Sarah stayed on in the station's west ranch house. The first station manager for the company was Horace Wellman, who soon was joined by a gangling young man named James Butler Hickok, twenty-four years old, mild of manner and a loner who cut hay for the stock and lived by himself in a dugout close to the stables. Hickok had been mauled in Raton Pass on the Santa Fe Trail by a grizzly. The bear had ripped his scalp and lacerated his left arm and body. The company had sent him to Rock Creek to recuperate.

All might have gone well at the station except that Russell, Majors and Waddell were slow to pay McCanles for the property. McCanles made frequent visits to Wellman to demand his money. Each visit was stormier than the one before. For good measure he took to twitting the young stable hand. He called him "Duck Bill," because he had a slightly protruding upper lip, and often he flung the meek young man to the ground in spite of his injured arm.

Finally Wellman went to Brownville on the Missouri River to try and persuade the company to pay McCanles the money due to him. During his absence "Duck Bill" Hickok became acting station manager, a status which did not protect him from daily abuse from the angry McCanles. McCanles became still angrier when Wellman returned without any funds to pay him. He threatened to take back the station by force.

On July 12, 1861, McCanles appeared at Rock Creek with his cousin James Woods, James Gordon, a ranch hand, and his own twelve-year-old son, Monroe, McCanles pounded on the kitchen door until Wellman's common-law wife asked what he wanted.

"I want to settle with your husband!" he shouted.

"He won't come out!" she shouted back.

"Send him out or I'll come in and drag him out!"

Wellman did not come out; instead young Hickok, speaking from behind the barred door, tried to quiet McCanles down.

"All right if you want to take a hand in this, come out, and we'll settle it like men!" cried McCanles to Hickok.

Hickok knew he was no match for the burly McCanles. He hid behind a calico curtain which screened a bedroom from the sitting room. McCanles, moving around to the front door, caught a glimpse through a window of the young man hiding behind the curtain.

"Come out and fight fair!" he demanded.

Then he pushed open the door and started into the room. Hickok fired his pistol from behind the curtain, and his shot struck McCanles in the heart. Woods and Gordon, hearing the report, rushed toward the house. Hickok shot and wounded both. As they fled, the cowering Wellman became a lion. Snatching up a hoe, he chased Woods into a patch of weeds at the east end of the station and hacked him to death. Another station employee, Doc Brink, also hiding within the ranch house, seeing Gordon limping away, raced after him, brandishing a shotgun. He caught up with Gordon in the creek bottom and killed him at the foot of a tree.

98

Running to his dying father, Young Monroe cradled his head in his arms and sobbed.

Wellman's wife stabbed a finger at the boy.

"Kill him, kill him!" she screamed to Hickok, but the young man was suddenly sick. He had already killed his first man and wounded two others. He put his revolver back in its holster and shook his head. The men at the station wrapped Gordon in a blanket and buried him beneath the tree where he had fallen. They hammered together a double coffin and buried McCanles and Woods together on nearby Soldier Hill. The actual events of that day in July were sordid, but this did not keep frontier storytellers from spinning a heroic tale in which young Hickok killed ten ruffians attacking the post and in so doing defended the U.S. mail. "Duck Bill" Hickok grew a mustache to cover his protruding lip and as "Wild Bill" Hickok went on to become the West's top gun with the law at the point of his gun.

During the remainder of the day, we traced the Oregon Trail to Fort Kearny on the Platte River. Most of this part of the trail has been long since plowed up, but north of Fairbury on State 15 we found the Smith Lime Kiln, built in 1872 close to where a kiln was erected in 1848 by a company of soldiers. The soldiers burned lime for the construction of Fort Kearny. Old-fashioned dooryard flowers grew wild around a nearby abandoned homestead built of the same stone as the kiln. Doubtless the flowers are the descendants of blooms set out by a pioneer woman.

A marker on a county road helped us to locate the Big Sandy Station. A passing hunter, perhaps frustrated in the chase, had shot the sign full of holes with a twenty-two. From Big Sandy Station the trail once led along the divide separating the valleys of the Big Blue and the Little Blue. Dropping into the valley of the Little Blue it passed between low bluffs. It dipped into gullies washed out by the torrential rains of the prairies and in places slipped beneath the welcome shade of the cotton-woods and willows which then as now grew along the river. Five miles northwest of Fairbury we came upon a rock set up along the trail by the sons of George Winslow of the Boston and Newton Joint Stock Association, a company which journeyed over the trail in 1848 bound for the gold fields of California. On July 8 of that year Winslow died of cholera and was buried here, lucky only in that he had left two sons to mark his resting place.

Low sandy hills separate the headwaters of the Little Blue from the Valley of the Platte. Francis Parkman, in his classic of pioneer trail travel, *The Oregon Trail*, reports that he found the hollows and gorges of the hills gloomy. Our truck sped through them in a matter of minutes, and we had scarcely time to think of the hills at all. We emerged from them, as had Parkman, to look out over the Platte.

"For league after league, a plain as level as a lake was spread beneath us," wrote Parkman. "Here and there the Platte, divided into a dozen thread-like sluices, was traversing it, and an occasional clump of wood, rising in the midst like a shadowy island, relieved the monotony of the waste. No living thing was moving throughout the vast landscape, except the lizards that darted over the sand and through the rank grass and prickly pears at our feet."

The river that we saw before us was unchanged, but farmhouses were tucked among the clumps of wood, and fences ran to the horizon closing in a patchwork of fields. A pick-up truck stopped ahead of us. A small boy jumped down from the back door and scuffed his shoes through the soil by the road. He sprang ahead a few steps and plucked a small wriggling lizard from behind a tuft of grass. He held it up to us as we drove slowly past him for proof that lizards still live along the Platte.

Most of the pioneer journals and diaries agree that the valley of the Platte was scarcely grand and scenic although it had a monotonous beauty of its own. To the Omaha Indians and their cousins, the Otoes, the river was "Ni bthaska" or flat water, a name that some early maps gave to the Platte and that ultimately was given to the state of Nebraska. In 1739 two adventuring French brothers, Pierre and Paul Mallet, came up the river and named it "La Rivière Plate," which is French for the "Flat River." Platte River it became, and flat river it most decidedly is.

"In fact," said Val, looking upon the river with the uncompromising eyes of youth, "it is the flattest river I've ever seen."

In May, 1846, Congress passed "an Act to provide for a regiment of Mounted Riflemen, and for establishing military stations on the route to Oregon." The Mexican War stopped the actual building of the forts to protect emigrants on the Oregon Trail until the spring of 1847, when a battalion of Missouri Mounted Volunteers arrived on the Platte and began to construct a fort on the south bank at the head of Grand Island. Daniel P. Woodbury, a lieutenant in the Corps of Engineers, supervised 175 men in making adobe bricks, cutting timber and milling it in the sawmill, carpentering, and erecting sod houses. The buildings were built surrounding a parade ground of four acres with a flagstaff in the center. The soldiers planted cottonwood trees around the parade

ground as shelter from the high plains sun in the summer and the blizzards of the winter.

We parked our truck beside the stockade erected by the State of Nebraska where Fort Kearny once stood. State archaeologists found six of the old support posts when they constructed the replica. The wind soughed through the leaves of the cottonwoods, which are all that is left of the original fort. It was a nostalgic sound, which goes deep into the memory of any man who has had a midwestern boyhood, a sound suggesting endless summer and no school, but somehow with an overtone of an ultimate end to carefree days.

Fort Kearny was one of the most important posts on the Oregon Trail. Emigrants stopped at its adobe storehouse to buy supplies that the commanding officer was authorized to sell to them at cost. If the westering families were in want, the soldiers at the fort often gave them provisions free of charge. When in 1850 a stagecoach began to run over the Oregon Trail from Independence as far as the junction with a route to Salt Lake City, mail service was also provided. Pioneers could mail letters to folks back home to let them know that they had safely reached the banks of the Platte.

The Indians may have pondered making an attack on Fort Kearny which was defended only by a garrison of two companies, but they never did. Even in 1854 when the Cheyenne and the Sioux struck furiously at the trail along the banks of the Little Blue and the Platte, they kept their distance from the fort. Wagon train after wagon train was overwhelmed. Pioneers were killed and scalped, their belongings looted and their wagons left in flames on the prairie. Settlers as far east as the Missouri River fled before the Indians, but Fort Kearny remained unscathed.

During the next decade of warfare on the high plains, soldiers rode out from the fort as escorts for stagecoaches and wagons. They succored the survivors of massacred trains. Fort Kearny was a haven on the bloody frontier. By 1865 the Indians had moved farther west and the fort became inactive. In 1875 the buildings were torn down. When in 1876 the military reservation was turned over for distribution to settlers under the Homestead Act, only earthworks built in 1864 remained.

The state of Nebraska has in recent years excavated these earthworks and has plans to restore the once strategic post. A fine museum has already been completed. Close to the site of the fort the state has already established a campground, and here we parked our truck for the night. In the morning we were aroused early by a bulldozer grunting beside our truck from the labor of pushing a sandy hill around. The state was building a beach on the pond so that campers could swim. We had already finished breakfast when a ranger rapped on our door.

"Would you mind moving your camper?" he inquired. "They're going to do some blasting here in a few minutes."

When we spotted the crews arranging their dynamite in uncomfortable proximity to us, we got our camper moving with something of the haste that the occupants of a covered wagon would have shown if they awoke one morning to find themselves camped next to a hostile Indian village.

We drove west along the south bank of the Platte, which pioneers sometimes called the Coast of Nebraska. On either side of the river at a distance of from one or two to perhaps a dozen miles, sandy hills limited the valley. The pioneer wagons fanned out over the grassy bottoms between the hills and the bank of the river. Each wagon found its own way, except where hilly tongues of land reached toward the river. There wagons came together to jolt over deep ruts through the defiles. Our route took us along farm roads among fields of corn and alfalfa, occasionally crossing irrigation canals brimful with water sliding just beneath the floor of the bridges. During the days of the Oregon Trail the appearance of the valley was different. Long coarse grass covered the hills and the plains behind them. Buffalo skulls lay whitening. Circular wallows churned into the sandy soil by buffalo bulls were everywhere. Parkman wrote:

From every gorge and ravine opening from the hills descended deep, well-worn paths, where the buffalo issue twice a day in regular procession to drink in the Platte. The river itself runs through the midst, a thin sheet of rapid, turbid water, half a mile wide, and scarcely two feet deep. Its low banks, for

102

the most part without a bush or a tree, are of loose sand, with which the stream is so charged that it grates on the teeth in drinking.

The construction of diversion dams on the Platte to irrigate fields of corn and alfalfa has made the stream even more shallow and robbed it of its current. Today's highway bridges pass over barren sandy banks and dry river channels before they reach the water.

We crossed tributaries of the Platte on concrete bridges, but the wagon trains either forded the streams or crossed on makeshift bridges such as that described by Enoch Conyers in his diary:

The bed of the creek was cut down into the soil by the freshets to the depth of about eight feet and about twelve feet wide with abrupt banks and bordered with a narrow strip of willows. These willows the emigrants cut and piled into the creek level with the surface thus forming a temporary bridge for their teams to cross. The company that had done this work on the willow bridge, after crossing laid by and collected toll at the rate of 50 cents per wagon until they had received what they considered sufficient pay for the labor performed, then left the bridge and went on their way.

After the bridge-builders left, the Pawnees took possession of the bridge and demanded one steer of each team that arrived.

"This demand was refused," wrote Conyers. "We offered to give them some flour, rice, and sugar, but these articles they indignantly spurned."

"Help Pawnee. Much hungry!" cried the old chief. He pointed to a steer in the team.

So many heavily loaded wagons had already crossed the bridge that the dirt and willows of which it was made had been pressed down almost into the rushing water. The bridge appeared about ready to wash away.

"Nevertheless cross we must and cross we did," wrote Conyers. "Our captain gave the order to proceed, and I started our team on the bridge, whilst the Indians on the opposite side were taking off their blankets, intending to shake them in front of our cattle to run us off the bridge into the water."

The pioneers pointed their rifles at the Indians.

"Pawnee heap good," said the chief. The guns had tempered the hunger in his stomach. He contented himself with pointing to the sun and swinging his arm around to show its course to the west. Then he laid his head on his hands to let the pioneers understand that they would all be dead men by the setting of the sun.

103

At Fort McPherson National Cemetery we stopped to see the graves of soldiers and Indian scouts who died during the frontier wars which raged over the now peaceful valley. Many of the soldiers were originally buried at other forts in the West closer to where they fell, but their remains were moved to Fort McPherson as the old posts were abandoned. At Fort McPherson rows of corn crowd the well-kept graves. The living green ranks are as military as the rows of stones honoring the dead. A little farther up the river we discovered that the soldiers' adversaries also are honored by today's Nebraskans. From a high hill Indian lookouts once watched wagon trains creeping along the Platte. Today a statue of a Sioux crowns the lookout point.

Once the valley was buffalo chip country. Since there was little wood to be found, pioneers cooked over fires built with the chips. Parkman claimed that they burned like peat and produced no unpleasant effects. He might have had a hard time maintaining his viewpoint before the party of pioneer women described by Conyers.

"Many of the ladies can be seen roaming over the prairie with sacks in hand, searching for a few buffalo chips to cook their evening meal," he noted in his diary. "Some of the ladies are seen wearing gloves, but most of them have discarded their gloves and are gathering the buffalo chips with their bare hands."

At least, the pioneers discovered that a steak cooked over a buffalo chip fire required no pepper. We were happy to do our own cooking over a gas stove and then season to taste.

A few miles above Fort McPherson Cemetery we passed the forks of the Platte. The Oregon Trail continued along the south bank of the South Branch, a river that pioneers claimed contained superior water. It was muddy, but a man could always drop a handful of corn meal into a bucket and let it settle overnight. Still, even in the morning the water was likely to have an alkali flavor and be full of miniscule wildlife. A slouching pioneer, gazing at the river water in his tin cup, called to Parkman as he passed.

"Look here, you," he said, "it's chock-full of animals!"

Parkman observed that the cup "exhibited in fact an extraordinary variety and profusion of animal and vegetable life."

At first pioneers were able to drink from prairie lagoons, which then lay upon the grassy bottomlands ablaze with golden coreopsis blooms. The water was clear and fresh, but later the lagoons became polluted with cholera and other diseases. Then emigrants dug wells, eight or ten feet deep in the sandy soil. Many of the wells also became tainted, and wagon trains had to look farther and farther afield for safe water.

The trail up the South Platte may have been better supplied with water, but it was scarcely a stream of beauty to pioneers and stagecoach travelers. Mark Twain in *Roughing It* describes the river as "the shallow, yellow, muddy South Platte with its low banks and its scattering flat sand bars and pigmy islands—a melancholy stream straggling through the center of the enormous flat plain, and only saved from being impossible to find with the naked eye by its sentinel rank of scattering trees standing on either bank."

Mark Twain's coach floundered through quicksand in crossing the river.

"Once or twice in midstream," he wrote, "the wheels sunk into the yielding sands so threateningly that we half believed we had dreaded and avoided the sea all our lives to be shipwrecked in a 'mud-wagon' in the middle of the desert at last."

A few miles above Brule, a town named for the Brulé tribe of the Sioux, is where the wagons forded the South Platte at the Lower California Crossing. We drove west of town on U.S. 30 to the point where the wagons crept up from the river bank and over California Hill, which can be seen to the right of the modern highway. A local entrepreneur has erected a lookout tower from which tourists may view the ruts of the trail leading up the hill to the northwest. Two old Army wagons once used at Fort Robinson and a covered wagon in which freight was hauled over the trail are displayed nearby. Nobody was present collecting fees, and judging from the dilapidated condition of the tower, all is not well with this enterprise. We waved to a knot of men busy loading sheep into a stock truck and climbed the tower with impunity.

From the top of this tower the trail can plainly be seen passing over the hill to table land for sixteen miles to Ash Hollow close to the North Platte. Indian boys in Brule directed us along a gravel road which runs north at the foot of the table. We could make out the trail along the rim of the table with the help of our field glasses. At one place a gravestone stands by the ruts, but we could not read the legend on it with our glasses and did not want to cross a large pasture in which cattle were grazing under the supervision of a suspicious bull. Studying it from afar, I did not notice until too late that I was standing close to an ant hill. In this way I became personally acquainted with the wicked dispositions of western Nebraska ants. I danced with pain and swatted at the small invaders who after a few venomous practice nips were attempting to scale my pants legs.

The trail reaches Ash Hollow through a jumble of rocks and bluffs. It skirts the edge of the table looking for an easy descent into the hollow and then in despair plunges down Windlass Hill in the most dangerous descent east of the Rockies. Wagons were windlassed down the hill. Sometimes they broke loose from the ropes and careened to the floor of the hollow, three hundred feet below, where they splintered against the rocks. Beasts and men were often crippled.

We camped in a grove of ash and hiked along the trail into the bluffs. The Oregon Trail is easy to trace through this rugged terrain. It struck us as ironic that the Indians and then the wagons followed a buffalo trail, and today a century after the Oregon Trail fell into disuse, only cattle now in their search for grass and water follow the ruts of the wagons. Erosion has cut deeply into the trail where it runs down hillsides, and we often had to clamber through cuts which would have swallowed a wagon. Grasshoppers jumped around us in a shower at every step. Gophers sped away at our approach.

Ash Hollow reaches from the bluffs down to the banks of the North Platte. It is a valley of meadows and woods with a stream purling through it, and it must have been a sweet respite to the wagon trains after the dry trail across the table to the south. Here, too, cholera searched out the weak and the strong. On June 18, 1849, eighteen-year-old Rachel Pattison of Illinois and her husband reached Ash Hollow with a party of relatives on their way to Oregon. The next morning she was sick with cholera. That night she died. She was buried on a small hill at the mouth of the hollow, and there we found her grave. Ash Hollow has grown up around her resting place. The original stone placed by her grieving husband still is upright, but after one hundred years of wind and rain, it has been enclosed in a concrete and glass case to protect it against further weathering.

During 1855 the Brulé Sioux harassed the migrants trekking along the Oregon Trail through western Nebraska, and General W. S. Harney and six hundred men marched out from Fort Leavenworth to the rescue. The soldiers camped at Ash Hollow on September 2. Scouts brought word that the village of Little Thunder's band of Brulé Sioux was located six miles north on the Blue Water. Little Thunder insisted that he and his people were friends to the emigrants, but Harney refused to believe him. In the morning he gave orders for the attack on the village to begin.

106

Soldiers struck from two sides, killing eighty-six warriors and capturing at least that many women and children. For a while wagon trains moved unchallenged along the trail, but soon winter blizzards struck the high plains and stopped them. Winter accomplished what the Indians in the vicinity of Ash Hollow no longer had the warriors to do.

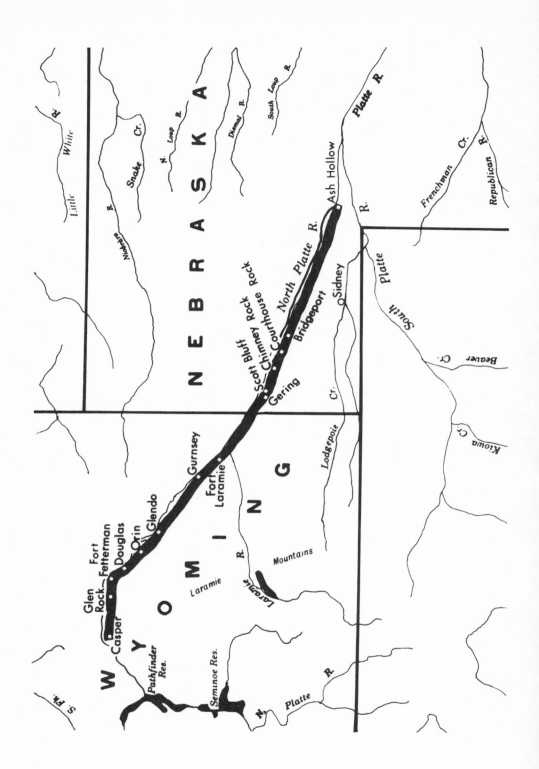

8

Oregon Trail:
The North Platte

●

We drove up the North Platte. The country became higher and drier the farther west we went. This is the land where the plains are rumpled into the first craggy outposts of the mountains. Our road passed Brady's Island, where two trappers, one named Brady, camped one night. They fell to quarreling, and Brady's partner later claimed Brady's gun accidentally went off and killed him. Farther along the Oregon Trail poetic justice took effect. The surviving partner accidentally shot himself. As he lay dying, he confessed that he had killed Brady.

Close to where Brady was murdered, we saw a plane dipping and swooping over the fields. The pilot was dusting crops with an insecticide powerful enough to eliminate all the creeping and crawling bugs that once plagued the frontier farmer. A short distance farther we had to wait while a cowboy on a horse and another in a truck drove a herd of cattle down the road toward us. The lowing herd told us far more eloquently than did the rising bluffs that we were leaving the land of corn, alfalfa, and soy beans for the range country.

The old stations mentioned in diaries and journals as having been situated on the stretch of the Oregon Trail we were now following have all vanished, but we did locate the trail itself. It passes approximately 1,750 feet south of the intersection of State 88 and U.S. 26 in Bridgeport. The town grew up around a pioneer bridge built over the North Platte to speed stagecoaches on their way from Sidney, Nebraska, to Deadwood in the Black Hills of South Dakota. Bridgeport was a hub of the pioneer trails, for the Pony Express Trail passed six miles south of the town, and the Mormon Trail was located one mile north on the opposite bank of the North Platte.

Courthouse Rock looms over today's modern highway as it loomed over the Oregon Trail. Its castellated summit rises four hundred feet above the plain about five miles south of the river, but so clear is the dry air of western Nebraska that every fissure was easy to make out as we started over the highway toward it. We turned aside onto a dirt road which looped up through the brush to the foot of the rock.

Both boys squirreled up the rock, Val to get a photo of the spreading plain beneath him, and Rick to climb higher than Val. More than a century before Rick and Val, thousands of westering boys and men had climbed where they now found footholds for sneakered feet, because most passing wagon trains paused so that emigrants could inspect at close hand this dramatic promise of the mountains yet to come.

Courthouse Rock and the smaller Jail Rock, which rises nearby, were created over sixty million years ago when sand and gravel were washed here from the Rocky Mountains then being thrust up to the west. Volcanic action flung ash and lava over the valleys. Most of the soft material was soon eroded away by the pitiless high plains weather, but where hard caps protected the softer material beneath, high bluffs were left standing. Not only Courthouse and Jail rocks, but other great rocks mentioned in pioneer accounts farther up the valley were formed in this way.

"It doesn't look like a courthouse to me," remarked Rick.

Richard Burton did not think it looked like a courthouse either. "The Court-house, which had lately suffered from heavy rains, resembled anything more than a court-house," he wrote.

It might be argued that Burton, an Englishman, would not have recognized an American courthouse if he saw one, for pioneer after pioneer expedition solemnly agreed that the rock definitely was like the courthouse back home for which here on the western plains they discovered they held a nostalgic affection. Arguments broke out as to exactly which courthouse it resembled the most.

Emigrants on the Oregon Trail camped for two different nights with Courthouse Rock in view, although in between the camps they made twenty to twenty-five miles along the Platte. Even as they set up camp at Courthouse Rock, pioneers could also look up the Platte to Chimney Rock, the next great natural landmark on the Oregon Trail. Chimney Rock is a spire of Brulé clay with interlayers of volcanic ash and sandstone which today rises one hundred feet above a conical base. The three of us truck campers agreed that it does indeed resemble a chimney, which put us in happy agreement with almost all the early travelers over the trail, including Richard Burton, who conceded, "The name is not, as is that of the Court-house, a misnomer: one might almost expect to see smoke or steam jetting from the summit."

The sight of this towering rock formation ensorcelled pioneer families for two entire days as the slow wagon trains rolled up the Platte to camp at a spring which bubbled near its base. Once the camp was established for the night, men and boys hiked the two miles from the trail to the curious rock. Viewing it in the clear, high plains air, they variously estimated its height at anywhere from fifty to seven hundred feet high. Most climbed the base to dig their names into the soft rock with their knives.

Today Chimney Rock is a national historic site. A National Park Service ranger on duty at an information center on Nebraska 92 directed us over a gravel road to a point only a half-mile from the rock.

"You'll have to hike from there," he said. "Look out for the sword-plants and the rattlesnakes."

We found an easy trail leading from the end of the road to the rock. Stepping gingerly among the sword-plants, we arrived at its foot without seeing a single rattler. Long before our arrival the weather had erased all the names of pioneers from the soft Brulé clay. The Chimney rose above us fragile and seemingly about to tumble down onto the plain where we stood. So it also appeared to the pioneers. The missionary, Father DeSmet, seeing it in 1840, wrote, "A few years more and this great natural curiosity will crumble away and make only a little heap on the plain."

Geologists are convinced that, in spite of appearances, the rock will last for many hundreds of years. A study of early sketches of the Chimney suggested to us that it has indeed weathered away to some extent, but there is plenty of rock to go before it becomes a "little heap on the plain."

Our meditation on the pioneers who had camped at the spring, the lost graves of cholera victims, which we knew from old journals and diaries were scattered about the plain between the rock and the river, and the ultimate fate of the rock itself, were broken by the splutter of a light motorcycle. A fifteen-year-old ranchboy, bow and arrows on his back, came bouncing up through the sword-plants. He swung a heavy shoe down onto the ground to stabilize his cycle and grinned a Westerner's friendly grin.

"I've just got to be hunting," he said, "but I don't see much except you fellows."

The boys snapped out of our somewhat mournful speculation about the fate of man and rock to chatter with our visitor about motorcycles, bows and arrows, jackrabbits and things. Their lively talk of hunting at first caught me up, but then I was lost again in the past. I recalled that on the banks of Kiowa Creek, a few miles farther west, archaeologists found vestiges of the chase left by hunters who brought down their quarry some ten thousand years ago.

In western Nebraska the Oregon Trail passed through badlands similar in origin to those of South Dakota. Just as in South Dakota, there are intriguing fossil remains in the soft Brulé clay. Even the early mountain men and fur traders taking the trail noticed the remains of huge pig-like animals called "oredonts," saber-toothed tigers, rhinoceroses, and camels.

In 1847 a fur trader brought the jawbone of a Titanothere to Dr. Hiram Prout of St. Louis. The doctor described the discovery for science, but the Indians of the Badlands of western Nebraska had long before this found the giant fossil teeth of the Titanothere. They came to different conclusions than did Dr. Prout. To them the teeth were those of a fierce beast that came to the earth during the tumult of a storm when the lightning was blazing among the bluffs by the Platte and the thunder was reverberating through the passes. The thunder horse chased and killed the buffalo, who were known to stampede before him in such terror that they often plunged over cliffs to their destruction.

As the stagecoach carrying Richard Burton approached Chimney Rock, forked lightning played about it and a huge black cloud billowed down the valley. By the time Burton reached Scotts Bluff the storm was roaring through the pass at its foot. Their oxen blinded by the gale, a company of emigrants which he overtook were bringing their wagons together in a corral. They herded the livestock inside the corral for fear that they too would stampede before the ravening thunder horse whose screaming neigh was the wind and whose thudding hooves were the thunder.

From Chimney Rock westward the trail clung to the Platte until the Badlands closed in so tight upon the river that it had no alternative but to plunge into the hills. The original Oregon Trail left the river about six miles east of modern Gering and skirted Dome Rock to the south. It cut through a pass named for Joseph Robideaux, who established a blacksmith shop there in 1830. Wagons paused for repairs and oxen were given new shoes if the emigrants had money to pay the smith and his Sioux wife. Today a marker shows where the long vanished smithy stood. The trail itself is clearly visible as it crosses sod which to this day is unbroken except where it was removed for the graves of pioneers now marked by a memorial.

Later a new trail was cut to the north of Dome Rock through what was called Mitchell Pass after the stockaded Fort Mitchell was erected by fur traders and named for David Mitchell, one of their friends. The trail through Mitchell Pass can also be recognized today. Nebraska 92 cuts back and forth across it inside of Scotts Bluff National Monument.

Scotts Bluff, the next great landmark on the Oregon Trail, first appeared to westering families as a blue mound on the horizon. It grew ever larger as the wagons moved along the Platte until at last it rose up as massive as a fortress overlooking the plains. Richard Burton's imagination compared the great rocky formation to the "Arabs' City of Brass, that mysterious abode of bewitched infidels, which often appears at a distance to the wayfarer toiling under the burning sun, but ever eludes his nearer search." Wagons toiled beneath the high plains sun for a month after leaving Independence before they arrived at this great bewitched fortress which, upon closer approach, turned to yellow boulders and crags of marl covered by dwarf cedar and shrubs.

To our party of three the bluff had an ominous look befitting the origin of its name. It was named for Hiram Scott, mountain man, who died at its foot. There are as many stories of how he died as there are storytellers, but it is certain that Scott who, together with Jim Bridger, Jedediah

Smith, William Sublette, and Thomas Fitzpatrick, worked for fur trader William Ashley, became ill in the autumn of 1828 as he was returning with a party to St. Louis. The mountain men camped at Laramie's Fork, a tributary of the Platte about sixty miles west of the bluff. A canoe mishap had drowned their powder, and the men could not hunt. They searched the area for wild fruit and edible roots while waiting for Scott to recover enough strength to go on.

According to a French-born West Pointer, Captain Benjamin Bonneville, who took the first wagon train along the trail in 1832:

While they were searching round in quest of edible roots they discovered a fresh trail of white men, who had evidently but recently preceded them. What was to be done? By a forced march they might overtake this party, and thus be able to reach the settlements in safety. Should they linger they might all perish of famine and exhaustion. Scott, however, was incapable of moving; they were too feeble to aid him forward, and dreaded that such a clog would prevent their coming up with the advance party. They determined, therefore, to abandon him to his fate.

Pretending to look for food, the others left Scott and hurried off down the trail. When they caught up with the strangers, they told them that Scott had died of his illness, a fate that they were confident would soon overtake him.

The next summer as the trappers took the trail back up the Platte to the annual fur rendezvous in the mountains, they were horrified to come upon Scott's remains sixty miles from where they had left him. At

Wagon trains toiled for a month to reach Scotts Bluff, a towering landmark on the Oregon Trail, now protected in a national monument in western Nebraska.   *Old West Trail Photo*

the foot of the highest bluff they discovered the bones and grinning skull that they knew to be his. He had died at the foot of a bluff which ever since has borne his name. Tradition has it that he was found at a spring from which visitors to the national monument now drink, but a park ranger whom we asked about it did not think so.

"There's not a shred of evidence," he said, "where the bones were found and where they are buried; and many historians doubt that he crawled sixty miles before dying."

It took Captain Bonneville a month to bring his twenty wagons from Missouri to Scotts Bluff, while we made the same journey in a few days. To get his wagons through the wilderness the captain and his men corduroyed soft spots with timber and cut half-roads called dugouts. They windlassed the wagons down precipitous slopes. At rivers that were too deep to ford they took the wheels off and sheathed the wagon boxes with hides to convert them into bullboats. Bonneville's wagons were fortunately smaller than those the emigrants were to use later on, and he got them safely over the rough terrain. When Washington Irving wrote about his exploits in *The Adventures of Captain Bonneville*, it not only made him a hero but created a popular interest in the Oregon Trail as a practical wagon route to the Northwest.

Indians built signal fires atop Scotts Bluff, and pioneers climbed it for the view. Today tourists drive up a toll road that corkscrews and tunnels its way to the top. To our surprise we found ponderosa pine towering out of the thin soil atop the bluff. Parking our truck in the parking area, we set out along the Saddle Rock Nature Trail among stands of Rocky Mountain juniper, which the westering pioneers called cedar. They used the wood in repairing their wagons and later as fence posts because it resisted decay. We ended up among the grotesque spires of Saddle Rock, which to wagon trains seven hundred feet below in the valley seemed to be the battlements of a fortress. Looking out over the panorama of the Platte, we saw irrigated fields ranging back against the tawny hills and the several thousand homes of Scottsbluff, Terrytown, and Gering. Far to the east we could make out the thin pencil of Chimney Rock twenty-three miles away, a solid proof that this populous valley before us was once the valley of the covered wagon trains.

Driving back down to Mitchell Pass, we parked the truck again and set out along the ruts of the Oregon Trail on foot. A short hike brought us to the spot where on August 2, 1866, William H. Jackson, bullwhacker, camped with a freight outfit. Jackson was also a painter and he sketched the view of the perpendicular bluffs from the campsite. The sketch is now

115

in the park service museum in the Scotts Bluff National Monument. A room has been set aside for his pictures because Jackson went on to become one of the West's most remarkable pioneer artists and photographers. He carried his heavy camera far along the frontier shooting stereoscopic pictures for the viewers which nineteenth century Americans were fond of looking into on rainy Sunday afternoons. Year after year Jackson returned to the Oregon Trail and particularly to the part of it which ran through western Nebraska. He died in New York City at the Explorers' Club in 1942, nine months before he was to attend a dinner at Dearborn, Michigan, that Henry Ford planned to give in honor of Jackson's one hundredth birthday.

At Reynal's Station west of Scotts Bluff, Reynal, son of one of Napoleon's soldiers, and his wrinkled Sioux wife kept an untidy inn. Richard Burton wrote:

The house boasted of the usual squaw, a wrinkled old dame who at once began to prepare supper, when we discreetly left the room. These hard-working, but sorely ill-favoured beings are accused of various horrors in cookery, such as grinding their pinole, or parched corn, in the impurest manner, kneading dough upon the floor, using their knives for any purpose whatever, and employing the same pot, unwashed, for boiling tea and tripe.

In the town of Scottsbluff, the boys, tired of their own cooking, lured me into a hamburger emporium. There we discovered morosely that the cook, muttering over the grill, must have been a lineal descendant of Reynal's ill-natured wife. Bad cooking, I am certain, is passed down from generation to generation through the genes.

Our stomachs sulked as we drove westward into Wyoming and camped on a ranch near Raw Hide Creek, along which cowboys drove cattle over the Texas Trail into Montana from 1866 to 1897. As Rick and I advanced upon a fishing hole, a brace of skunks blocked our path. They lifted their tails and glanced coyly at us over their shoulders. We withdrew and tried another path to the pond where we soon learned that grasshopper bait would hook a fish almost at the first wriggle but that the mosquitoes outnumbered the fish by at least one thousand to one.

Wagon train masters generally yoked up the oxen at five A.M. and after a grub pile of bread, bacon, and coffee moved out with the crack of bullwhips. The boys and I got out of our sleeping bags about seven A.M., cooked, ate breakfast and did the dishes, and were on our way in about half an hour. Both the wagon trains and we usually got off the trail by sundown.

116

Structures remain from Fort Laramie. Nowhere else in the West do the Indian wars seem closer. *Photo by Val Schaffner*

Across the high plains of eastern Wyoming wagons rolled with ease along the Oregon Trail, but the mountains were still to come. *Wyoming Travel Commission*

Close to Register Rock, wagon wheels cut so deep into the sandstone that their tracks will remain long after modern highways have broken up. *Wyoming Travel Commission*

We drove away in the chill of a Wyoming morning and found it only a short trip from our camp to Fort Laramie, the most important military post on the Oregon Trail. Before we broke camp, the boys and I washed with particular care and put on clean clothing because most westering pioneers did so. After all, Fort Laramie was not only the greatest military bastion on the trail, but it was also the social center. It was the post from which young Lieutenant Caspar Collins wrote to his mother: "They make the soldiers wear white gloves at this post, and they cut around very fashionably. A good many of the regulars are married and have their wives and families with them."

Pioneer wives did not want officers' wives looking down on them, so many of them wore gloves, though perhaps soiled from picking up buffalo chips, as they rode behind their oxen to the fort. Once at the fort the pioneers strolled as we did across the parade ground to the trader's store. There they bought such things as Arbuckle's coffee, Gladstone's celery, pepsin compound, and New England pickles. We found the store still stocked with the merchandise and foods of the frontier.

After a visit to the store, the men went to the enlisted men's bar where wine and beer could be had. If they were men of consequence or were acquainted with a post officer, they also might be invited to the officers' club where not only beer and wine, but whiskey, champagne, ale, and brandy were served. Both the enlisted men's bar and the officers' club have been restored as they were during the days when a man might one evening play billiards in the billiard and card room of the club and the next night be freezing to death in a mountain blizzard or recline on the turf beneath the western stars with an arrow in his chest.

"Old Bedlam" is the most dramatic of the restored fort buildings. It was built in 1849 as the officers' quarters, but for many years the post headquarters were located on the first floor. It was here at midnight on Christmas Eve, 1866, that Portugee Phillips staggered through the door out of a blizzard and into a boozy party. He gasped out the news that Captain William Fetterman and his eighty men had been ambushed and annihilated by Sioux led by Crazy Horse and Red Cloud. Out on the parade ground his horse lay dying after a furious 236-mile ride over storm-swept plains. A relief expedition was soon on its way to Fort Phil Kearny, at the foot of the Bighorn Mountains, which the Indians threatened to overwhelm.

There is nowhere in the West today that the Indian wars seem closer. From Fort Laramie troopers rode out to the relief of other forts and to the aid of beleaguered wagon trains. The fort which began as a fur traders' stockade in 1834 was strengthened until when it was finally abandoned in 1890 there were sixty-five buildings to be auctioned off to homesteaders. Settlers bought them for lumber. Only twenty-one structures still remained when the old fort was made a national historic site. Today ten of these are in ruins, but eleven have been restored and refurnished so that Americans can see firsthand how the army lived while guarding the Oregon Trail through hostile country.

"Did Indians ever attack Fort Laramie?" Rick asked a ranger on duty in the old fort commissary, which is now a visitor center.

"Not in force," he replied. "But once a detachment of troops returned from a three-day scouting trip in which they kept their eyes peeled for the hostiles. They unsaddled their horses and let them roll on the parade grounds. Suddenly at noon thirty warriors, who had been watching the party during the entire scout, rushed into the fort and halooed the horses off. This sort of thing drove Major Wood, the fort commander, right up the wall."

From Fort Laramie the Oregon Trail followed the valley of the North Platte northwest through a rocky desert. Sage and greasewood prosper in this dry land of gullies and knife-edges through which the modern highway runs close to the old trail. In downtown Guernsey we turned south from the Oregon Trail Monument to cross the Platte and drive east on an easy road to Register Rock, the site of the first wagon camp west of Fort Laramie. Rancher Frederick Guernsey has given Register Rock to the state. A caravan of Wyoming ranch families motored ahead of us over the ranch road to the foot of the cliff. We joined the tour as Frederick Guernsey's son pointed out the over five hundred pioneer names carved in the chalky cliff beneath a colony of mudbirds' nests. Large, raw-boned women and weather-beaten men stood together at the foot of the cliff and studied the names of men and women who must have in many ways resembled them.

We followed the caravan of ranch people back to Guernsey, where they drove off toward Fort Laramie in search of their pioneer heritage. We headed out of town on a ranch road to the west and then south in search of a hot springs which one of the ranch women had called the "emigrants' wash tub."

"The water stays at 70 degrees the year around," she said, "and the wagon-train women used to do their laundry in it."

We lost our way, but a cowboy, rockhounding on the gravelly shore of the Platte, put us on the right road. A geologist's hammer hung from his belt where, according to Western movies, a six-shooter should have been suspended.

"Just keep closing the range gates after you as you go," he said. He added as an afterthought, "The National Guard is using the area as a firing range for machine gun practice, and I don't know how far you can get."

The pots and pans in our camper's cabinets clattered and banged, and provisions sprang about in our icebox as we jolted over a ranch road made easy to follow by the jeep and truck tires of the guardsmen. We opened and closed gates as we went. Fortunately the guardsmen had long since left, and only a sprinkle of discarded shells remained. We reached the hot springs, which proved far too tepid for any laundering we might have had in mind.

The boys and I were eating lunch when the cowboy drove up in his venerable car, for which he showed an affection that in another day he would have reserved for his horse.

"This is a good place for Indian arrowheads," he announced. "The Indians liked the hot springs, too."

U.S. 26 runs northwest along the route of the Oregon Trail, and we followed it to the Cold Spring Camping Ground, where on August 1, 1876, the Sioux killed and scalped George Throstle and wounded a teamster of Heck Reel's freighting outfit. The Indians slaughtered four horses and ten oxen and burned three wagons before whooping off into the hills. Rifle pits dug to defend the campgrounds against renewed attack can still be seen on the knoll five hundred feet north of the highway.

A road runs west out of Glendo past the site of the old Horseshoe Station, from where Alf Slade ruled the Rocky Ridge Division of the Overland Stage. In Slade's kingdom, remarked Mark Twain in *Roughing It,* "after a murder, all that Rocky Mountain etiquette required of a spectator was that he should help the gentleman bury his game—Otherwise his churlishness would surely be remembered against him the first time he killed a man himself and needed a neighborly turn in interring him." Slade was judge and jury along this portion of the Oregon Trail, and his Navy revolver was the executioner. Doubtless Mark Twain exaggerated in his remark that Slade had killed twenty-six men, but when the stationmaster offered the author a second cup of coffee, he dared not refuse for fear he would be number twenty-seven. He drank the brew to the last bitter drop.

Richard Burton, who also visited the station, was less perturbed by

Slade than by his wife, who was "cold and disagreeable in manner, full of 'proper pride,' with a touch-me-not air." Burton noted:

One of our party who had ventured into the kitchen was fiercely ejected by the "ladies." In asking about dormitories we were informed that "lady travelers" were admitted into the house, but that the ruder sex must sleep where it could— or not sleep at all if it preferred. We found a barn outside; it was hardly fit for a decently brought-up pig; the floor was damp and knotty; there was not even a door to keep out the night breeze, now becoming raw, and several drunken fellows lay in different parts of it. Two were in one bunk, embracing maudlinly, and freely calling for drinks of water.

It would seem that Burton had good reason to fear Slade's wife. Once the station employees got drunk and dumped one barrel of liquor into the well so that they would have a perpetual supply of refreshment. They drank another. Then someone suggested that they burn the buildings. Virginia Slade drew a revolver and promised to shoot down the first man to strike a match. The party sobered up in a hurry.

The fur traders and trappers first explored the country through which the Oregon Trail ran. When arbiters in the East and in Europe dictated that beaver hats no longer were the epitome of fashion, many of the mountain men turned to guiding wagon trains. Others operated ferries on rivers that the trains had to cross. Among these was Jim Bridger, who in 1864 established a ferry across the North Platte, fifteen hundred feet up the river from where U.S. 26 crosses it today.

The boys and I went into the town of Orin to find how to get to Bridger's Crossing. A man fixing a windmill told us to turn right at the first road past the bridge.

"You'll have to go through some people's yard, but there's nobody living there so they won't be bothering you much," he concluded and waved a wrench in the direction we should take.

We drove through a ranch yard and down along the riverbank to the spot where the ferry had once landed. Irrigation pumps were lifting water from the river and passing it down through a ditch in a cultivated field where the old mountain man once carried wagons and oxen, men, women, and children with all their goods to the opposite shore.

From Douglas we drove out past another spring enjoyed by wagon-train families and across Bed Tick and Wagon Hound creeks. The trail can still be made out stretching across the Wyoming range country. We detoured to the remains of Fort Fetterman, founded to protect the trail from Indian incursions from the north. An ordnance warehouse and a

Modern Casper keeps alive the early trail days with restored Fort Caspar, named for a lieutenant killed by Indians while he was rescuing a fallen trooper.
Wyoming Travel Commission

restored officers' quarters are all that is left of the post from which General George Crook led three of his Powder River Expeditions during the last big Indian fights. Until the state of Wyoming took over a few years ago, cattle and sheep sheltered in the officers' quarters.

West of Glen Rock oil jacks creak in the Big Muddy Field discovered in 1916. We drove out Thirteenth Street among oil storage tanks on the west side of Casper to reach the famed Upper Crossing of the North Platte. As early as 1847 Brigham Young's Mormons fastened together two large cottonwood canoes with cross pieces and covered them with slabs of wood to make a ferry. They rowed the contraption with oars. The Saints ferried pioneers across the Platte until 1858, when a wooden bridge was built by Louis Guenot from Quebec. Guenot charged fifty cents a crossing as a rule, but he asked as much as five dollars when he thought he could get it.

Colonel W. H. Collins brought the 11th Ohio to erect a post at the strategic crossing in 1861, and the Indians seemed helpless to prevent the military from clamping down a tight control over the riverbanks. Then on July 26, 1865, Sergeant Custard and a detail of twenty-three set out west of the fort with a wagon train. The Indians attacked within eyesight of the fort. All but three of the soldiers were killed before a party came galloping to the rescue, led by Lt. Caspar Collins, son of the colonel and the young man who had written home to his mother about the need to wear white gloves at Fort Laramie. Just beyond the bridge two hundred Indians ambushed the rescue column. Four more soldiers dropped from their horses. The young lieutenant was killed when he stopped to lift a toppled soldier back to his saddle.

122

The post was renamed Fort Caspar for the dead lieutenant and he was given a decent burial. The graves of Sergeant Custard and eighteen of his men have never been found, but this did not keep the United States from providing gravestones. They are set up in a cemetery in a valley northwest of the old fort against the possibility that the remains might yet be found.

In 1867 the fort was abandoned and the Indians promptly burned both the fort and the bridge. It wasn't until 1936 that the WPA built a replica of the fort on its original site to give the modern city, which misspells the trooper's name as Casper, a link with the days of Indian fighting along the Oregon Trail.

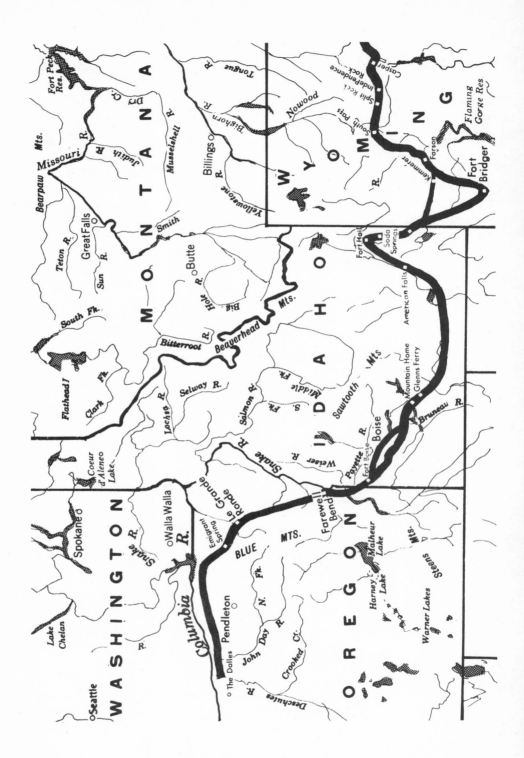

9

Oregon Trail:
South Pass and Beyond

●

From the Upper Crossing the Oregon Trail ran through a dry land
of alkali creeks and swirling dust storms to the Sweetwater River, so called
because a mule with a party's pack of sugar stumbled and fell into it.
We drove out of Casper on the Poison Spider Road and turned aside
just before Emigrant Gap to follow a ranch road which runs over the
ruts of the Oregon Trail itself. By stopping to ask directions at first one
ranch house, then another and finally at a consolidated school, we managed to keep on the right route and in time came to Wyoming 220 and
the old Sweetwater crossing.

Independence Rock, a giant whaleback of red and white feldspar and
mica, appeared only a short distance down the road. Geologists say that
the rock is of igneous origin, but we preferred Jim Bridger's explanation
of how it came to be. Jim claimed that he tossed a stone across the
Sweetwater. When it hit the far side, it just grew and grew and grew!
Jim probably also claimed that he scratched his name onto the rock with
some 50,000 others that once decorated its surface. His name appeared
on the rock all right, but someone else cut it there because he could not
write.

Some prosaic folks say that Independence Rock was named because
it stands independent from all other rocks and mountains. Actually it
was named by fur trappers who celebrated the Fourth of July there in
1825. Wagon trains that arrived in the vicinity during early July either
hastened or lingered so that they too could celebrate the nation's birthday

125

Pioneers scratched their names on Independence Rock, a giant whaleback named by trappers who celebrated the Fourth of July in its shadow in 1825.
Wyoming Travel Commission

in its shadow. The pioneers had few fireworks, so they filled the hubs of broken wagon wheels with gunpowder and gingerly placed them inside cracks in the rock. The explosions gave a very satisfying salute to the nation whose Manifest Destiny many pioneers felt it was to settle the Pacific Northwest.

Five miles from Independence Rock the Sweetwater tumbles through a four hundred foot deep chasm in a granite ridge known to the pioneers as the Devil's Gate. The Oregon Trail detoured around the chasm. The train with which E. W. Conyers traveled reached Independence Rock on July 2, but they did not linger. They pressed on to the Devil's Gate where a Frenchman named Schambau, who had been with Fremont's expedition, was building a trading post with timber hauled from the Sweetwater Mountains six miles away. Schambau took one look at Conyer's faltering old ox Dick.

"Who does that ox belong to?" he demanded. "Well, had I been here twenty minutes sooner I would have saved that ox for you. He has been alkalied. When I was with Fremont, we lost quite a number of our oxen before we discovered a remedy."

The remedy Schambau told Conyers was to take one-half pint each of lard and syrup and warm the ingredients just enough so that they mixed well.

"If the animal is bloated," concluded Schambau, "add to this one-half pint of good vinegar and drench them immediately."

The wagon train stopped to celebrate the Fourth of July. While the boys hunted game, the men took apart the wagon beds to use as long tables.

126

"One lady brought forth a sheet," wrote Conyers in his diary. "This gave the ladies an idea. Quick as thought another brought a skirt for the red stripes."

Another girl ran to her tent and brought out a blue jacket. The girls sat on the grass and manufactured Old Glory. Small boys ran to cut a liberty pole and to gather wood for a dinner fire. When the hunters returned with antelope, sagehens, and jackrabbits, the pioneers prepared to enjoy an Independence Day feast.

At dawn on July 4 the men fired off their small arms and raised the flag. The people circled the flagpole singing the "Star Spangled Banner." There were three rousing cheers and a tiger for Old Glory, and then a newspaperman, R. L. Doyle of Keokuk, Iowa, read the Declaration of Independence. Rough hands hoisted Virgil Ralston of Quincy, Illinois, who had been drinking freely of liquor bought from Schambau, atop a table decorated with evergreens and wild flowers and steadied him as he delivered a spirited oration. Then everybody sat down to a feast of roast antelope, sagehen and rabbit stew—of antelope pot pie, of fried sagehens, fried rabbit, and treasured Irish potatoes brought from Illinois, Boston baked beans, rice, and pickles. There were white bread, graham bread, and warm rolls fresh from the camp oven, and for pastry, pound cake, fruit cake, jelly cake, Sweetwater Mountain cake, peach pie, apple pie, strawberry pie, and custard pie. Coffee, tea, chocolate, and cold mountain water fresh from the brook washed the feast down. The hunters had brought back a huge ball of snow on a pole, and this was used in making ice cream, a last dessert for a wilderness banquet.

Today's highway also bypasses the Devil's Gate and hurries on to Split Rock, where during pioneer days an ice slough existed beneath a layer of peat at the depth of a man's arm. Even in July there was ice to be dug from the earth. Henry Tappan, a 49er, wrote that he found the ice perfect for a julep after crossing the scorching mesquite stretch just before Split Rock. Today the slough is gone, and as we drove past horses were grazing where it used to be.

The valley that we drove our truck through is serene if sere, but once it was one of the bloodiest sections of the Oregon Trail. Indians delighted in seizing Ben Holladay's Overland Stages, which forded the river eight vulnerable times in forty-six miles. White bandits also hid in the hills and swooped down on eastbound coaches to steal their boxes of California gold. The depredations grew so fierce that in 1862 Holladay shifted his stageline to the Overland Trail in southern Wyoming.

The modern highway and the Oregon Trail weave back and forth together along the Sweetwater as it makes its way through the mountains. Wagons that rumbled through the choking dust of the mesquite plains here ground over mountain gravel. Pioneers felt refreshed. They stopped to shorten wagon beds and took off any side projections so that their laboring oxen would have less weight to pull up the long climb toward South Pass.

The pass itself proved easy, for it is a mesquite saddle stretching twenty miles between the Wind River Mountains and the Antelope Hills badlands. The modern road twists up the pass through the Red Canyon past the winter game preserve of the Wyoming Fish and Wildlife Restoration. Once at the pass we jolted over a washboard road to camp in the almost deserted mining town of Atlantic City, which is on the Atlantic side of the Continental Divide. In the winter when the temperature falls to 50 below zero and the roads are closed with snow, the mail still comes to Atlantic City on snowshoes. The only shower in town was constructed by some young U.S. Geological Survey geologists who attached a big can to a post. The sun heats water in the can. At the yank of a cord it drizzles down onto the bather.

"It can be a bit breezy taking a shower," Doug Fox, a college student from Atlanta, Georgia, working for the summer, told us. "When the chemist's wife came out to join us, we put up tarps for privacy and this also cut off some of the breeze."

We parked our camper beside a stream where gold tracings still show. After dinner I hiked down the deserted main street of this once flourishing town. A lone bull eyed me evilly where gunfighters had once unlimbered their weapons, then snorted and rammed off into the dark. At the geologists' trailer we talked. Uncle Sam, it appears, is making drillings in old gold-producing areas to see how much gold may still be left.

"We look for arsenic traces," explained the geologist. "Arsenic is usually found with gold."

Doug Fox and Ed Leyden, another college student from Lahaska in Pennsylvania's Bucks County, had the next day off. In the morning the boys and I piled into a four-wheel-drive vehicle with them, and went grinding up the steep trails to where we could get a fine view of the Oregon Buttes, past which the covered wagons once rolled. This tertiary cliff which forms the south wall of the pass signaled the downward descent of the wagon trains toward the still-distant Pacific and is mentioned in most of the diaries and journals.

Our vehicle lurched over the trails to an abandoned mine. Clambering along the tunnel, our flashlights stabbing into the gloom, we slipped on the floor ice that never melts. "A guy could put on ice skates and skate to the mine head," said Rick.

"Fellows chop it off to cool their drinks in the summer," commented Doug Fox.

"Poachers also hang their venison in mines like this," added Ed Leyden.

The hills are populated with deer and antelope, just as they were in wagon-train days. The day before the hunting season opens, the sourdough prospectors of the pass, who do most of the out of season poaching, go out into the hills and fire off their guns. The fusillade warns the deer and antelope that the hunting season is about to open and that they had better take cover.

"The fellows around here figure that they need the game to live and that sportsmen from the outside are only trying to show off what hairy-chested he-men they are when they gun down a deer with a telescopic sight," said Doug. "They see no reason to let the outsiders get a shot at their meat supply."

We explored the crumbling town of Miner's Delight, where two old miners still live with their eighty-three-year-old Edison phonograph and boxes of ragtime cylinders. In several places we could see where a modern-day prospector had dug along a vein of quartzite looking for gold. Tailings and ripped-up rails attracted us to old workings. At one mine we saw an underground bunk house that was cool in summer and warm in winter.

Climbing Peabody Ridge to the eighty-five-hundred-foot level, we came across heavy workings. It had taken twenty-eight horses to pull the huge timbers of the old mine to the top of the hill. A little farther along the trail we came upon a family living in a sheep wagon. A flock of sheep grazed in a mountain meadow nearby.

"The sheepherder there also works in the new U.S. Steel taconite plant here in the pass," said Ed Leyden.

When we returned to town we found that the U.S. Geologists had struck their service flag and hoisted the Star Spangled Banner in its place. The ghost town was holding an election, and ancient miners and prospectors from all over the hills were filing into the trailer, which was being used as a voting place. An octagenarian pulled his hoary beard with a small boy's glee.

"Most fun electing a mayor that this old town's had since we held the big dance over there at Hyde Hall," he said.

We pressed for details of the dance.

"Well, sir, they were all whooping it up and cavorting around like they've got the long john winter itch and there comes a big roar! It was an earthshake, and it shakes so hard that it takes the whole second floor off. It falls down on the veranda, and those dancers were so hopped up that nobody even noticed. That was some party, but this electing folks beats all."

When we drove away, the citizens of almost deserted Atlantic City were debating furiously what to do about ghost voters. Only a few miles down the gravel road we came to South Pass City, a twin mining town nearing extinction, through which Mark Twain passed on his stagecoach ride west. Mark Twain noted four log cabins by the trail. A few years later in 1867 a gold strike on the upper Sweetwater boomed the population to seven hundred by snowfall. Atlantic City, Miner's Delight, and other mining camps sprang into existence. By 1870 South Pass City had a Main Street a half-mile long with thirteen saloons and five hotels, to say nothing of a beer garden, a bowling alley, a gun store, and two doctors' offices. Stagecoaches carried shipments of gold over the Oregon Trail.

We found one of the hotels, the Eclipse, still standing. A store built in 1869 is now a museum showing such things as an opium bowl used by Chinese miners and a ladies' charming brass knuckles. The storekeeper handed the boys square nails which he had pulled out of old boards.

"You can easily make five or six dollars a day panning gold in the crick today," he told them, "but it doesn't pay a man."

We rummaged among the homemade skis and ski poles, a barber chair which doubled as a dental chair, muffin tins made out of assay office trays, and a hotel tub for which a man paid four bits for two buckets of water and tub-sitting privileges. The miners of South Pass City had a fine appreciation for object lessons, it would appear. We discovered a two-room building, one end of which was fitted with heavy wooden doors and bars. This end obviously was the jail. The other end of the building was the school where children studied only a wall away from the pass's most objectionable citizens.

South Pass City and Atlantic City are as fragile as old men. They recall the last days of the Oregon Trail when freight wagons and stagecoaches had joined the pioneer trains on the historic trail. In fact, most of the men who rushed to the gold field in South Pass were construction crews building the Union Pacific Railroad through Lone Pine Pass to the south. Despite the desertions, the Union Pacific was at last completed, and the decline of the Oregon Trail was made certain. Every winter the heavy snows press relentlessly down upon the dilapidated buildings of the old mining towns, and every spring finds more of them crumpled to

All summer long ice coats the floor of abandoned
mines in South Pass. Poachers hang their venison
in the chilly gloom of the shafts.
Photo by Val Schaffner

South Pass City is as fragile as an old man remembering the trail days.
Wyoming Travel Commission

the earth. If these towns, a heritage of the old West, are to survive, they require urgent attention from the state of Wyoming.

Pioneers surmounting the South Pass and the Continental Divide were delighted to see that the streams now flowed toward the Pacific. They felt the worst of their journey was over. Then they learned that their troubles were only beginning. Oxen and cows grew weaker, grass thinner, and game harder to kill as they struggled forward over a sagebrush plain. Even the waters of Pacific Springs proved a mixed blessing. The springs covered half an acre of alkaline swamp. A tough sod had formed over the surface of much of the springs, so that a man could walk to the fresh water, even though the "ground" quaked for forty feet around him as he went. Sometimes cattle ventured after the men and fell through the sod and drowned.

In 1962 when the Union Pacific built its seventy-six-mile spur line from the main line near Rock Springs to the U.S. Steel taconite project in South Pass, engineers dug drains and poured fill to cross the swamp. At several points the railroad's high iron passed near the deep wagon ruts of the Oregon Trail. Work crews carefully avoided disturbing them because of their historical importance.

From Pacific Springs the Oregon Trail ran westward along Pacific Creek. Descending from the pass, Mark Twain noted "long ranks of white skeletons of mules and oxen" left by the wagon emigrants. Up-ended boards and small piles of stones marked the graves of those who had crossed the Continental Divide only to die before the snowcapped Wind River Range had disappeared from view. Wyoming 28 led us along the same route. Sage and thistles spread over the alkali flats. We paused at a rest stop by the road where tourists are invited by a sign to walk through a gap in a barbed wire fence to inspect the very spot where the trail to Fort Bridger and California and the trail to Oregon separated. The true spot where wagon trains turned left to California or continued straight on along the trail to Oregon is farther to the west.

The gravel Blue Rim–Farson Road leads across the empty tablelands from Farson close to the route of the Oregon Trail, and we set out over it. Dust whirled behind us in a cloud and penetrated into the camper where it settled down as much as an inch thick before we reached the banks of the Green River. Antelope raced ahead of us, wheir white rumps flashing warning to their fellows that our strange contraption was hurtling over the plateau where wagon trains once crept. The hot sun beat down, and the crossing became unpleasant even in a rapidly moving truck. It must have been hellish in a wagon or plodding on foot beside the oxen. Dust stung eyes and gritted between the teeth. Oxen tongues were blackened by it.

Near Simpson's Hollow just off the road the remains of freight wagons tell of a violent incident on the trail in 1857, for which the Indians for once could not be blamed. During that year Mormons and the U.S. Army were in conflict. Captain Lot Smith of the Utah militia fell upon three trains of seventy-eight Majors and Russell wagons hauling army supplies over the trail and burned all but two. Captain Smith, honored among the Saints for his hard riding and gallantry, spared two wagons so that the drivers would be able to reach their homes. No blood was shed, but without his supplies General Johnston's soldiers were unable to advance into Utah. They had to winter at Camp Scott on one-quarter rations.

When we arrived at the old Dodge Suspension Bridge over the sun-dappled Green River, we clattered to the middle of it before we learned from a fisherman angling over the side that the bridge had been condemned and was closed to vehicular traffic! Rather than back off and drive back to Farson, we continued on to the far bank. We arrived safely with no damage to the bridge or the truck. During the crossing I knew exactly how an elephant walking tightrope must feel.

As the pioneers approached the Green River, the oxen bawled and ran towards the water. The trains forded the river or were ferried across at the cost of $3 per wagon. At that price the pioneers had to swim their own cattle. Once across the Green the wagons rolled on to Emigrant Springs. There the trail pitched down over such a hazardous slope that Conyers wrote, "If a tin cup should accidentally fall out of the front end of the wagon, it would fall over the heads of the tongue yoke of cattle before it would reach the ground," Emigrant Springs still bubbles close to U.S. 189 near the intersection with a paved road leading to the Fontanelle Dam on the Green.

From the springs some wagons went south to the security and supplies of Fort Bridger, before turning again northwestward toward the still far-off Columbia. Other wagons took a trail westward from the springs that passed north of today's Kemmerer. The routes came together east of U.S. 30N south of Cokeville and crossed into Idaho immediately north of what is now Border Junction. Over the years still other routes were opened up by guides who led columns of wagons through rival mountain passes. Landers Trail, the Hudspeth Cutoff, and the South Alternate along the Snake River were each taken by hundreds of emigrant trains. The routes of these trails through the mountains and plateaus can be traced today, but we decided to stick to the main trunk of the great "white-topped wagon road" itself. We took U.S. 30N through Border Junction into Idaho.

The Oregon Trail ran a short distance to the north of the highway as we followed the Bear River westward. The wheels of emigrant wagons and of the freight wagons and stagecoaches which followed them cut deeply into the earth. Across Idaho the old tracks have been obscured by irrigated farms and city streets, but in range country they still can be traced for miles at a time. Sometimes the modern road follows close to the trail, but elsewhere it seeks a longer but easier way to cross the mountains. As an example, just within Idaho the trail cuts through rugged Emigrant Canyon, while the highway dips south to follow the gentle valley of the Bear. The roads—the old and the new—come together again at Smith's Fort, where covered-wagon oxen once paused to graze in the lush meadows.

"If this country were ever settled, fine farms could be had here," Enoch Conyers wrote in his diary.

Mountain man Thomas Long Smith, known on the frontier as Peg Leg, was of the same view. He packed a plow and implements from Salt Lake City and tried to farm the valley in 1848. Peg Leg failed, but today there are rich farms along the Bear River. Probably Peg Leg's failure as a farmer was more a matter of temperament than anything else. After all, this was the same two-legged cousin of a grizzly bear, who as he trapped beaver in the mountains was struck in the leg by an Indian bullet. It smashed his leg. Smith should have died, but he wrapped a tourniquet of buckskin thongs around his thigh and amputated with the aid of his companion's hunting knife. He clamped off the severed arteries with a bullet mold. He whittled himself a leg of hickory. At Smith's Fort pioneers found him stamping about his settlement of four log cabins. Peg Leg may have failed as a farmer, but wagon train diarists noted that he made one hundred dollars a day profit trading with passing emigrants.

The Oregon Trail continues northwest through Montpelier near where we tried to camp on the flanks of Geneva Summit in the Caribou National Forest. It was dusk, and we found all the camping sites already taken. A storekeeper in Geneva from whom we bought supplies directed us to the school yard where we parked our camper for the night in the lee of the village schoolhouse. When we walked over for a bedtime snack, two teen-aged boys from Shabona, Illinois, revved their motorbikes outside of the store. One boy's headlight was out, and the boys were uncertain that they should try to ride the dark mountain road with only one light for two of them. They kept peering down the dark road to the west with a westering hunger that seems part of the fiber of Americans. But there was more than a westering instinct in one of the boys.

"I've got to get to Montpelier," he told me. "I can get a phone booth there and phone my girl back home. She was out last night when I phoned, and if she's out tonight, it's all over."

Many a wagon-trail youth must have fretted about the girl he left behind him. It was inevitable that finally the boys got up enough nerve to go sputtering off up the mountain, their one headlight making a pinprick of light in the night.

In the morning we drove to Soda Springs where the Soda Point Reservoir on the Bear River has flooded Beer Spring, which pioneers claimed tasted like lager beer although disappointingly flat. Steamboat Spring, a mile farther on, is also flooded. Before the days of irrigation reservoirs, water at Steamboat Spring collected in a crevice and then spurted up to a height of about four feet, making a noise resembling steam escaping from a pipe on a Mississippi River steamboat. When Enoch Conyers arrived at Steamboat Spring with his wagon train, the Keokuk newspaperman, R. L. Doyle, bet that he could stop the flow by sitting on the crevice. When other emigrants covered his wager, he took off his pants and sat on the hole just as the spring began to flow.

"Doyle soon began bobbing up and down at a fearful rate," wrote Conyers. "At this stage of the fun several of the boys took hold of Doyle and tried to hold him on the crevice, but in this they failed, for the more weight they added to Doyle the more power the spring seemed to have, and Doyle kept on bobbing up and down like a cork."

Finally Doyle cried out, "Boys, there is no use trying to hold the devil down. It can't be did, for the more weight you put on, the more the devil churns me. I am now pounded into a beefsteak."

The Oregon Trail turns to the right around the Soda Springs Hills, and we left U.S. 30N on a ranch road to try to follow it. At one point we pulled off the road to hike through the fields to find the trail running next to an irrigation ditch. Our road wound among foothills and across dusty deserts where wind devils danced. Somehow we took a wrong turn and ended up on a track that plunged down into an arroyo through which our truck wallowed to the opposite side. At last we came across a wiry sheepherder, Ernie Romero, who came out of his wagon with a scowl on his face. He brightened when he saw the boys.

"Thought you was cattlemen," he told us. "This morning they drove a herd of cattle right through my camp. They trampled the camp and fouled my drinking water."

Romero's sheep graze far off on the range, but at the end of the day he saddles his old horse and rides out to bring them back to graze overnight near his camp. He showed us how to find the road we wanted. We lunched on the range while a herd of cattle collected around us to see what we were doing. Wind devils whirled and shook the camper and blew dust in its open windows.

We found the road, only to lose it again. This time a young Mormon mechanic at Chesterfield pointed out the correct way to go, and we followed the trail to where it is now drowned by the Portneuf Reservoir. At first I was bothered that so much of the Oregon Trail through Idaho is now submerged beneath reservoir waters. This is so because the trail followed the rivers. Then I reflected that the pioneers would have cheered at the sight of irrigated fields and comfortable homes where they crossed a cruel desert. Narcissa Whitman, wife of Dr. Marcus Whitman, the medical missionary to the northwest tribes, passed along the trail in 1836 and described this part of it. "Truly I thought," she said, "the heavens over us were brass and the earth iron under our feet." Because of the dams and reservoirs, this world of hard metal is now a land of farms and towns.

The inhospitable desert was not the only problem that travelers over the Oregon Trail encountered. At Hell's Acre near Fort Hall, a robber band regularly ambushed stagecoaches. One day they dashed out of the brush firing a fusillade of buckshot. The driver, Frank Williams, dropped wounded from his seat and four passengers were killed. Two unhurt passengers jumped into the brush and ran for their lives. One uninjured man crouched at the bottom of the coach covered with blood from his dead comrades.

"Gentlemen," he cried to the bandits who brandished their guns at him. "I am dying. Don't mutilate my face."

They left him unhurt but went off with some sixty thousand dollars in loot.

Wagon-train pioneers and stagecoach travelers breathed a sigh of relief when they reached Fort Hall, over which the British flag was flying even though it was in American territory. The fort was founded in 1834 by Nathaniel Wyeth of Boston, but it was bought by the Hudson's Bay Company four years later. British Fort Hall was the only outpost along hundreds of miles of dusty trails, and travelers were given a hospitable welcome. We drove through the Fort Hall Indian Reservation, where Shoshone and Bannocks live in desolation, to find the site of the adobe fort. A furious dust storm blew up out of the west, and we jolted and tossed through its vehement gusts as coveys of Indians fled toward their shacks. The women had a daunted look. The children had pinched faces. All signs of the fort have vanished, and we were morose as we drove back to the main highway.

From the site of Fort Hall the Oregon Trail struck out across the Michoud Flats, which since the construction of the American Falls irrigation dam in 1925-27 are mostly under water. The trail runs directly beneath the dam itself and continues on along the south bank of the Snake River. We camped that night on the edge of the reservoir, where a number of fishermen angled from the stony beach with little luck. The impounded waters of the Snake lapped on the cheerless beach much as the imprisoned spirit of the frontier West presses against the bonds of the pragmatic modern American mind. The American Falls, once the wonder of trappers and emigrants, is a depressing place even if it does make possible the livelihood and well-being of thousands of families.

Not far west of American Falls U.S. 30N and the Oregon Trail come together to pass between the Snake and a jagged tumble of rocks. The Shoshone had an observation post atop the rocky hill on the south side of the trail. On August 10, 1862, braves fired from behind the rocks overlooking the trail and killed nine and wounded six of an emigrant party. We drove through the defile at sixty miles per hour.

Farther along the road our wheels sloshed through a black stream of Mormon crickets. Sometimes traffic on a western road will mash so many of these crickets that the road will become slippery with death and cars will flip off into the ditch as if they had hit a glare of ice. I've driven through migrating crickets elsewhere in the West, so I slowed. The wheels made a thick and sticky sound on the crickets.

Along this stretch of the trail, Enoch Conyers also encountered herds of crickets. He reported that the Digger Indians spotted the crickets with glee. They filled holes, three feet across and two feet deep, and in them kindled hot fires of sagebrush and willow wood. Bucks, squaws, and chil-

137

dren whipped the grass in a circle to drive the crickets into the heated holes. There they sizzled and fried, swelled up and burst something like a roasted chestnut. The squaws mashed the insects, mixed them with roots and herbs, and kneaded the mixture into flat cakes, which they dried in the sun for a winter snack.

The highway crosses the Raft River about two miles north of where the California Trail branched off the Oregon Trail. We took ranch roads that traced the Oregon Trail through deserts and through fields of Idaho potatoes. Often we could make out the trail across a field of alfalfa because the crops grow with a deeper color where the oxen once walked. A gravel road follows the trail where it skirts the black-rocked canyon of the Snake and offers a spectacular ride to a motorist who does not mind dust and a washboard surface.

Two and a half miles beyond Twin Falls is Desert Station, where in 1869 Stove Pipe Sam, having failed at cards and gold digging along the Snake, took his first step toward becoming a clergyman. He rigged up two dummies from sagebrush and driftwood and placed them near the trail. At dusk the stage came thundering up to the station.

"Halt!" cried Sam. "Throw out the treasure box."

The driver, seeing what looked like three bandits about to fire at him, tossed down the box and whipped his horses to make his escape. Alas for Sam. He talked too much around trail campfires. He was arrested for a $750 reward and imprisoned in the new penitentiary at Boise. There he got religion. He sang hymns from his cell and shouted until the other prisoners called him "Preaching Sam." Boise ministers came to hear him and were moved at his eloquence. In 1875 they obtained a parole for him so that he could do his preaching and hymn-singing on the outside.

We stopped at an observation point on U.S. 30 beyond Desert Station to watch the Thousand Springs gushing out of the lava walls on the opposite side of the Snake River Canyon. The phenomenon marked by most Oregon Trail pioneers was caused by volcanic flows over the Snake River plain, which forces the river to arc southward. In time, underground channels and reservoirs formed in the spongy lava to allow torrents of water to pass beneath the surface and burst into the open air at the Thousand Springs.

At Upper Salmon Falls pioneers fished or traded with the Indians for fish to augment their dwindling supply of salt bacon. In the canyon of the Snake River just before the falls the pioneers found the going grim. Henry H. Gilfry wrote in his narration, "Foul odors were everywhere from the dead cattle, and the air was rife with disease, destruction and death, and its treacherous waters claimed many victims. The rocks and hillsides destroyed the wagons, and gloom was again everywhere around us."

A modern highway bridge lifted us over the canyon to the north bank, which in pioneer times was the route of the North Alternate trail, sometimes called the Kelton Road. The main trail crossed the Snake at Three Island Crossing near present-day Glenns Ferry. Sometimes when the water was too high for wagons to ford the river the pioneers continued on along the south bank of the river on the South Alternate trail to a point just west of Fort Boise, where they were able to cross and rejoin the Oregon Trail.

We followed ranch roads over the rugged hills along the route of the Oregon Trail to Rattlesnake Station, also known to the pioneers as Mountain Home. We drove over gravel and concrete to Boise, the state capital, where we talked to a teen-aged boy working in a gasoline station who spends his weekends on a motorbike following the Oregon Trail along the canyon rim. He picks up artifacts—ox shoes, wagon bolts, sometimes knives or pieces of broken crockery.

"Landslides have dropped some of the trail into the river," he told us. "Those places I make a big detour, and that's where it gets hairy."

We drove up the north side of the Boise River to the Lucky Peak Reservoir. At places we could make out the Oregon Trail on the south canyon rim. We camped close to the reservoir so that we could swim in its chill mountain waters and wash off the dust of the trail. After swimming we watched men panning for gold in Boise River sands.

"Nobody's going to get rich at this," one fellow told us, "but there sure is gold here."

West of Boise the trail and the modern highway run close together along the Boise River to a spot where people now picnic in a pleasant meadow. Grasshoppers jump and zip through the air. At this place on August 20, 1854, Alexander Ward's twenty-member party, Oregon-bound, was attacked by the Indians. Only two boys were spared. The Army struck back against the Indians, who then became so enraged that both Fort Boise and Fort Hall had to be abandoned. Troopers escorted wagon trains along the Boise River for the next eight years. Sometimes the trains pressed on without soldiers, which invited the Indians to attack. This stretch of the Oregon Trail became one of the most tragic.

Cattle fed on the wild rye grass that grew five to six feet high in the Boise Valley and grew fat even as the trains moved forward. But sometimes they drank of alkali water and died a bloated death. Indians feasted on the dead cattle until emigrants cut open the carcasses and inserted strychnine with the intention of killing off some of the coyotes that pestered the wagon trains at night. Indians died by the scores instead. Enoch Conyers reported that the Indians tried to cure their poison victims by putting them in sweat-houses built with sticks and then covered with dirt.

"These sweat-houses are built near the bank of the river," he wrote in his diary. "When they imagined the patient had been sufficiently sweated, they would suddenly open the door, when the patient would make a desperate rush for the river, plunging into the cold water head foremost. Under this treatment the patient invariably died within a few minutes after coming from his cold bath."

At the Hudson's Bay Company's Fort Boise, situated where the Boise River flows into the Snake, the trail crossed the Snake into Oregon. Here some of Conyer's train grew tired of their irksome progress by land and decided to descend the Snake by boats made from wagon beds.

Quite a number of emigrants took some discarded wagon beds at our last crossing on the Snake River, near Fort Boise, calked them with strips of rags, loaded their provisions and blankets and started down the river. They reported the river as very swift and filled with large boulders and perpendicular cliffs of rocks, towering up 400 and 500 feet on either side, and exceedingly dangerous to navigate. One of the wagon beds struck a rock and capsized. They lost all their provisions, bedding and clothing, the occupants barely escaping with their lives. They became frightened by their dangerous adventure down the Snake River in a wagon bed and concluded to desert their boats and take the emigrant road for the balance of the way.

Most wagon-train people took one look at the raging waters of the Snake and chose to follow the Oregon Trail, which ran down the Snake River, although at some miles distance from the waters, to Farewell Bend. There the families camped for their last night on the banks of the river where modern travelers picnic and swim at an Oregon State roadside park on U.S. 30. The Oregon Trail struck off across the Snake River Plains as does today's U.S. 30, called "The Old Oregon Trail Highway."

The wagons rolled down precipitous grades into La Grande Ronde, named by a Canadian voyageur because of its circular shape. The lush grass of the valley was beautiful to the emigrants. While the Conyers party camped for the night, Indians stole among the wagons and made off with a horse, "rope and all," although it was tied to the back end of a wagon only a few feet from a sleeping emigrant. In the morning a group

The James Smith Store at South Pass City is now a museum, containing such things as a lady's brass knuckles and a Chinese miner's opium bowl.

Photo by Val Schaffner

Some wagons turned aside to the Whitman Mission to obtain medical help from Dr. Marcus Whitman or to rest from the long journey to Oregon.

From a painting by William H. Jackson, National Park Service Photograph

The surgeon's quarters remain from Fort Dalles, which was built on the banks of the Columbia River at the western end of the Oregon Trail.

Oregon State Highway Travel Division

of men set out in search of the missing horse but could not find it.

"While out in the valley, they heard a number of persons singing an old Methodist hymn," wrote Conyers in his diary. "Thinking it was some emigrant company that was holding a meeting, they approached the grove where the meeting was being held, and to their surprise discovered that it was a large body of Indians who had met in the grove for the purpose of holding a religious meeting. Not desiring to disturb the services, the boys withdrew and returned to camp minus the horse." Doubtless these Indians were converts either of Dr. Marcus Whitman or more likely of the Rev. Henry Spalding, who was a Methodist.

Harvey and A. B. Meacham run a trading post at "Mountain House" near Meacham Meadows, a favorite camping place for the emigrants. Here Major A. G. Lee camped in 1844 on his way over the trail, and here on July 3, 1923, Warren G. Harding came to celebrate the eightieth anniversary of the great covered wagon migration of 1843. We bought gasoline from the Meachams and drove up through the Blue Mountains to camp at Emigrant Spring State Park. In the mountains the pioneers found themselves at last in a great pine forest where the wind swept through the branches with a soothing sound, and the heat of the trail

142

could be forgotten. They filled their water barrels in the spring which still flows in the park and rested for a few days before pushing on towards the Columbia.

At what is now Pendleton the wagon trains camped beside the Umatilla River and climbed the same precipitous hill that U.S. 30 climbs today. Twenty miles farther west the Oregon Trail crossed the Umatilla at Echo, from where its ruts still may be easily traced for miles. A short distance from the village of Biggs the trail at last came out on the mighty Columbia where the grandeur of the bluffs and the broad flood filled the weary families with awe.

There were still obstacles to overcome before the wagons could reach The Dalles now so hard at hand. To cross the Deschutes River the pioneers floated their prairie schooners and swam their livestock. Indians ferried women and children across in canoes in exchange for bright-colored shirts. Now a pleasant state park is on the banks of the river where pioneers calked their wagons for this final dangerous river crossing.

The wagon trains rolled on unvexed toward Mount Hood's great snowy cap. Our truck sped along the Columbia River on a highway which runs beneath beetling cliffs to The Dalles, which is the sort of town where peach trees bear fruit in dooryards, and a girl rides her horse across a schoolyard without fear of censor. Tumbleweeds rolled unnoticed along the street ahead of our truck. In City Park at Eighth and Union Streets we found the lump of basalt which marks the end of the Oregon Trail, half a continent away from Independence, Missouri, where the trail began.

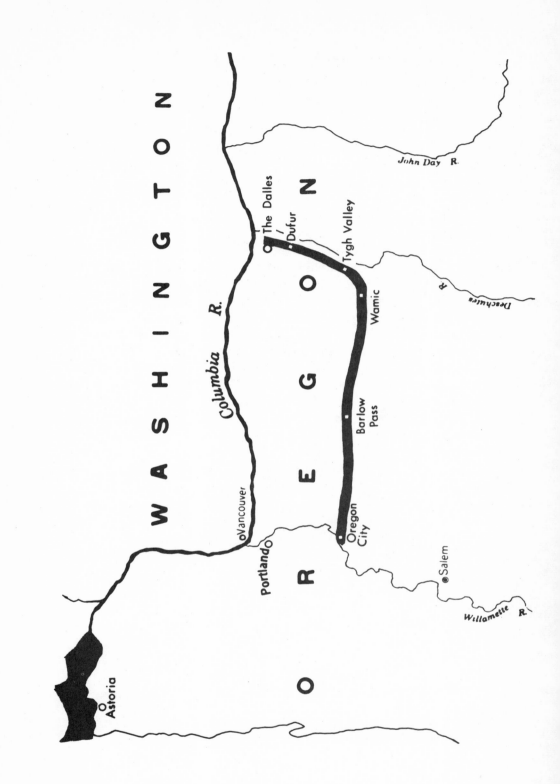

10

Barlow Road

●

"God never made a mountain that he had not made a place for some man to go over it or under it," Captain Samuel Kimbrough Barlow told the Oregon provisional legislature. "I am going to hunt for that place."

The legislators stirred in their seats and murmured to one another. Barlow was a redoubtable man. That they knew, but the mountain in question was Mount Hood, a colossus of rocky slopes and forests, of upswept ice fields and perpetual snow. The frosted extinct volcano shouldered down to the Columbia west of The Dalles and prevented pioneer wagon trains from following the river west to the Willamette Valley and the sea beyond. Most emigrants took to boats on the Columbia. In the turbulent current many drowned in the waters of the river that they had crossed half a continent to find.

Samuel Barlow wanted authority from the legislators to scout a way through the Cascade range south of Mount Hood. He planned to build a wagon road and charge tolls. Already Barlow had led an emigrant party over the Cascades. He had left The Dalles at the end of the Oregon Trail with nineteen persons, seven wagons, and livestock on September 24, 1845. When winter snows had blocked his way in the mountains, he had ordered the company to leave its goods with William Berry, a member of the party, at Fort Deposit. The pioneers had then slogged ahead through the drifting snow on foot using oxen and horses to pack

145

vital supplies. Barlow had led them safely through the high spectral world of blizzards and hunger to the Willamette Valley. If anybody could build a road through the mountains, it would be Samuel Barlow. The legislators agreed to let him try.

Barlow went into partnership with Philip Foster. The paper read, "The said parties to agree to make and open a wagon road between Oregon City to the foot of the Cascade Mountains on the east side, agreeable to an act of the legislature of Oregon."

The partners astounded the legislature by quickly finding a way over the apparently impregnable Cascades. Their work teams felled trees and cut through the dense undergrowth to build the first wagon road in Oregon. Looking for a way to skirt the towering mountain to the west, the Barlow Road ran south from The Dalles to Fifteen Mile Crossing at what is now Dufur. It climbed Tygh Grade into the Tygh Valley. Then it angled to the northwest keeping to the north of the White River, a foaming tributary of the Deschutes. It climbed without pause until it reached the summit of the Cascades in a high craggy saddle between Mount Hood to the north and lofty Mount Wilson to the south. After crossing the divide it descended westward to the Sandy River and on down through the ancient forests, ever lower until it reached the open valley of the Willamette. In 1846, the very first year, 145 wagons and 1,559 horses, mules, and cattle, and droves of sheep passed over the Barlow Road.

Today a modern highway has been blasted out of the rock westward along the Columbia River from The Dalles, but the boys and I ignored it in favor of putting our truck camper over as much as we could of the original Barlow Road. We camped on the flanks of Mount Hood and talked it over. We knew that the forest service has kept much of the old road open as a fire road and that there were some improved wilderness campsites strung out along it.

"Oh, we'll get half a dozen campers every month," a ranger had told us. "I don't think you'll have to worry about being overcrowded. You'll have no trouble in getting through."

Close to where our truck rested underneath the great trees, several families of migrant field workers set up camp. As each ramshackle car drove up, a tumble of barefoot kids fell out of the back seat. Mom and Dad climbed stiffly out, tired from the day's pear picking in the orchards of the Hood River Valley. The forest glade rang with the laughter and shouts of the boys and girls as they searched for firewood and helped their parents get ready for the night. Weary men and women snarled at one another and at the tumult of kids, cuffed a child here and furiously ordered another there. A few boys went to a rushing stream with cane poles and worms dangling on their hooks and soon came back with trout, which made a mouth-watering aroma frying in the skillet.

My boys and I clambered along the rocky stream with some of the migrant boys.

"Got to look lively," said Billy, a twelve-year-old youngster from the Missouri Ozarks. "Last year the water rushed a man over the falls."

As we returned to our camp we saw signs of grizzly bear, which frequent the falls near the campground.

"Got to build a fire to keep away the bears," said Billy's dad, a whiplash of a man. We all fell to work, and as soon as the cooking was over and the dishes washed we kindled a roaring fire, which although most likely not needed to keep away the bears at least served to keep off the mountain chill that settled down in the forest once the sun had set.

Rick got out his guitar and played and sang three or four songs mainly for the benefit of two beautiful girls, a blonde thirteen-year-old and a chestnut-haired fifteen-year-old, who had gone to the stream and carefully washed the day's grime from their faces and their bare legs when they saw that this strange boy from the camper had a friendly grin and was a new acquaintance of their brother, Billy. They listened to Rick singing by the fire and asked shyly for the same songs over and over. Finally the father took the guitar and strummed out the heartfelt old songs of the frontier.

"I planned on being a guitar picker back home in Missouri," he said, "and I ended up a pear picker."

His songs all had sadness in them, just as when he laughed at one of his children's pranks, there was sadness beneath his laughter. As we sat by the fire listening to the "old-timey" songs, the flaming fire in the lowering forest, the bright-eyed, barefoot children seemed a scene drawn out of the trail past. The boy, Billy, came to sit at my side. He held a stick out towards the flames with his bare toes until it caught fire.

"My dog cured my asthma," he said. "I'm in fourth grade, and I would have been higher, but we move so much, and I missed school because of asthma."

"Your dog, Billy?"

"Yes, my dog." He had a pleased, excited look on his face as he undid a button on his shirt. A chihuahua's pert head popped out and yawned. The dog reached up lovingly to lick the boy's chin. I had noticed the bulge in the child's ill-fitting shirt earlier in the evening but had not suspected there was a dog concealed beneath it.

"I keep him warm at night because he hasn't got much hair," said the boy. "I used to be right bad, but the doctor said I needed something to love. My daddy got me this dog, and my asthma went away."

I wondered how many beans, peaches, apricots, or pears had to be picked to pay for the little dog snuggled at the boy's breast. The mother and father looked at their son.

"Billy wants to be a doctor," said the father. "Sometimes I think he might be at that."

Before long the chill grew deeper and we left the fire for the comfort of sleeping bags and blankets. The night claimed us all. I wondered just before I fell asleep how many beans, peaches, apricots, or pears had to be picked to send a boy through medical school.

U.S. 197 follows the route of the Barlow Road south out of The Dalles. Our truck camper surmounted the Tygh Grade with ease and rolled down into the Tygh Valley where a log pond lies full of logs. As we climbed the hill on the far side of the valley, the only danger was the log trucks, which careened around the sharp turns in the road on their way to the log pond. We paused on the mountainside above to watch the trucks dump their loads into the pond. There was a distant metallic rattle of chains being loosened, the thumping of the logs, and the splash of water.

The tollgate set up by Sam Barlow and Philip Foster was at Wamic, where the town dogs wag their tails and nose visitors who stop to read the sign marking the spot. Here wagons were made to pay a five-dollar toll. The charge for each horse or cow was ten cents. Sometimes emigrants

arrived at the gate and found nobody there to collect the fee. Then they cracked their whips over the oxen's backs and rolled on over the road without asking any questions.

Just beyond Wamic, the Barlow Road, here paved with gravel, leads across Smock Prairie and into the forest where pinecones carpet the ground. There a dirt road winding among the trees was three inches deep with dust that whirled up into a choking cloud behind us. Soon the interior of our camper was buried beneath a thick powder that we never entirely succeeded in sweeping out during the remainder of the trip. Each loop through the enormous pines carried us higher up the mountain slope.

At Klip Creek the early pioneers lowered their wagons down a steep grade with cables. The trunks of the trees at the top of the hill still show the scars left by the rubbing cables holding back the weight of wagons and household goods. At one point we stopped to follow fresh bear tracks by the road, and at White River Station we could see where a female and a cub had clawed at a tree in a campsite that had been laid out by the forest service where the pioneers once camped. The dirt road beneath our wheels, the tall trees, the presence of bears all conspired to make pioneer days seem close as we drove on. We crossed the White River and Barlow Creek on bridges, but wagons forded the stream. We parked our camper at Hay Burner's Station. Here Louis Klinger, trapper and hunter, and his wife, Melissa, sold hay and supplies to emigrants. Part of their fireplace remains, but that is all.

By the rail along the East Fork of the Salmon River we also found a pile of rocks marking the grave of a pioneer woman. Then the primitive road we were following emerged from the forests and joined the pavement of Oregon 35 to climb on over Barlow Pass. Mount Hood towered over us, wrapped in the smoke eddying up from a forest fire to the southwest. Soon we reached Laurel Hill, so named by pioneers because the leaves of the trees growing on the Pacific slope of the Cascades resembled the laurel trees of home. Here too wagons were snubbed to trees by ropes. Going down Laurel Hill, Enoch Conyers and his party ran into trouble.

"We locked both wheels and then rough-locked with chains," he wrote in his diary, "and then came very near killing one of our wheel oxen. Something had happened to one of the teams ahead of us, which caused a stoppage of all the teams on the hill back of them. When our leaders stopped, and the hill being so very steep, the other oxen in the team telescoped them, caused by our wagon running onto them. In the mix-up, one of our wheel oxen had his neck so wrenched that a stream of blood about the size of a lead pencil spurted from his nose."

The ox bawled but went on, apparently no worse from the wrench. Conyers found the road down Laurel Hill worn down five to seven feet by the skidding, bouncing wagons and so narrow that a man could not walk beside his oxen without leaning on them.

To slow his wagon's descent, Conyers cut down a small tree about ten inches in diameter and forty feet long. This he fastened to the rear axle with chains, the top end first. Dragging the tree behind it, the wagon plunged down the slope. At the foot of Laurel Hill, Conyers removed a similar tree left in the middle of the road by the preceding wagon but in turn cut loose his tree for the next emigrant party to wrestle aside.

Today a paved road ascends Laurel Hill, and skiers drive up it to the Government Camp winter sports areas. Their mind on snow conditions on the slopes, they scarcely notice the bridges over the Little Sandy and the Big Sandy where the wagons zigzagged through the boulders that blocked the stream beds. At Foster Ranch, now vanished, most trains stopped to pay 50 cents for a dinner that Enoch Conyers noted included "hot biscuits, cold slaw, fresh beefsteak and boiled potatoes served with hot coffee or tea." One young man in Conyers' party ate three full meals before Foster sent him away in disgust. As his wagon again rolled down the road, the youth became violently sick because of his gluttony. After five lean months and five days on the Oregon Trail and the Barlow Road, the temptation of good food had been too much for him.

That night the Conyers party pitched their tent near the new wooden Methodist church in Oregon City, where people already painted their houses white. For our part we drove down the paved highway that has now obscured the last fourteen miles of the Barlow Road. By that night we had driven the remaining miles to the ocean, where we slept on the beach at the sunset end of the continent that the pioneers had made their own.

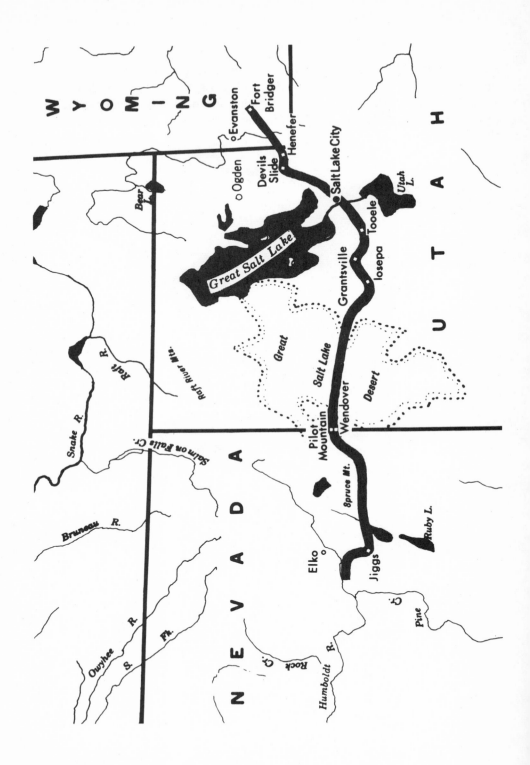

11

Hastings Cutoff

●

Thirteen-year-old Eddie Breen fell from his horse and broke his leg. He was with the party led by George and Jacob Donner and James Reed, and at the time the emigrants, having crossed the Wyoming desert, were resting for four days at Fort Bridger. Men shook their heads, for frontier medicine demanded that the boy's leg be removed. His mother would not agree. She cried that no knife was going to cut her boy. When faced with such a determined if misguided female, the men put his leg in rude splints. The poor kid would never walk again, it was certain.

Eddie Breen's accident was not the only problem confronting the party as the post blacksmiths worked on the wagons. The season was advancing, and the Donner Party was weighing the advantages of leaving the Oregon Trail at this point and traveling the Hastings Cutoff. It was said that the cutoff saved from three to four hundred miles over the established California Trail, which left the road to Oregon at Fort Hall. James Reed, the leader of the train, had read the *Emigrant's Guide to Oregon and California* by Lansford Hastings.

"The most direct route, for the California emigrants," wrote Hastings, "would be to leave the Oregon route, about two hundred miles east from Fort Hall; thence bearing west southwest to the Salt Lake; and then continuing down to the bay of San Francisco."

When he wrote this book, neither Hastings nor anybody else had been over the route. Hastings, whom Bernard DeVoto called a Fremont in

153

miniature, was one of the first of a long and continuing series of California boosters, part real estate promoter, part politician, a self-styled explorer and guide.

John McBride met Hastings in 1846 on the Oregon Trail and described him as "a tall, fine-looking man, with light brown hair and beard, dressed in a suit of elegant pattern made of buckskin, handsomely embroidered and trimmed at the collar and openings, with plucked beaver fur." McBride and other emigrants thought him the perfect figure of a brave mountaineer and listened eagerly to his tales of how earlier in the year he had crossed the Sierras from California and ventured across the desert and through the Wasatch to Fort Bridger. His new cutoff would keep them from the bitter miles that stretched ahead on the Oregon Trail to Fort Hall.

Jim Clyman had made the journey with Hastings. Old Jim had been born in 1792 on a Virginia farm belonging to George Washington, and he had seen the first President when he was a boy. He had gone westering with Jedediah Smith and Thomas Fitzpatrick, and had been with their party when they first crossed South Pass. Around a campfire at Fort Bernard on the upper Platte he sat with the leaders of the Donner Party and told them about the cutoff so glowingly described by Hastings. He told them about the desert, the heat, the Digger Indians, the Wasatch canyons, and the high Sierras. He told them about how his little dog who had trotted with him through the wilderness had rushed panting into a desert spring to cool off, only to find that the spring was boiling hot with the fires in the earth. His dog had been scalded to death. As for the trail itself, he said, "It is barely possible to get through it if you follow it."

He urged the Donners to take the California Trail from Fort Hall. James Reed feared the snows that he knew fell early in the Sierras. The cutoff would save hundreds of miles.

"There is a nigher route," Clyman remembered his saying, "and it is no use to take so much of a roundabout course."

Reed took out Hastings' book and showed it to Clyman to prove that he was right. The word of a rough-spoken mountain man could not be taken against that of a well-dressed man who had written a book. The Donner Party continued on to Fort Bridger, where they expected to meet Hastings himself, but the prophet of the cutoff had gone on ahead along his trail with the Harlan-Young Party. The Fort Bridger where the party tarried was a fort in name only.

"Fort Bridger is a small trading post," wrote Edwin Bryant, "established

The Donner Party took the Hastings Cutoff at Fort Bridger and met their grim fate in the High Sierra snows. The Army buildings still standing at Fort Bridger were built in 1857 during the Mormon War.

Wyoming Travel Commission

and now occupied by Messers. Bridger and Vasquez. The buildings are two or three miserable log cabins, rudely constructed, and bearing but a faint resemblance to habitable houses. Its position is in a handsome and fertile bottom of the small stream on which we are camped, about two miles south of the point where the old wagon trail, via Fort Hall, makes an angle, and takes a northwesterly course."

Fine grass and clumps of cottonwoods grew in the bottomlands along Black's Fork of the Green River, and the water of the stream was cold enough that trout lived in it. Despite Edwin Bryant's opinion, by frontier standards the buildings were serviceable enough. Jim Bridger had built them of poles cut from the slopes of the Uinta Mountains and daubed them with mud from the banks of the fork. The Mormons took the post from Old Gabe and his partner in 1853. When four years later Albert Sidney Johnston's U.S. troops arrived during the Mormon War, the Mormons burned it before they fled. The soldiers built officers' quarters

155

and barracks around a parade ground, and the post began to look more like it does today.

Joan and I—with three of our children, Nancy, Jim, and Jeff—arrived in our station wagon to explore Fort Bridger before we set out over the route of the Hastings Cutoff. A museum is in the old barracks. The Pony Express stables, the family milkhouse, and the trader's store all remain. So does a school erected in 1860 by Judge William A. Carter for his four daughters and two sons, as well as other children living at the post. A boy was sitting beside the trader's store painting a picture with watercolors. Surely, we thought, he is picturing the old post; but when we asked to see his work, he proudly showed us a vase of flowers done from his imagination.

The trail ran behind the barracks and crossed the stream. It was over this trail that the Donners set out on the morning of July 31, 1846. Eddie Breen gritted his teeth at the pain which shot up his leg with every jolt of the wagon. Across the tableland known as Bridger's Butte the trail is to the left of Interstate 80. The first pioneers forded the Little Muddy, which turned out to have a deep mud bottom through which oxen floundered. When Mose Burns opened ferry service across the Little Muddy in the 1860's, he found that emigrants gladly paid a dollar a wagon to cross, not out of fear of the shallow water but of the deep mud.

From the Little Muddy the wagons rolled on west to Sulphur Creek, which took them down through what is now ranch land to the Bear River. In Evanston we turned south to drive eight miles out Highway 89 past the Myers Ranch to a marker that tells where the trail came up from the river and crossed today's road. There are some pioneer graves nearby, and the ruts of the wagons can easily be made out ascending a ridge west of the road. The Evanston Junior Chamber of Commerce maintains a picnic grove on the grassy banks of the Bear near this point. We parked our car where an Evanston man was fishing and hiked a short way up the river to the place close to the onetime Myers Ranch house where wagons forded the river. The ford is paved with rounded stones, and it seemed easy considering the troubles that befell pioneers crossing it.

When the '49er William Kelly's mule team was crossing at this point, a man on horseback tied a rope to the lead mules and then rode across the river to the opposite bank so that he could pull on the rope if a fractious mule tried to turn downstream to avoid the current. One unhappy mule fell in the deepest part of the stream. Trampled and drowned by the other mules, the mule had to be dragged lifeless, by brute force, to the shore before he could be removed from harness.

In the 1860's a toll bridge was built over the Bear. When the Millington family reached the river, they paid for their wagon to use the bridge, but they were too short on cash to pay the toll for their herd of cattle. The hired man drove the herd into the river as the wagon started across. Panicking in the water, the cattle stumbled and swam, bawling, to the bridge where they spied the wagon that they had been following across the plains and through the mountains. In their anxiety to crowd close to the familiar wagon, they almost pushed it off the bridge into the rushing current. People like the Millingtons complained that bridge builders often placed a bridge across the only practical ford over a river.

As we drove into Echo Canyon, great earthmovers were gouging turnouts off I-80 for tourists to stop and walk to viewpoints overlooking the spectacular red rock cliffs that so fascinated the pioneers. The trail reached Echo Canyon by way of Cache Cave and the Needles. In the canyon it crossed and recrossed the creek a score of times. Bryant and his pack train easily wound their way along the canyon floor among great rocks, but the wagon trains that followed had a bitter time among the boulders. A man could easily jump across the creek, but the wagons had to plunge through it. Early trains also found bears to be numerous in the canyon. They ignored the wagons, but they tried to eat some of Thomas Flint's sheep. The Donner Party, weary and heedless of the passing summer, halted for five days just west of the mouth of Echo Canyon, but on August 12 they began to roll westward again.

It took the Donners six and a half days to reach the crossing of the Weber River near where the village of Henefer, Utah, now is located. Weber Canyon leads on through the Wasatch, but three miles beyond the crossing it was choked by the great avalanche of rocks known as the Devil's Slide. The Bryant pack train, detouring over a rough mountain route around the slide, made its way down the canyon. The Harlan-Young Party also managed to take its wagons on down the Weber. They windlassed them over the rocks and climbed high on the walls of a cliff. When oxen lost their footing, they dragged the wagons after them to death and ruin on the canyon floor. Later engineers put the Union Pacific Railroad through the canyon, but it was almost impassable for pioneers.

When the Donner Party reached the crossing of the Weber, they found a letter from Hastings thrust into a cleft stick by the trail warning them of the perils of the canyon ahead. They camped at the crossing while Reed and two others rode through Weber Canyon in pursuit of Hastings, who was somewhere ahead. Surely he would be able to guide them out of the canyon in which they were now caught. Five days later, the men returned without Hastings. He had hurried on with the Harlan-Young Party, and the Donners had no choice but to use their best judgment. They ascended Little East Canyon Creek and made their way over the mountain shoulders.

Utah 65 follows their route today past where East Canyon Reservoir has flooded the trail. The Donners found Little Dutch Hollow choked with stones and willows through which they had to slash their way. They riprapped swamps, bridged brooks, and three different times they were completely stopped by towering canyon walls. They had to turn back over the road that they had just built to find a better cleft. More precious days were lost before the party could reach the top of 8,200-foot Big Mountain. We were slow in climbing the mountain, too, because two sheepherders on horseback and a pair of very clever dogs were working a large herd of sheep up the road ahead of us. Atop Big Mountain itself another shepherd drove sheep from a meadow just below where we picnicked beside a trail marker.

The modern road hairpins down Big Mountain where the ruts of the trail still can be seen. The road follows the trail through Pine Creek Canyon. There is no following the route of the tortured Donner Party, which descended Big Mountain into Mountain Dell Canyon, then wound down Parley's Canyon only to find they could not go farther. They returned up Parley's Canyon and through Mountain Dell Canyon again to cross over Little Mountain into Emigration Canyon. The trail wound down Emigration Canyon, but we could see no traces of it as we drove along the highway to where a tall apartment, an outpost of Salt Lake City, rises atop a steep hill. This is the place where on August 22, 1846, the Donners gave up fighting the boulders on the canyon floor and hauled their wagons up over the hills. They doubled teams on every one of their twenty-three wagons to make the pull. It wasn't until September 3 that the weary pioneers reached the banks of the Jordan River and camped where the North Temple Street bridge now crosses. Traffic snarls on the busy street, and the river is sludgy and evil-looking with industrial waste that the otherwise clean citizens of Salt Lake City allow to drain unchecked into the now polluted Great Salt Lake.

The early pioneers following the Hastings Cutoff had to slosh through marshes through which the Jordan flowed. On the west bank of the stream

Jed Smith made a raft of cane grass. He loaded his belongings aboard it and swam the stream, the raft pulled by a cord which he held in his teeth. On the far side he built a fire of sedge to dry his clothes and cook his meal of horsemeat.

Beyond the Jordan, alkali flats lie blistering in the sun. John Craig, never one to mind his spelling, wrote in his journal that "with a few exceptions a more dry Sandy and barren country doze not (in my opinion) exist on Gods footstool. Excepting the great african desert. The intire county having a Streaking and volcanic appearance and abounding with hot and even boiling Springs. And if the different parts of our continent is cursed in proportion to the Sins of the inhabitants that formerly dwelt on them. Then indeed must those ancient inhabitants have been awfully wicked, for this is truly a land that the Lord has cursed."

Across these searing flats the Hastings Cutoff ran to the northern tip of the Oquirrh Mountains, into which miners have dug the world's largest opencut copper mine at Bingham Canyon. Once grass grew by a spring where now black slag from a smelter adds a man-made evil to the "land that the Lord has cursed." On Black Rock the army explorer Captain Howard Stansbury erected an observatory in 1849. He corned beef by tying it to a rope and dropping it into the salt lake. Today the rock is nowhere near the lake, which recedes farther and farther every year.

Only two miles past the Black Rock the cutoff curved southward around the northerly point of the Oquirrhs into Tooele Valley, named for the tule plants that grew around a spring-fed pond. The modern highway curves even farther south and then heads west to Grantsville, which grew up around the springs that the Donners called Twenty Wells. Lombardy poplars line a side road leading to the springs where wagon trains camped. Here Luke Halloran, a sick youth befriended along the trail by the gentle Tamsen Donner, died of tuberculosis with his head in her maternal lap. Young Halloran left $1,500 in gold coins and his Masonic insignia to George Donner. The Masons in the party convened and buried Luke with appropriate ritual in a grave dug in the salt mud close to the upper wells.

Willow Creek flows through Grantsville. Many wagon trains camped on its banks. The Bryant Party camped there too. When Colonel Russell left his nine-shooter in camp, a young Ute brave stole it. After the Bryants had gone on west, the Indian shot himself in the leg, which so disturbed his fellow tribesmen that they handed the dangerous weapon to the next group of white men to come along the trail. This was the Harlan-Young Party. Later in California the pioneers returned the gun to its owner, who had long since given up any hope of seeing it again.

The trail and the highway circle the rugged tip of the Stansbury Mountains; then they part. The trail runs along Skull Valley, where it was ninety miles from fresh water to fresh water. Men filled their canteens, buckets, and their boots with water. They tied their oilcloth pants together at the ankle so that they too would hold water, and set out across the wastes which Bryant described as "covered with a saline efflorescence of a snowy whiteness. The only vegetation is wild sage; and this is parched and shrivelled by the extreme drought."

A blacktop road now leads down the center of the valley to Iosepa, which was the Kanaka Ranch of pioneer times. Here the Donners found scraps of a note from Hastings tacked to a board. A bird had torn the note apart. Tamsen Donner carefully pieced the paper together and the pioneers learned that the crossing of the desert ahead of them would take not just one day, as Hastings had originally said, but two days and nights. It took the Donners, who traveled almost all of every night, six days to make the journey.

From Skull Valley the trail makes a thousand-foot ascent over Hastings Pass in the Cedar Mountains to the west. It can still be followed with four-wheel-drive vehicles. We stopped at the ranch house at Iosepa to see if we could make the drive in our station wagon. A woman and two boys were setting a table for a score or so of big eaters, and a lean, sun-browned man was bolting down huge mouthfuls of chocolate cake.

"You can't make it this year," he said, "and you can't make it in most years. You can get to Hastings Pass from the west over the old aragonite mine road if you want."

We drew a mixed chorus of rude and friendly remarks from the cowhands working in the corral as we got in our car and started back down the road. Farther south on this road is the Skull Valley Reservation where descendants of the Diggers, who offered Bryant mashed grasshoppers and sunflower seeds in trade, now live. There is life in the valley that the pioneers found so forbidding.

Beyond the Cedar Mountains the road to the aragonite mine turns off U.S. 40. We bounced over the Western Pacific Railroad crossing at a flagstop called Aragonite, where a few boys were clambering atop a forlorn shed. The trail passed close to the flagstop. We followed back along it on the road to the mines which are high in the pass leading over the Cedar Mountains. We found deep pits gouged in the mountain, their sides gleaming with the crystalline calcite that chemists prize. When the road became too deeply rutted for our car to go farther, we got out and hiked over a rocky trail and at last reached the top of Hastings Pass.

Far out in Skull Valley ahead of us we could make out the ranch where we had stopped to ask for directions. We could also make out the trail crossing the flats and climbing the mountain pass to where we stood. Facing west we looked through Hastings Canyon and across the desert to Pilot Peak, seventy-five miles away on the edge of Nevada. The desert was a blistering sight. When the mountain man Hudspeth led the Bryant Party to the top of the pass, he refused to go any farther.

"How do we get across the desert?" Bryant shouted after Hudspeth, who was already riding back down the trail.

Hudspeth turned in his saddle.

"Put spurs to your mules and ride like hell."

We hiked on down the mountain to our car and returned to the main highway. No sooner had we reached the road than a tire blew out to let us know that driving over the Hastings Cutoff still can present problems. After changing the tire we went on to the village of Knolls to have it repaired. Signs at the gas station tell tourists not to waste the water which is trucked in for fifty-eight miles.

The summer sun glared down on the Great Salt Lake Desert. Mirages danced in the heat waves eddying off the highway ahead of us as we drove on west. Here as the Donner Party struggled over the packed salt, William Eddy saw a file of men coming and thought it must be Hastings returning to rescue them. His spirits quickened, only to sink again when he realized that the file of men was actually himself projected twenty times by the shimmering light. Thirty-six oxen died in the desert, but no persons. Half of the dead oxen were James Reed's. He abandoned two wagons, shared surplus food with other families, and pressed on. The hard salt was terrifying, and the soft salt was maddening. Some men stopped and dug holes in the sand and lay in them for an hour hoping to cool their burning bodies. Lips and noses of men and ox alike were caked with salt. Children suffered horribly with thirst.

Stronger men, such as James Reed and William Eddy, pressed on ahead to the springs at the foot of Pilot Mountain and returned with water for the wagons that were still anywhere from twenty to forty miles out on the desert. In the crossing of the Great Salt Lake Desert, men and animals who reached the shadow of Crater Island, a great hulk of rock rising from the desert floor, would lie down in the relative coolness to rest and often to die. Henry Bloom noted in his journal:

"Got to the Rock of Misery, sixty-five miles, our water all gone and our horses nearly famishing for water. Teams giving out, men lying by the side of the road in the hot sun speechless for the want of water. Some lying in the shade of the rocks nearly dying from thirst. Men offering, one, ten, twenty and five hundred dollars for a single drink of water."

In 1850 a water wagon drove out from the springs at Pilot Mountain to succor those dying of thirst. The water wagon drivers found a nightmare of suffering on the desert. In the gap through the great rock called Silver Island an old lady wandered with a coffeepot of water for her husband who, somewhere in the desolation, had lain down to die. Farther along a woman sat in the shadow of her stranded wagon, trustfully waiting for her husband, who had gone for water, to return. Usually the water wagon went only as far as Silver Island. Since there was scarcely enough water for the dying people, the animals had to be left thirsty. Many died, and their bodies mummified in the heat in the gap of Silver Island.

There in the shadow of Silver Island the palatial parlor wagon, built so that Grandma Keyes could ride comfortably in her rocking chair, was finally abandoned. Grandma had died far back on the trail at Alcove Springs, Kansas, but the Donner Party had hauled her great coach along with them until now they could haul it no farther. In 1927 Captain Charles E. Davis, tracing the Hastings Cutoff, came upon the remains of the vehicle at Silver Island. It is now in the museum on the site of the Donner starvation camp.

The water for Wendover on the Nevada border comes from pioneer springs. Where wagon trains once labored over the salt flats, some of the fastest land vehicles in the world now race the clock, and the restaurant in Wendover where we dined was decorated with the pictures of celebrated drivers. To get to Silver Island we drove north on the road to the McKellar Ranch. We could see the gap in Silver Island through which the wagon trains had come to the parched flats east of 10,074-foot Pilot Peak. Melting snows trickling down the mountain from a series of springs. These brought an end to the terrible thirst of the desert.

Pilot Peak, toward which the thirsting wagon trains rolled from the distant Cedar Mountains, was properly named by John C. Fremont. In 1845 Fremont, leading his expedition across the desert, sent his scout, Kit Carson, ahead to find water. Carson found the springs at the foot of the mountain and piloted the explorers to it by lighting smoke signals atop the peak. In the days before souvenir collectors, this last stretch of the desert was strewn with the wreckage of man's hopes, but we found it empty of any sign that so much tragedy had occurred within its confines.

From the springs the trail leads west to Silver Zone Pass in the Toano Range through which U.S. 40 also runs. The modern highway has destroyed all signs of the historic trail, but a sign along the road advising motorists of a spring still indicates where the pioneers found the first water after leaving water at Pilot Peak. The trail runs on to Johnson Spring, which supplies water to Wendover, and Flower Springs, over Flower Pass, and through the Ruby Valley to the Ruby Range, where it turns south to take advantage of the snow-fed springs at the foot of the mountains. It crosses the mountains at Overland Pass near the place where the Shoshones stole George Donner's cream-colored horse and turns north again in Huntington Valley, holding to the sagebrush slopes above where the modern highway runs. If the wagons followed too close to Huntington Creek, they ran the risk of being mired in the mud.

In the valley, the Digger Indians tried to show pioneers how to survive in the wilderness. They demonstrated to Lienhard how to dig roots, catch a grasshopper and pop him between the tubers to make a tasty sandwich. They also raided camps at night to drive off the stock. The trail runs on past the present-day town of Jiggs at the end of the paved road leading south from Elko, and through the canyon of the South Fork where rocks still show the scoring of wagon wheels.

West of Elko a deep canyon opens onto the Humboldt Valley, through which wagons following the California Trail made their way. The South Fork of the Humboldt surges through the canyon, and along its banks ran the Hastings Cutoff. Out of the canyon mouth came the Bryant Party and their mules, the Harlan-Young wagons, and finally the wagons of the Donner Party. There were meadows along the Humboldt, and to the Donners, not knowing anything of the future, the sight of the California Trail was almost like reaching California itself. Moreover, Eddie Breen's leg had knitted perfectly, and he was walking and riding his horse after strayed oxen as if nothing had happened.

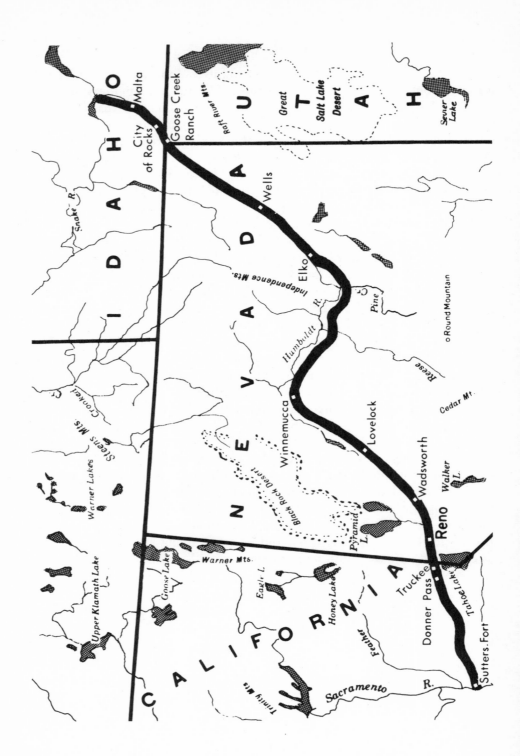

12

California Trail

•

California emigrants had already traveled fourteen hundred miles from the banks of the Missouri when they reached the Raft River in southern Idaho. They had followed the Oregon Trail over the rolling prairies of Kansas and Nebraska, up the Platte and over South Pass. They had descended the Snake until here, just before the Oregon Trail forded the Raft, they must turn their wagons on the trail to California. The weariness and suffering of fourteen hundred miles turned with them. They did not pause for lingering farewells, but cracked their whips over their oxen and pressed on up the Raft over what most of the journals called a good road.

The trail runs close along the river past today's hamlet of Yale and crosses U.S. 30S north of Malta. Both the Hudspeth Cutoff and the Salt Lake City–Oregon Connection then join the California Trail, which runs up Cassia Creek. Idaho Highway 77 from Malta to Elba and on to Almo follows where once the wagon wheels turned up clouds of dust.

My son Rick and I stopped at a store in Almo to provision our truck camper. Here in the range country the store stocked Brazilian corned beef. On the edge of town a historical sign told of how three hundred westbound emigrants on the California Trail were massacred, with only five escaping. When they saw us reading the marker, some village boys came over and read it, too. They seemed to be reading it for the first time.

The boys did know the way to the City of Rocks, great titans of granite carved by erosion. Weary as they may have been, wagon train people paused here as their tourist descendants do. They fancied that this rock resembled a camel, and that another resembled twin sisters. Many of the youthful pioneers climbed two hundred feet to the top of Bath Rock. The rock in no way resembles a bathtub, but a hollow depression on the top collects rain water. An Indian legend says that a bath in this water will restore youth. Since only a very few old people manage the climb, the legend has gone largely untested. Less agile pioneers contented themselves with writing their names on the rocks with wagon grease, which has weathered so slowly that the names and dates now stand out in relief.

The wagons did not tarry long, because California called. Soon the teams were laboring up the steep grades through Granite Pass, which is today on the Utah-Idaho border. Today's Goose Creek Road follows the trail across into Utah. Water from the Goose Creek Reservoir irrigates fields in Idaho, but once we had crossed into Utah we found ourselves in rough country that in turn gave way to the neat buildings and fertile pastures of Goose Creek Ranch. We camped on the range that night, and a herd of cattle gathered around us. The cattle bawled to one another their curiosity and concern that we were there, until they finally slipped away silently in the moonlight to where the grazing was better.

The California Trail crosses only the northwest tip of Utah and then heads southwest across Nevada to the Humboldt River. At Record Bluff men once again fell to carving their names or painting the rock with wagon grease in an effort to leave some memory of themselves in this inhospitable wilderness. The wagons rolled along Thousand Springs Valley for twenty miles and descended Bishop Creek, which now flows into a reservoir. At last they reached the sluggish Humboldt near Wells. For two hundred miles the California Trail and the Humboldt are inseparable, for, sluggish as the river may be, it at least offered water and intermittent meadows for the oxen.

Fremont had named the river for the German naturalist, Baron Alexander von Humboldt. Thomas Ambrose Cramer following the trail along the river in August, 1859, felt that the river did Humboldt little justice.

"It does him little credit here," he said. "He was filled with wisdom and goodness; it only with mineral and vegetable poisons."

At least the river flowed more or less westward toward California, even though by the time of the '49ers emigrants knew that it was destined to sink into the barren wastes of the Forty-mile Desert. Mark Twain portrayed the river more pointedly. He said a man could easily jump back and forth across it until he was thirsty enough to drink it dry.

The country along the river lies withered in the sun. Ochre hills and cliffs of the badlands look down on alkali flats. It is a land in which the

Digger Indians said a man must be able to sleep in the shadow of his arrow to survive. Yet when Fremont passed along the Humboldt, he found the valley "rich and beautifully clothed in blue grass and clover." Pioneers who read his lyric descriptions of the river found that the hungry livestock of preceding trains had eaten the grass and clover. They renamed the river "the Humbug." Along it they dug shallow graves for their dead, and as their animals perished they abandoned wagons and household goods. In one forty-two-mile stretch more than one thousand wagons were abandoned, and for generations afterward the skeletons of oxen and mules and crumbling wood and rotting canvas remained.

In places the river ran through shoulder-high grass and tule. The Indians cut the tule to gather honeydew. Pioneers bought balls of the sticky goop from friendly Indians until they learned that it was the excretion of aphids. Most Indians offered little opportunity for trade even for honeydew because the Diggers were decidedly unfriendly as a rule. They peered from the long grass at the passing trains or lurked behing crags and waited for a chance to discharge a volley of arrows into the emigrants' oxen. A dead or badly injured ox had to be left behind where it could easily be cut up for Indian cooking pots.

Sometimes the Indians aimed their arrows at the emigrants. Often the arrows were poisoned. The Indians would capture a rattlesnake and tease it until it struck at a piece of liver. When the liver was saturated with venom, the Indians rubbed their arrowheads in it. It is no wonder that in August, 1846, Jesse Boone, grandson of Daniel, shot and killed a Digger with his shotgun—probably the last Indian to be killed by a Boone. By 1849 the Diggers had exchanged their bows and poisoned arrows for rifles, and until the 1870's they kept up a deadly harassment along the trail.

U.S. 40 and I-80 carry auto traffic along the river today. Just west of Elko the Hastings Cutoff emerges from a deep canyon and joins the main road to California. From that point on the old trail, the modern highway and the railroad weave in and out along the valley into which fingers of sand and rock reach down from the badlands.

Each mile along the trail carries the weight of comedy and tragedy. Near Winnemucca at Iron Point is where James Reed of the Donner-Reed Party knifed John Snyder, who was unmercifully whipping both Reed and his wife in a quarrel over oxen. At the bend, J. Goldsborough Bruff found a red-painted barrel standing where the trail forked.

"It was a nice new barrel, about the size of a whisky-barrel, iron hoops, and a square hole cut in the head," he wrote in his journal, "and neatly painted in black block letters, upon it, POST OFFICE. On looking in, found it half full of letters, notes, notices, etc."

Buzzards wheeled overhead when an ox was dying. They settled down on a carcass even before the dust of the passing train had settled. When an emigrant died, men cut wood from the tailgate of a wagon to make a gravemarker and cut wagon chains into the right lengths to enclose the grave. The wagons had barely passed out of sight when the Diggers dug up the grave in search of valuable clothing. The buzzards waited impatiently until they also had gone. Far from marking graves, later emigrants drove their wagons over their dead to hide where they lay.

The alkali in the river water made it taste like bile. People put vinegar or citric acid in it to make it potable, but those who drank water with too much alkali were stricken by nausea. Cattle, their tongues parched, lapped up the water, too. Men fed the sick cattle a plug of tobacco between two slices of bacon in a vain attempt to save their lives. One emigrant saw fifteen hundred dead animals in fifty miles of trail.

Finally the river that they were following sank exhausted into the desert. Mark Twain came to the spot and wrote, "We tried to use the strong alkaline water of the Sink, but it would not answer. It was like drinking lye, and not weak lye either. It left a taste in the mouth, bitter and execrable, and a burning in the stomach."

Mark Twain put molasses in the water and finally a pickle to try and improve its taste. He announced that coffee made with it was ghastly.

Near present-day Lovelock, pioneers paused among meadows of rye and grass. Here they could cook their meals over sagebrush fires, care for their sick, fix their wagons, and cut wagonloads of grass for the passage of the Forty-mile Desert. Many pioneers attempted to cross the desert in the night to avoid the inferno of heat that was the desert by day. Wagons stuck in the loose sand and had to be abandoned. Household goods were jettisoned, and even today once-prized keepsakes of emigrating families can be found where they were flung in the terrible heat.

"Boys," exclaimed Bartleson of the Bartleson Party, "if ever I get back to Missouri, I'll never leave that country. I'd gladly eat out of the troughs with my hogs."

Then the ordeal was over, and the wagons came out of the desert to the Truckee River, which they discovered flowing northward into Pyramid Lake. Not far to the south, where Wadsworth now stands, the river turned west and along it the emigrants journeyed towards the Sierra Nevadas, craggy ramparts of snow and rock that rose ever larger on the horizon. At Truckee Meadows they paused to gather strength for the high pass that after 1846 carried the fateful name of Donner. In 1852 a man named Jamison set up a station in the meadows, and by the 1860's there were a bridge over the river and a small inn operated by a Mr. Lake. Jamison's Station became Lake's Crossing and then Reno.

The provisions of many wagon trains were running low as they rested beside the Truckee. Niles Searls of the Walker Train wrote that on the trail to California, "rancid bacon with the grease fried out by the hot sun, musty flour, a little pinoles and some sacks of pilot bread, broken and crushed to dust and well coated with alkali, a little coffee without sugar—now constitute our diet."

Hungry wagon-train families ate wild parsnips. These were safe when cooked but poisonous when raw. A mixture of bacon grease, whiskey, and gunpowder was considered the best antidote. People also sliced steaks from dead oxen lying along the trail and ate the often putrid meat raw.

Unsavory as such provender may have been, the families camped at Truckee Meadows feared that if they were trapped by autumnal snows in the mountains ahead they might be reduced to worse. The banjos strummed about the campfires and the men got out their decks of cards that some now forgotten wit labeled California prayer books. But who could rest, listen to music, and play cards with the most fearful of all the trail's ordeals looming ahead? Even the by then legendary Jedediah Smith was known to have lost seven horses and a mule loaded with provisions when in 1826 he crossed the High Sierras from California.

With such fears fretting in the camp, few wagons rested long before beginning the ascent. Their prairie-bred beasts climbed a trail which led along sheer cliffs. Some emigrants roped themselves together out of dread of the precipices, but soon most grew accustomed to the dizzy heights and pressed on. Their route still led up the Truckee, which alone offered them a way through the gorges, blind canyons, and twisting ridges that still today make the Sierra Nevada a baffling barrier along the eastern border of California.

The wagons finally arrived at what the emigrants called Truckee Lake, but which is today known as Donner Lake. On the north shore of the lake, Mrs. Graves of the Donner Party, not trusting her companions, hid her money in the woods. She died in the Donner Camp in the summit valley which still lay ahead, and her money was lost until 1891, when it was discovered by chance. An 1826 half dollar from her cache is displayed today at Sutter's Fort in Sacramento.

The last of the Donner Party's draft animals had died or wandered off by the time they reached Truckee Lake, and the wagons had to be abandoned. Little food of any kind remained. The cruelest fate to overtake any of the wagon trains was about to overtake the Donners.

Speeding along Interstate 80 it is hard to imagine the hardships of the emigrant trail through the Sierras. It is only a short drive from Reno to the turnoff to the Donner Memorial State Park. There we found fishermen angling in the Truckee River which purls through the sun-dappled forest where in the winter of 1846 forty-two men, women, and children died of starvation and exposure. Stumps of trees felled by the Donner Party still stand in the forest. The stumps are twelve feet tall, which indicates the depth of the snow at the time they were cut. The monument surmounted by figures of the pioneers is twenty-two feet tall: the depth of the snow that finally piled up around the marooned emigrants.

Six miles northeast of the campsite an axle broke on George Donner's wagon. He stopped, felled a tree, and was shaping it into an axle when his chisel slipped and gashed him. The wound became infected, and he died in the camp. In 1961 a tree was chopped down on Alder Creek near where he fixed his wagon. A chisel inscribed "L&I J White—Buffalo, N.Y. 1837" was found in the heart of the tree. Other Donner Party belongings have been found in the campsite. In fact, Charles F. McGlashan, who published the *History of the Donner Party* in 1879, sold relics of the party found there to raise money to build the monument.

Rescue parties from California coming to the relief of the stricken Donners came upon a scene of incredible horror. The dead were being devoured by the still living. Each eyewitness account of the terrible fate of the Donner Party is more ghastly than the other. The most hardened frontiersman became sick with disgust to find children devouring the heart and liver of their father who had just died, and the limbs, skulls, and hair of half-eaten bodies scattered in the snow among the cabins where survivors were barely alive.

To James Reed, returning with a rescue party, it must have been more horrifying than to any other man. If this clear-minded man had not been exiled after killing young John Snyder on the trail along the Humboldt, he might have been able to check the series of blunders that led the Donner Party to its doom. When he brought the relief party up from the Sacramento Valley, he found the bones and skulls of his old friends in camp kettles. At least he had already come upon his wife and two of his children staggering through the snow away from the camp and knew that they lived. He had hurried on to the camp where as he approached he saw his little daughter Patty sitting upon the corner of the roof of a cabin. When he went inside the cabin, he found his son, Thomas, still alive.

We visited the museum at the Donner Memorial and found there a tear-stained doll cherished by Patty Reed during the ordeal, and we walked the trails that lead to the great boulder that was the north end of the fireplace of the Murphy cabin. On June 22, 1847, General Stephen W. Kearny and the army reached the site and buried the bodies beneath the floor of the cabin.

As we stood before the boulder, we could hear children merrily calling from the picnic grove nearby. Often it is hard for a person interested in the history of our land to visit a place where stirring deeds happened and see how oblivious to the past so many Americans, young and old, can be. At the Donner Memorial it seemed better that the picnickers did not know what had happened where they frolicked, and when some boys climbed up the very boulder at the Murphy cabin, I was thankful that they knew nothing of what happened at their feet.

Beyond the place where the Donner Party met its grim end, emigrants still had to climb through Donner Pass and track their way down almost impossible slopes to the Sacramento Valley. From Emigrant Gap wagons were lowered by ropes to the floor of Bear Valley. The trials of the trail were scarcely over. On the banks of the Yuba River, Nicholas Carriger's wife gave birth to a baby girl, and within the hour both his father and his sister-in-law died. He buried his dead beside the river.

"While I engaged in paying the last tribute to the dead that I hold so dear," he wrote in his journal, "my oxen strayed and ate poisoned weed." Both oxen died, but Carriger reached Johnson's ranch, which was the first house on the Bear River, and bought oxen to finish the journey.

As they reached the gold fields, emigrants left the main trail to find their way to this mining camp or that. Many continued on to Sutter's Fort, where a house was set aside for their use. Men slept on the floor in an attic at the fort. The charge for a three-foot by seven-foot space was one dollar. Wrapped in their own blankets, their boots for pillows, 250 men would crowd into the attic for the night. One traveler reported "the combined smell of boot leather, tobacco smoke, sweaty clothes, sweating bodies, garlic breaths . . . . If you raised up on your elbow and looked around, it was just like looking over a rolling ocean of men—twisting, turning over, talking in their sleep, mumbling prayers, others sobbing, others cussing, some all of these, and Good Lord, how they snored!"

At least this was the end of the trail, and the lonely plains, the deserts and the mountains, the suffering and death lay behind these men, who could now begin a new life in California.

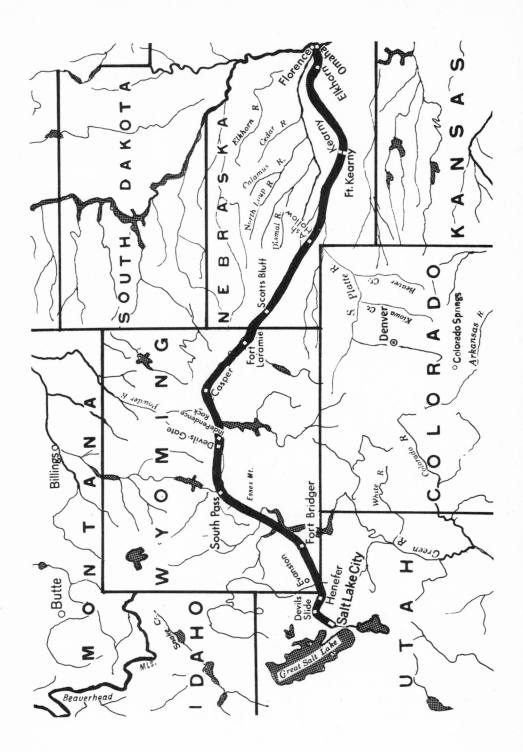

13

Mormon Trail

●

Two fellows with electronic detectors were going over the turf in the park at State and Thirtieth in Florence, Nebraska, and we were certain that they were looking for Mormon artifacts buried beneath the surface. What might they turn up on the historic spot on the northern outskirts of Omaha where the Saints set up their winter quarters that bitter year of 1846-47?

"Have you found anything left by the Mormons?" I asked. "They were desperately poor, so they couldn't have left much."

"What Mormons?" one fellow, who operates a lawn service, replied. "We're looking for coins. They fall out of people's pockets in parks. The best pickings are beneath slides and swings where kids play, but this should be pretty good too."

Our family watched as they found several pieces of tinfoil and one nickel. This on Missouri Bottoms, which the Mormons called "Misery Bottoms," a place that knew suffering and heroism. The Mormons picked it because it would be easy to defend with John Scott's homemade three-pounder. Thirty-five hundred men, women, and children packed into the six or seven hundred log huts, sod houses, and dugouts. They starved and they froze in the damp cold beside the Missouri River.

Behind them lay a long and cruel journey through America that started in 1830 in Fayette, New York, a year after Joseph Smith followed the instructions inscribed on ancient plates of gold buried in a hill, and founded the Church of Jesus Christ of Latter-Day Saints. The Saints were driven from New York to Kirtland, Ohio, and from there to Jackson County in western Missouri, and then to Nauvoo on the Illinois shore of the Mississippi. Other Americans feared the growing political power of the Mormons and suspected them of criminal activities. They resented the prosperity that the hard-working Mormons achieved, and they talked darkly about the polygamy that they were said to practice. When a people are feared and judged both immoral and prosperous, they become an enemy, and with the lynching of Joseph Smith in Carthage Jail near Nauvoo, Mormons understood that they must move again. As Smith was dying, a watching Mormon elder thought: "It seemed to me that he was indispensable. What could we do without him? He has been the brain, the eye, the ear, the mouth, and hand for the entire people of the Church of Jesus Christ of Latter-Day Saints."

Smith had planned to flee to the Rockies, and now Brigham Young decided to act on the dead leader's plan. The elders approved, and on February 10, 1846, flatboats carried the first Mormons across the Mississippi. Within a week the Saints had left Nauvoo. They trekked across Iowa, and most of them camped on Misery Bottoms where the river ran cold with icy slush.

We drove up State Street to the hill where six hundred Mormons who died beside the river lie buried. The graves are scattered beneath the shady trees on a peaceful hill where on that summer day birds were singing. The suburban tranquillity was broken only by the stutter of a power motor from down the street. A metal marker listed "Deaths and Burials in the Camps of Israel." The names of many infants and children were on the list.

Throughout the long winter as the roll of the dead lengthened, Brigham Young, aged forty-six, one-time Methodist, a work-a-day carpenter, glazier, and mechanic, was the brain, the eye, the ear, the mouth, and hand for the people of Zion, and the people remained faithful despite the terrible suffering. Between April 7 and April 15, the first party, later called the Pioneer Band, left winter quarters for the rendezvous at the Elkhorn River. There were 143 men, 3 women, the wives of Brigham Young, of his brother Lorenzo, and of Heber Kimball, and 2 children. There were 72 wagons, carrying plows, farm implements, anvils, spinning wheels, looms, grain, a year's supply of provisions, and people too sick or judged too weary to walk. There were 93 horses, 52 mules, 66 oxen, 19 cows, 17 dogs, and some chickens.

There on the banks of the Elkhorn about midway from winter quarters to the Platte River, Young exhorted the people not to bicker and warned them about drinking and gambling in the evenings after the day's journey was over. We followed where the Mormons had once gone through what are now the suburbs of Omaha, past Elkhorn, and along the north bank of the Platte.

The Mormon Trail from winter quarters reached the Platte just beyond the Loup Fork and followed the north bank where the grass was more plentiful, and the Gentiles were in scarce supply. Brigham Young did not fear the Indians, but he did fear the Missourians and Illinoisans, whose enmity was all too certain. He ordered the men to keep their weapons loaded and ready for use at all times, but to keep them hidden so as not to trigger incidents.

For most of the way our road was U.S. 30. The trail ran between the highway and the river, but there is little to be seen of it today. At Clarks on U.S. 30, about thirty miles west of Columbus, the state of Nebraska has established a Mormon Trail state wayside area and indicated that the trail ran about a mile south of the intersection of U.S. 30 and U.S. 30A. We drove over to look at the trail, which turned out, of course, to be along the banks of the Platte. Some girls were fishing for catfish. Puffs of clouds rode the horizon, and it was a lazy prairie day.

That night we stayed at Kearney, a town which grew up in the 1870's on the Mormon or north bank of the Platte almost opposite to Fort Kearny on the Gentile or south bank of the Platte. The Oregon Trail ran along the south bank from this point westward, and the Mormons looked apprehensively at the shallow waters that kept them apart from their enemies.

Across Nebraska, Interstate 80 follows the trail closer than does U.S. 30, but it gives a motorist far less feel for the land and its alfalfa fields. It misses the alfalfa pellet processing plants where great cylinders roll over roaring fires amid an all-pervasive spinach odor of cooking green things. Brigham Young had directed five men in the Pioneer Band to keep journals, and there is an accurate record of when the party reached what point on the Platte. By May 14 they were in the area of Paxton on the North Platte, by May 15, near Roscoe, May 16 near Keystone, May 17 near Martin Bay, May 18 between Martin and Lemoyne, May 19 near Belmar, May 20 near the famous Oregon Trail camping site of Ash Hollow, and on May 24, about a thousand feet west of the Platte bridge at Bridgeport. Another man was given the task of making latitude and longitude observations for each camp, and another counted the revolutions of a red cloth tied to a wagon wheel, three hundred and sixty to a mile, to give a reasonably accurate estimate of the distance covered every

175

day. He kept his eye on the wheel until Orson Pratt rigged up a crude odometer, which did the job more accurately.

The Pioneer Band awoke every morning at five to the sound of a bugle, which called them to prayer. There was breakfast, and at seven the day's journey began. At night there was a private prayer in each wagon, and on Sunday the caravan stopped the whole day for prayer. The day's journey of twenty miles or so was long and hard, the religious fervor for the emigrants high, the discipline strict, but even so, men danced and played cards. Opposite Scotts Bluff, Brigham Young halted the train and denounced the company for practical jokes, too much dancing, cards, dominoes, and checkers. He sent each man off into the hills to pray. In a chastened mood the emigrants started on.

In early June the Pioneer Band reached Fort Laramie. They halted to hunt for elk and buffalo and to dry the meat for the journey ahead. They fattened their horses and livestock and asked the Gentiles for information about the trail. They repaired their wagons and started on again.

The Mormons cut a new road just south of the Oregon Trail on up the Platte to the crossing where Fort Caspar was later built. The river was high, and they helped Gentile wagons cross the swollen waters in exchange for food or cash. Mormon blacksmiths set up their forges and shoed oxen and fixed wagon hardware for Gentile pioneers who could pay. Mormons were short of both food and cash, and when the Pioneer Band reached Independence Rock, Brigham Young set two men to work chiseling the names of more affluent Gentile travelers into the cliff at a price. Their attention to business in the middle of the wilderness failed to win them friends among other emigrants. At the same time their superior organization and apparent ability to take care of themselves intimidated Gentiles who otherwise might have continued in the West the persecutions begun in the East. Mormons, it was rumored, murdered men, stole women for their harems, and kidnapped children to raise in their own faith, but not many pioneers felt that they should try and do something about it.

As the Pioneer Band traveled, it paused to plant crops that would mature and succor later Mormon caravans. That July of 1847, 1,553 people with 560 wagons set out from winter quarters in the wake of Brigham Young's party. They made the journey with no greater hardships than those of the Pioneer Band. The 2,500 more who set out with Brigham Young for Utah in September of 1848 made the journey without serious loss, too. In 1856 things went just about as well for the first

two brigades of handcart pioneers. The first brigade of 497 people with 100 two-wheel handcarts loaded with supplies and provisions set out in May. They sang a song as they went:

Some must push and some must pull
As we go marching up the hill
As merrily on our way we go
Until we reach the valley, oh.

They made the fourteen-hundred-mile trip as fast as had the wagon trains. The second brigade also safely made it to Utah late in 1856, although carpenter Archer Walter's journal makes it clear that the trail was not without hardship. On June 4, Archer noted, "Made coffin for a child in camp." On June 6, he made another coffin and repaired the handcarts. As the days and miles passed, he made a series of coffins, mostly for children. Then on July 26, Brother Henry Walker was struck by lightning in the very middle of the train and killed. There no longer were any boards to fashion a coffin, so Brother Walker was lowered into his grave without any shelter from the cold earth.

The Martin and Willie handcart brigade starting late in July had a grim experience. They too sang the handcart trail song to make the miles pass faster. They were short of supplies from the start and lived on a pound of flour a person. At Fort Laramie they stopped to trade their watches and rings for provisions. Even so, they cut their rations to three-quarters pound of flour, then to one half pound, then still lower. The handcarts split on the rocky trails. At the Red Buttes the first storm of the threatening winter struck on October 19. At the last crossing of the Platte, the women had to lift their skirts and wade through the icy water. A blizzard blew up as the Mormons were huddling about their warming fires.

Tugging and pushing their heavy carts through the deepening snow, the pioneers struggled up the Sweetwater toward the Devil's Gate. Every morning men, women, and children were found frozen in their blankets. The higher the pioneers climbed, the deeper the snow, until they could no longer go farther. They cleared the snow with frying pans and tin plates to make way for their tents. They splintered their pegs in the frozen earth. The party was marooned in the snow, unable to go ahead or go back. The people dined on the few draft animals they possessed. Every morning there was the grim business of finding just who had died during the night. At least two hundred died before supply wagons sent from Salt Lake by Brigham Young reached them.

The rescuers and the rescued crossed South Pass in a blizzard on November 18. Children froze to death in the lurching wagons. It wasn't until Sunday, November 30, that the suffering Saints came down out of the snowy Wasatch Mountains into the warmth of Salt Lake Valley.

In western Wyoming the Mormon Pioneer Band of 1847 turned south along the trail to Fort Bridger. While they camped beside the Green River, mountain fever brought aches, burns, and swellings to the pioneers. One day Jim Bridger rode into camp, and at last the band reached Fort Bridger.

Undismayed by reports of the hardships encountered in the Hastings Cutoff, the first Mormons set out over it. They chopped down trees, hacked through brush, pried boulders out of the way, and leveled and graded so that wagons to follow would be able to pass through the Wasatch. The trail that the previous year had so taxed the unlucky Donner Party was made wide for the people of Israel.

The Mormons pioneered the trail past the Cave and the Needles. At the foot of the Needles, President Young fell ill of mountain fever. Eight wagons stayed with him as he waited a few days for the fever to go down, but the rest of the band pushed on to the head of Echo Creek. It was here in Echo Canyon that the stricken handcart pioneers paused while a woman gave birth to a baby. When both mother and baby lived, the pioneers counted it a good omen, and the child was appropriately named "Echo."

In Hennefer, where the Hastings Cutoff crosses the Weber River, there is a monument to both the Mormons who passed this way and to the Pony Express riders who galloped through the ford a decade and a half later. We stopped in at Al's Mercantile to buy the makings of a picnic lunch. A Mormon woman at the checkout counter told us how Mormons had bluffed the U.S. soldiers under General Albert Sidney Johnston during the Mormon War of 1857. The soldiers were advancing along the trail, harassed by Mormon guerrillas.

"Fifty men barred the path of a whole army!" said the woman, and a listening Mormon boy's eyes sparkled with the adventure of it. He'd heard his mother tell the story many times before. "The fellows got up on a cliff and marched around the top carrying their guns so that it looked like a long column of militia, but there were only fifty men!"

"If you want to learn more about the Mormon pioneers and the trail they followed, take Highway 65," she added.

We did, for this highway follows the Hastings Cutoff to Lone Tree Camp, where the Mormon advance company camped on July 16, 1847, and built a bridge across the creek. From Hogsback Summit, on July 19, they got a discouraging view of the seemingly endless ranges of mountains ahead of them. Then they were atop Big Mountain, from where the still-ailing Brigham Young got his first glimpse of the promised land beside the Great Salt Lake.

The Pioneer Band came down through the canyons. In Emigration Canyon they encountered the boulders that had blocked the Donner Party in the previous year. The Donners had climbed the mountain at great effort and with a tragic loss of precious time. The Pioneer Band cleared the boulders from the canyon so that they could take their wagons down to the mouth in only four hours. Explorer Post 436, doubtless boys from a post sponsored by a Mormon church, has marked the place with a tall cairn. It was July 24, 1847, that Brigham Young, still weak with mountain fever, riding on a stretcher in a covered wagon, came over the last rise in the canyon. The caravan stopped as the emigrants stared out over the valley. Young sat up in his stretcher and gazed out over the vast distances.

"This is the Place!" he said, and to the twelve to fourteen thousand Mormons who were to come over the Mormon Trail in the next ten years, this place was the Promised Land.

179

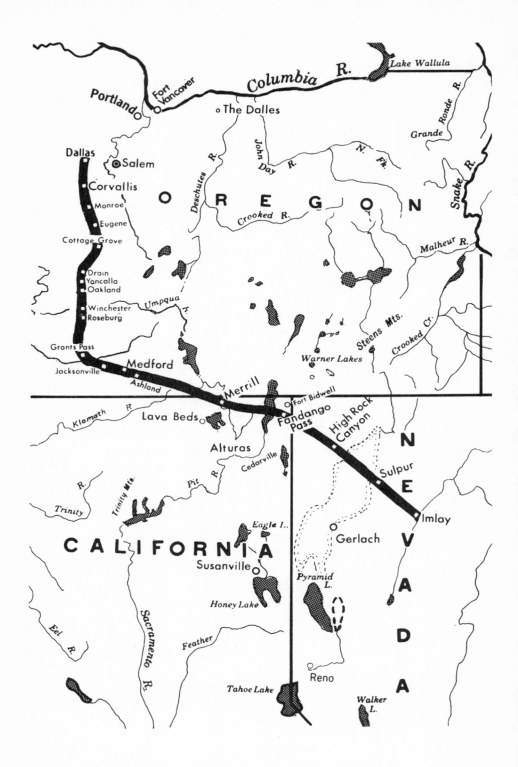

14

The Applegate Road

•

The Applegate brothers, Charles, Lindsay, and Jesse, trekked with their families over the Oregon Trail with the Great Migration of 1843. They arrived at last on the banks of the Columbia at Fort Walla Walla. Lindsay wrote:

Having a whipsaw and other tools with us, we hunted logs from the masses of driftwood along the riverbanks, hewed them out, sawed them into lumber, and built boats, and with our families and the contents of our wagons, commenced the descent of the river. Dr. Whitman procured us the service of two Indians to act as pilots to The Dalles. From there we thought we would have but little trouble by making a portage at the Cascades. We did well till we reached The Dalles, a series of falls and cataracts. Just above the Cascade Mountains one of our boats, containing six persons, was caught in one of those terrible whirlpools and upset. My son, ten years old, my brother Jesse's son Edward, same age, and a man by the name of McClellan, who was a member of my family, were lost. The other three who escaped were left to struggle the best they could until we made the land with the other boats. Leaving the women and children on shore while we rushed to the rescue, it was only with the greatest effort that we were able to keep our boats from sharing the same fate. William Doake, a young man who could not swim, held on to a feather bed until overtaken and rescued. W. Parker and my son Elisha, then twelve years old, after drifting through whirlpools among cragged rocks for more than a mile, rescued themselves by catching hold of a large rock a few feet above water at the head of Rock Island.

The bodies of the drowned were never recovered from the river although the Applegates offered a reward and the Indians of the region searched the rushing waters and the backwashes for months. The survivors reached the shelter of Lee's Old Mission, ten miles down the river from where Salem now stands. There they mourned their drowned boys.

"That long and dreary winter, with its pelting rains and howling winds, brought sadness to us. Under these sad reflections we resolved if we remained in the country to find a better way for others who might wish to emigrate," wrote Lindsay. Out of their loss the Applegates forged a resolve to open a new road up the Willamette Valley and around the far southern end of the towering Cascades. Then pioneers who had withstood the rigors of the Oregon Trail would not have to risk drowning in the Columbia while trying to pass the mighty bulk of Mount Hood which blocked the land route. Once they rounded the southern ramparts of the Cascades, the Applegates proposed to look for a "belt of country extending east towards the South Pass of the Rocky Mountains, where there might be no lofty ranges of mountains to cross."

The winter that found the sorrowing Applegates sheltering at Lee's Mission was also a time of trouble between Great Britain and the United States. Great Britain's right to Oregon was based on Sir Francis Drake's brief voyage along the coast in 1543 and upon the eighteenth century voyages of Captain James Cook. Captain Robert Gray, sailing the seas for Yankee merchants, ascended the Northwest's great river in 1792 and named it the Columbia for his ship. Only a few days later Britain's Captain George Vancouver dispatched Lt. William Broughton up the river to claim its shores for the king.

During the next year an adventurous Scot, Alexander MacKenzie, in the services of the British Northwest Company, crossed the continent to the Pacific. In 1805 Lewis and Clark led their expedition from St. Louis to the shores of the Pacific, built Fort Clatsop near the mouth of the Columbia, and wintered there. The skein of ownership to the Oregon country had become inextricably tangled, and in 1818 the United States and Great Britain signed a convention which arranged for its joint occupation by the two English-speaking powers.

For all practical purposes Oregon was in the hands of the British. The American Fur Company had established Fort Astoria at the mouth of the Columbia in 1811, but during the War of 1812 it had been yielded to the Northwest Company. The British Hudson's Bay Company and the Northwest Company shared the fur trade of the wilderness

The winter of 1846 came early and trapped westering pioneers on the trails. Many froze to death on the Applegate Road. *Courtesy Chicago Historical Society*

until 1821 when the Hudson's Bay Company took over its rival. From then on the Hudson's Bay Company and its chief factor John McLoughlin, whose headquarters were at Fort Vancouver on the north side of the Columbia opposite the mouth of the Willamette, ruled Oregon. American settlers coming over the Oregon Trail were often dependent upon the hospitality of British forts for their very survival.

Not all British were hospitable to the newcomers, particularly after the Great Migration of 1843, for they feared that the torrent of settlers now coming over the Oregon Trail would in time gain control of the territory. Reports of British hostility reaching the States struck upon the expansionist mood of the American people with the effect of flint on steel. "Fifty-Four Forty or Fight" became the battle cry of the Democratic candidate James K. Polk in the hot election of 1844, and the British became still more alarmed. The Democratic candidate and his vice-presidential running mate, George M. Dallas, were claiming all the territory as far as the northern border of what is now British Columbia.

The joint occupying powers of the Oregon Territory appeared on a collision course, and in 1845 the U.S. Department of War ordered the military explorer John Charles Fremont to search for a southern route to Oregon since the Oregon Trail could be easily cut off by the British at Fort Hall, Fort Boise, and Fort Walla Walla. Fremont diverted his attentions to the tumultuous situation in California and failed to carry out the mission.

The Applegates and their friends in the Willamette Valley also counted it important to discover a southern trail to Oregon in case of war with

183

Great Britain. They did not know that on June 15, 1846, the United States and England had signed a treaty setting the boundary line at the forty-ninth degree of parallel, which is the northern boundary of the present state of Washington. In June as the U.S. and British delegates were gathering to make peace, in the faraway Oregon Territory Jesse and Lindsay Applegate, Levi and John Scott (also 1843 immigrants), the celebrated mountain man, Moses "Black" Harris, and ten others gathered at La Creole near Dallas, named for the new war-hawk vice-president, in the county of Polk, named for the new war-hawk President. Each man had a saddle horse and a packhorse, a rifle, and his supplies.

On June 22 the trailblazers set out, and at the end of the first day they camped on the Mary's River near modern Corvallis. Hudson's Bay Company men who knew the valleys and the mountains to the south of the settlements on the lower Willamette had told the Applegates that the Cascades could be most easily crossed where the Klamath River cuts through the range, and the party, ironically enough, was relying upon British advice as they pushed to the south through immense forests of Douglas fir to find the Klamath River.

My son Rick and I, comfortable in our truck camper, followed their route on U.S. highway 99W which runs through the now prosperous valley. On the grounds of the Union High School in Monroe we found a prominent marker telling of the Applegate Road, but we found very few other markers in the towns that have grown up where it passed. In the late fall of 1846 the first settlers to straggle over the road that the Applegates surveyed stopped at the Eugene Skinner cabin to rest and thaw out after their hardships in the mountain passes which were now ahead of us. Today the city of Eugene, named for Skinner, contains upwards of 70,000 people, a university, art galleries, and a huge lumber industry made possible by the tall firs which impeded the pioneers' way.

On the second night of their expedition the Applegate party camped in the foothills of the Calapooya Range. They continued along the base of the mountains to the southeast past Spencer's Butte. In a little valley near the butte they came upon Indians digging camas root, which the redskins liked to mix with the fat grasshoppers still found on the hillsides and bake into tasty cakes. The camas diggers sprinted away through the trees, leaving one old man, whom the explorers captured.

When the white men signed that he should lead them, he took them for two or three miles and put them on a dim trail which the Indians had marked by twisting the tops of brush to show the way. The trail led to a prairie at the foot of low mountains and then on into the mountains themselves.

For all its present-day prosperity and civilization, the country through which the trailblazers traveled still has its share of hardships, as we discovered when we reached Cottage Grove, mining and lumber town south on U.S. 99W from Eugene. We approached the town through a great cloud of acrid smoke which swirled out of mountain canyons and eddied through the forests. The smoke stung our eyes as we stopped for gasoline. The attendent at the pump was smudged. His coat and hair were singed.

"She's under control now, but if you fellows had come along even this morning, we sure could have used you to help fight the fire!" he said.

A roaring timber fire had swept over 40,000 acres in the nearby mountains, and every able-bodied man and boy had been out fighting the flames that were turning the green forests to blackened stumps.

"But it's still burning," cried my son. "Can't we help?"

"She's under control now," repeated the attendant in a voice bleak with fatigue, "and there are enough men on the job, unless the wind rises. God, I wish it would rain!"

The smoke of a burning forest stayed with us for scores of miles as we drove on to the Yoncalla Valley. It was the middle of a beautiful June morning when the party of trail-finders reached this valley. Streams of cool water dashed down among meadows and forests of oaks and maples. Looking at the meadows, waist-high with grass, the explorers named it "horse heaven." Wild strawberries grew on the gentle hills, and game sprang away into the hazel thickets. It was so beautiful that in 1848 Jesse Applegate, with his family and all his possessions, returned to the valley to claim 640 acres for a farm. The next year Charles and Lindsay Applegate brought their families to claim farms, and Yoncalla, "Home of the Eagles," was founded. We stopped our camper at Front Street and Applegate Avenue in the town. The street signs had fallen on top of a trail monument at the intersection.

"The house by the side of the road where Jesse Applegate lived is back north of town," the town librarian told us as she checked out a book to a freckled little girl. "Jesse, who is just about the greatest man of old Oregon, is buried in the cemetery up on a hill. There are lots of Applegate descendants still living around here. Vince Applegate lives in the old Charles Applegate house, but there's a man named Payne living on the Jesse Applegate place."

We drove back to the Jesse Applegate farm. Born on a backwoods farm in Kentucky on July 5, 1811, Jesse was an uncommon pioneer. When

185

he was ten years old, his family took him to live in Missouri. At the age of sixteen, with one dollar in his pocket and the clothes on his back to last the winter, he studied mathematics and surveying from John Messenger at Rock Springs Seminary at Shiloh, Illinois, which is now the Shurtleff Campus of Southern Illinois University at Alton. In St. Louis he taught school and boarded at the Green Tree Tavern, where he met such mountain men as William S. Sublette, Jedediah Smith, and David Jackson back from the trackless wilds to talk furs with the city's businessmen. He volunteered to be their clerk and roamed the city with them listening to their tales. Although he became a surveyor, from then on he worked only for the day when at last in 1843, he started out with his family over the Oregon Trail to the country that his mountain men friends had told him about. Caught up in the Great Migration, he acted as captain of the cow column and cut the first wagon road over the western stretches of the trail so that wagons need no longer be left at Fort Hall. Although Levi Scott was nominally captain of the company which opened the Applegate Road, Jesse Applegate was its true leader, as Lindsay Applegate was its chronicler.

Driving up the lane which leads to the old Jesse Applegate house, we noticed that the back of the house faces the modern highway. The sun still shone bronze and baleful through the smoke from the burning forest. Darrell Payne, a lean, weathered man, had fought the fire for two days, but he came out of the house to talk to us.

"The old Applegate Road ran in front of the house," he said, "but folks put a new highway through around to the rear."

Payne, who grew up at North Platte, Nebraska, on the Oregon Trail, talked about the drought which was turning his fields to dust. Every gust of smoke-laden wind puffed away some of the soil of old Jesse's farm, upon which this young farmer's livelihood depended.

"Cattle prices are low. I worked in the lumber mill, but wages are low there too, and now the fire will bring harder times," he said. He stared moodily out over the fields.

"You'll find Jesse up in the old Applegate graveyard. Just close the gates after you as you drive up there."

We bumped over a farm road which is all that is left of the Applegate Road and climbed over a stile into the graveyard. There beneath a double tombstone we found Jesse buried on one side, dead in 1888, and his wife Cynthia on the other, dead in 1882. At the foot of their hill the Applegate Road still can be traced.

Even the creeks we crossed as we continued south on U.S. 99 tell stories. Cabin Creek is near Oakland. There a Presbyterian minister with the preposessing name of Josephus Adamson Cornwall built a rude cabin and spent the winter in the wilds rather than leave his precious books behind. The Rev. Mr. Cornwall had journeyed from distant Independence over the Oregon, California, and Applegate Trails. On the way he had conducted services for the dead when the occasion demanded, and with his wife he had shepherded his flock of four children, as well as four young men who accompanied him. In the dreaded Umpqua Canyon the minister lost his oxen, but was able to pack two cases of books and bedrolls out of the mountains to the shores of a small stream, where his son Joseph H. Cornwall, then thirteen, remembered later:

"Father having brought a crosscut saw and a frow with him and there being excellent cedar timber near our camp, we went to work in early winter to build a cabin. About Christmas it was completed, with excellent cedar shakes for the roof, and excellent cedar puncheons for the floor and a comfortable chimney." On the cold nights when the wind blustered about the family, they read the two cases of books by the light of flaring pine knots. They lived on camas that they bought from friendly Indians, venison that they shot in the forest, flour, and milk from the two or three cows that they had brought with them over the trail. In the spring men came to help them pack the beloved books down to the Willamette Valley.

In the vicinity of Roseburg we came upon Newton Creek. Here, as the bitter storms of the late fall of 1846 swept about him, John Newton and his wife met three Umpqua Indians. With a few English words and sign language, they let him know that he might as well camp here, for there would be no better place farther along the road. When he had set up his tent, the Indians begged first for something to eat and then for ammunition with which they promised to bring down a deer. Newton gave them three balls and some powder. The one brave who could speak English loaded his gun, but he did not leave the camp to hunt. Nor would he go away when Newton asked him to do so.

Newton, suspicious of his camp guests, watched them for hours, but as the night wore on he fell asleep. Instantly one of the Indians fired three balls into him. As he lunged inside his tent to get his gun, another Indian struck him with an ax and almost cut his leg off. Robbing the tent and taking Newton's mare, his guests hurried away. Newton died the next day.

The Indians of the southern Oregon country through which the Applegates opened their road plundered the wagon trains that followed later in the year and murdered the emigrants when they could, but they were peaceful when the first English traders came among them. They also were shy and fled the approach of the strange white men. Since this prevented trade, the traders became increasingly short-tempered. When in 1818-19 the Northwest Fur Company sent sixty men into the region to trade, the Indians once again slipped away into the forests. The traders attacked an Indian camp to seize their horses. This, they imagined, would force the Indians to trade with them. In the fight the whites killed fourteen Indians with their guns, and the rest fled in terrified confusion. After that the Indians were no longer either shy or peaceful, and they took out their vengeance on hapless wagon trains for a half-century. Jesse Applegate could only urge wagon trains that rolled over his trail to travel fast and in groups to avoid the marauders.

The Applegate Road crossed the North Umpqua River near the present Winchester and the South Umpqua River five miles farther on near the present Roseburg, named not for the roses it takes pride in growing but for a pioneer named Rose. The Applegates found the crossing of the North Umpqua to be dangerous. The riverbed was a mass of loose rocks, and the horses fell and tumbled their riders into the current. After crossing the south branch of the river the party camped on June 24 opposite Umpqua Canyon. Here about noon on November 5, later in the same year, Jesse Quinn Thornton, traveling westward over the new trail, arrived with his family, sick and embittered by hardship. Today the left bank of the river is serene, but to Thornton it appeared as follows:

Here I found the wrecks of all the companies who had been induced to enter upon the road along which our wagons were lying scattered in fragments, upon the side of the hills, from the tops of the mountains, and along the rocky glens, and the almost impassable canyons, which marked this disastrous cut-off. Some of the emigrants had lost their wagons; some their teams; some half they possessed; and some everything. Here were men who had a wagon, but wanted a team; there, others who had a team, but no wagon. Mr. Humphrey was the only man who, so far as I have since been able to learn, got to this point with a whole wagon and a complete team. All looked lean, thin, pale, and hungry as wolves. The children were crying for food; and all appeared distressed and dejected.

The Umpqua Range rises fifteen hundred feet over the valley floor where more than a century later we were now driving. On June 25 of 1846 the Applegate party started into Umpqua Canyon. As Lindsay Applegate later wrote, they "followed up the little stream that runs through the defile for four or five miles, crossing the creek a great many times, but the canyon becoming more obstructed with brush and fallen timber, the little trail we were following turned up the side of a ridge where the woods were more open and wound its way to the top of the mountains."

The trail petered out, and they cut their way through the underbrush until they at last came down into the Rogue River Valley. Rick and I found it an easy drive on a modern highway through the Umpqua Canyon, but pioneer wagon trains found the stretch of the Applegate Road through Umpqua Canyon almost impassable. Thornton wrote: "The canyon, which appears to have been rent asunder by some vast convulsion of nature, is about three miles long, having the whole of its width occupied by a very swift stream of cold snow-water, varying from one foot and a half to four feet in depth."

Young men with the Thornton party went ahead to cut brush and otherwise improve the road, but their labors were of little purpose. The oxen had to pull the wagons along the bed of the creek where many died in the icy water. The fall rains fell in blinding sheets. One man who had brought a hive of bees from Missouri lost them when his wagon overturned in the stream. Emigrants sickened, and some died.

Among those who died was William Smith, captain of a wagon train.

On November 15, 1846, his train entered the canyon. Driftwood, fallen-down timber, and huge rocks blocked the way as the train made its way down the creek. Exhausted by the labor of clearing a way through the rushing water, the party stopped at a wide spot in the canyon and built a blazing log fire to dry out. Most of the emigrants were certain that they could not continue, but Captain Smith was not ready to quit. He scolded the men for giving up when they were almost at the end of the road. He sank to his knees, looked up to the towering canyon walls and cried, "Lord, have mercy upon me." He fell forward dead. He left behind his wife and nine young children. They tore apart his spring wagon to make its box into a coffin, and buried Smith in it close to where he had fallen.

The ordeal of the Umpqua Canyon was particularly bitter because, for most of the wagon trains, the descent of the Rogue River Valley had been almost an idyll. They usually lingered in the beautiful valley to rest and often lingered so long that they were caught by the fall rains in the Umpquas. Lindsay Applegate became lyric in describing the beautiful valley through which the Applegates mapped their road:

"It seemed like a great meadow, interspersed with groves of oaks, which appeared like vast orchards. All day long we traveled over rich black soil covered with rank grass, clover, and pea vine." Today the valley is one of the gardens of the West. Rick and I found it aromatic with mint and bright with gladioli. In 1863 workmen improving the road were camped on the Rogue River when news reached them of Grant's capture of Vicksburg. Being forthright Unionists, the men named their camp Grant's Pass. My son and I drove through the modern town of that name and started up the Rogue River, the river on our left, over the old road which leads where the Applegate Road ran past present-day Jacksonville, Medford, and Ashland. We found the Rogue River Valley a hospitable country that treasures the pioneer past. Jacksonville sprang up as a boom town when gold was discovered there in 1852, but the strike proved longer lasting than most, and gold was taken out of the ground until the 1920's. Some antiquarians say that the town is the best-preserved pioneer community in the Pacific Northwest. We poked among the century-old buildings and were struck by the incongruity of listening to a trumpeter practicing in a pioneer house for the Peter Britt Music Festival that is held in the town in August.

What music is to Jacksonville, Shakespearean drama is to Ashland, where in Lithia Park there is a replica of London's Fortune Theatre of 1599. Where only yesterday pioneer wagon trains were attacked by the

Rogue River Indians, people now listen to the sweet accents of music or of the Bard. Yet it was from Jacksonville after the massacre at Bloody Point that miners rode out to patrol the trail. Finding still another wagon train under siege at the point, the miners attacked the Indians and drove them into the lava beds. They stayed at the point for two months to protect the emigrants. Even so, another wagon train was overwhelmed and the miners found the charred remains on the south side of Lower Klamath Lake.

The Rogue River Indians were as obstreperous as an Indian tribe could get. They preferred the scalps of redheaded woodpeckers, but since they failed to take enough of these, they contented themselves with lifting the scalps of pioneers. The Applegates came down out of the Umpquas onto a large creek which flowed into the Rogue. Later the stream was called Grave Creek for Martha Crowley, a girl of fourteen, who died of tuberculosis and was interred under an oak tree by its side. The pioneers dug Martha's grave deep and corraled the oxen over it that night to hide it from the Indians. In spite of everything, the Indians discovered the grave and dug up the body for the clothing and ornaments. A later party reburied the remains.

As the Applegate party descended the creek to the river, Indians watched them from the distance. They glided ahead through the pine and oak. Knowing that it was their horses that the Indians were after, the trailblazers picketed them with double stakes that night and mounted a watchful guard. The Indians, discouraged by the vigilance, kept away. In the morning the men discovered that the night dew had dampened the powder of their muzzle-loaders. They fired and reloaded and then advanced toward the river intending to cross in two divisions.

The Indians had gathered on the far bank of the river to enliven the crossing. When the first division reached the river, they drove all the pack animals across while the rear division covered them with their guns. Then the first division in turn covered the rear division's crossing, so that the Indians were not able to attack. All day the discomfited Indians kept pace with the party on the far bank of the river and tried to goad the men into a foray. That night the party camped on the stream now known as Emigrant Creek near the base of the Siskiyou Mountains.

Oregon Highway 66 follows Emigrant Creek past the Emigrant Reservoir and over Green Springs Mountain, where huge trucks speed with loads of logs cut in the Siskiyous. The Applegates arrived on the Klamath River on July 3, 1846. Lindsay wrote:

Afternoon we moved down through an immense forest, principally of yellow pine, to the river, and then traveled up the north bank, still through yellow pine forests, for about six miles, when all at once we came out in full view of the Klamath country, extending eastward as far as the eye could reach. It was an exciting moment after the many days spent in the dense forest and among the mountains, and the whole party broke forth in cheer after cheer. An Indian who had not observed us until the shouting began, broke away from the river bank near us and ran to the trees a quarter of mile distant. An antelope could scarcely have made better time, for we continued shouting as he ran and his speed seemed to increase until he was lost from our view among the pines.

State Highway 66 crosses the Klamath River eight miles downstream from the crossing used by Captain Levi Scott and David Goff and fifty wagons traveling over the Applegate Road in 1846. According to Thornton, boulders the size of barrels lurked beneath the surface at the crossing. Later Captain Scott relocated the ford to a spot only one-half mile north of today's highway bridge. By 1868 Brown's ferry had replaced the ford, and from the highway we could look over Big Bend Reservoir to the place where the ferry once ran. Cattle nosed around us.

The Applegates cut their track through the wilds to the shore of Lower Klamath Lake. There they turned south along the lakeshore into what is now California. Modoc smoke signals rose ahead of them. To the amazement of the explorers, they came upon a recently occupied white man's camp.

"We found pieces of newspapers and other unmistakable evidence of civilized people," wrote Lindsay.

The pioneer litterbug turned out to be the Great Pathfinder, John C. Fremont, coming from California, who had reached the point a few days before. Before he could continue on his exploration, he was overtaken by a rider who carried dispatches from California informing him that the Mexican War had begun. He returned to California, but not before the Klamaths attacked his camp. The Indians achieved a complete surprise and killed two of Fremont's Delawares. Only Kit Carson's daring had prevented a rout. The Applegates could easily make out the graves of the dead, although Fremont's soldiers had driven horses over them to conceal their location. The Applegates camped in open ground that night to prevent surprise. Lindsay said:

We were but a handful of men surrounded by hundreds of Indians, but by dint of great care and vigilance we were able to pass through their country safely. On every line of travel from the Atlantic to the Pacific, there has been a great loss of life from failure to exercise a proper degree of caution, and too often have reckless and foolhardy men who have through the want of proper care, become embroiled in difficulties with the Indians, gained the reputation of being Indian fighters and heroes, while the men who were able to conduct parties in safety through the country of warlike savages, escaped the world's notice.

The Applegates rounded the south end of the lake to the eastern shore. Our truck camper drove down a dusty road through the Lower Klamath Wildlife Refuge where signs advised, "Speed Kills. Watch out for birds." Another national wildlife refuge now surrounds Tule Lake, which the Applegates came upon as they pushed to the east. At first the pathfinders tried to go around the lake to the south, but they came upon the inferno of rugged lava ridges, caves, and crevices which is now part of the Lava Beds National Monument. David Goff chased a mountain sheep into the lava and soon got lost. Happily, he came out on the lakeshore and so surprised a band of lurking Modocs that they took to canoes and paddled furiously to an island in the lake.

The explorers turned along the lake and on northward up the Lost River looking for a place to cross. They came upon an Indian crouching under a bank. He led them to a sheet of water fifteen inches deep running over a huge rock in the river. On this "stone bridge" near today's Merrill, Oregon, wagons were to cross the Lost River for decades. The Applegate Road continued on past what is now Malin, Oregon, and on over the tableland between Clear Lake and Goose Lake across the border in California. The trail passed just north of Clear Lake and Blue Mountain. A dense cloud of dust swirled behind our truck as we took a forest service road through this juniper-dotted land in which Peter Skene Ogden, the mountain man, survived by sucking snow that he had stuffed into his pack in the Siskiyous. At Pot Hole Springs we stopped to prowl around in the rocks for the grave of a fourteen-year-old boy, who had died on the trail. We found it marked with boulders. That night we camped atop Blue Mountain at the foot of the Blue Mountain Lookout where grandfatherly Bill Harrington, of the U.S. Forest Service, and his wife, Gertrude, keep a sharp eye out for wisps of smoke. As we sat in the lookout and talked, a lightning storm moved across the tableland. The night wind rose, lightning cracked nearby, thunder pealed, and a few huge drops of rain pelted down. The lightning struck a single juniper near Goose Lake and set it afire. All told, the storm caused twelve smokes, but they all burned themselves out.

"Junipers are isolated from one another," explained Bill, "and the fire doesn't spread from one to another. The forest service rarely has to go after a juniper fire."

In the morning we found the six-inch-thick dust plotched with mud from the rain. We stopped to talk to a hunter who was scouting antelope in a pick-up truck against the opening of the hunting season on the next day.

"Those goats got great eyes," he complained, scratching his grizzled face. "I can see the herds with my glasses, but they can see me without glasses."

We stopped to look inside the pioneer Pease cabin on Little Grizzlie Spring situated on the Applegate Road, which can be traced across the barrens to the western shore of Goose Lake. We found Goose Lake lost in a fog, its brackish waters ghostlike in the gloom. The Applegate party passed around the south end of Goose Lake, but emigrants took seven different shortcuts across the dry lake bed when the water was low. Most emerged at the mouth of Mud Creek on the west side of the lake just beyond McGinty Point. Low water in the lake still reveals the ruts of the wagons, and sometimes a broken wheel or abandoned household article comes to light. We crossed the shallow lake on a causeway of dirt lined with rock.

Motorists on U.S. 395 driving north of Alturas come across a sign indicating where the Applegate Road crossed on its way east from Goose Lake. Today a gravel road leads up into Fandango Pass in the Warner Mountains, named for Captain W. H. Warner, who was shot full of arrows by Indians as he advanced into the region at the head of his expedition. His party fled while the Indians hacked at the fallen officer.

The pass proved a steep climb even for our powerful truck. Henry Minto wrote about his descent down the hill up which our truck labored. "The mountain being so steep the cattle could hardly step a'tall but just had to shove their feet along." The slope on the east side was perhaps even more difficult. J. Goldsborough Bruff, traveling over the Applegate Road in 1849 on his way to the Lassen Cutoff, which in turn was to take him to the California gold fields, described the east side of the pass as he found it:

In the center of a very broad, sandy and dusty road, men urging their heavy ox-trains up the steep hill with lashes, imprecations, and shouts, some riding up on horses and mules, and clouds of blind dust and sand flying. There rode up, an old man, on a jaded horse; a mattress covered the horse, the sick man astride and laying over on his breast; with a cover-lid thrown over him, and a

194

corner trailing in the dust, he looked pale and haggard; had his arms around the neck of the old horse. He was afflicted with the flux and scurvy. Another unfortunate followed him, on a mule, enveloped in a blue blanket, and barely able to retain his seat; he had the fever and ague. Some small boys, not over ten years of age, were leading jaded animals up. Women were seen, with the trains, occupied at chocking the wheels, while the oxen were allowed to blow, on the ascent. A man had a baby in his arms, and in midst of the thick dust, was urging up his team. Some wagons had as many as twelve yoke of oxen in them. One wagon, with women and children in it, when near the summit became uncoupled, and down hill it ran—stern foremost, with great rapidity—the women and children screamed, men shouted, and with all the rest of the fuss, there was a great clamor. A dead ox, a short distance in front of a heavy team, and men by them, brought up the backing out vehicle, most luckily without damage to any one.

From the summit of Fandango Pass the Applegates looked down into a paradise. "East and south of us, at the foot of the ridge was a beautiful valley, twenty or thirty miles in extent and containing a small lake. A number of small streams flowed from the mountain into and through the valley, affording an abundance of water for the wants of a settlement. This fertile valley on the border of the desert has since been called Surprise Valley."

The Applegate Road east of Fandango Pass ran between Middle and Upper lakes. When Upper Lake was dry, many wagons crossed over its sun-baked surface. Forty-Nine Lake across the border in Nevada was a salt lake in pioneer days, but today it is dry. The trail ran through the steep gorge of Forty-Nine Hill and past Forty-Nine Lake. We turned north from the Applegate Road on a paved highway which leads to the ruins of Fort Bidwell, erected in 1865 to protect emigrants from the Indians. Only the foundations of the fort survive in the yard of an abandoned schoolhouse where the windows are broken and the playground swings are missing their seats. The Fort Bidwell Indians and civic clubs have marked the site for visitors. Dogs barked at us and sheep stared as we walked among the foundations. Nearby an Indian boy was chopping wood for his family cookstove. When his father drove up in a Volkswagen, the boy threw down his ax and ran into his arms. After that demonstration of filial affection, it was hard to conjure up a picture of old Fort Bidwell beleaguered by savage Indians, so we drove off. That night Rick and I camped in the Stowe Reservoir campground west of Cedarville with a gang of jubilant rodeo cowboys.

East of Surprise Valley the Applegate Road traversed a desert of forbidding sand and gravel, broken by low mountain ranges and a towering volcanic wall through which a deep canyon wound. The Bureau of Land Management man in Cedarville warned us about the rigors of the desert and suggested that we keep out of the Black Rocks region because the Air Force was still using it for jet bombing runs. John Applegate, a descendant of the Applegate explorers, who followed the Applegate Road from east to west with his wife and four friends while Rick and I were following it from west to east, received the following advice in a letter from the Bureau of Land Management office in Reno:

"We could not guarantee your safety across the Black Rock Desert as there is a remote possibility of unexploded ammunition. The desert is also subject to periodic showers or cloudbursts. The soil composition of the old lake bed may make driving hazardous under these conditions. The soil becomes very slick and, depending upon the degree of saturation, can become very boggy."

Both the modern Applegate party and Rick and I gave the Black Rock Desert a wide berth. The prospect of being bombed by a jet while looking for the remains of an ambushed wagon train had a certain ironic appeal, but the appeal was decidedly limited. Rick and I were also bedeviled by two successive blowouts as we pursued the rough tracks across the Nevada desert skirting the danger area, and we retreated to the ranch town of Gerlach, Nevada, for new tires and more fuel and water, both of which are exhausted quickly in the searing heat and vast distances of the desert.

The Applegate Road ran where the modern road to Denio leads eastward past the Massacre Lakes and on southeast into High Rock Canyon, a fissure in the volcanic ridge from four to nine hundred feet deep, so narrow that the sun never strikes the bottom. Only one wagon at a time could follow the canyon. Digger Indians lived in a cave in the canyon and from ancient times chipped arrow heads of obsidian. Emigrants soon learned that the Indians could shoot a stone-pointed arrow through the backbone of an ox and six inches out of its other side.

To some wagon trains the narrow canyon was a place of terror, but to others it was a respite from the glare of the desert that lay to the east. At some points the canyon widened and there hungry oxen found patches of grass to munch in their parched mouths. To Bruff the canyon became the site of a celebration when five men stole the wine reserved for medical purposes. In the morning, reported Bruff, "they turned the bung of the keg down and swore the wine leaked out, though I noticed a great laughter and hilarity in their wagons at night."

Payute Peak was a landmark of the trail east of the canyon. Near the peak's western face in 1849 Peter Lassen, pioneer of the Lassen Road in California, was killed by Indians while prospecting for silver. Earlier in the year an emigrant named Harding had picked up a lump of what he took to be lead. He tossed it into his wagon. Later he melted some of the metal off and molded it into bullets which he fired at some game. When he reached the end of the trail, he discovered the metal was not lead but silver. He returned to search along the trail for the place where he had found the ore, but he never could discover it. Others took up the search. Among them were Peter Lassen and Clapper and Lemericus Wyatt, who was then sixty years old and weighed two hundred pounds. When the Indians surprised the prospectors, an arrow zinged through Lemericus Wyatt's clothes, but left him unscratched. He pumped his fat legs as fast as he could to cover. The party's horses bolted at the attack, but Wyatt's horse ran back to him, and he was able to get on its back. He galloped away bareback with the picket rope to guide his mount. He alone escaped 140 miles to Susanville, California, from where men rode out to bury the dead. In a few years the Masons of Susanville moved Lassen's body to an honored grave beneath a large yellow pine where he had camped at their town, in recognition of his having brought the first Masonic charter to California.

Coming from the east, modern travelers following the Applegate Road turn at Sulphur to take the road to Gerlach in order to avoid the Black Rocks Desert, which lies between Sulphur and the High Rock Canyon. Some few trucks and jeeps push on over the road which still leads to abandoned Harding City, named for the man who first found silver. Even though there are the ruins of a stamping mill near where the pioneers camped at Little Double Hot Spring, no silver except for Harding's solitary lump was ever discovered in the area.

Wagon trains found that the Black Rocks Desert was its own kind of inferno. J. Quinn Thornton noted in his diary:

Nothing presented itself to the eye but a broad expanse of a uniform dead-level plain, which conveyed to the mind the idea that it had been the muddy and sandy bottom of a former lake, and that after the water had suddenly sunk through the fissure, leaving the bottom in a state of muddy fusion, it was enlivened by the murmur of no streams, but was a wide waste of desolation, where even the winds had died.

Dominating the desolate scene is the Black Rock, which Lindsay Applegate described as "black volcanic rock and all about were vast piles of cinders, resembling those from a blacksmith's forge." Columns of steam led the trailblazers to hot springs. Once the water cooled, it was drinkable. Wagon trains reaching the springs later in the summer found that they could cook meat in a few minutes in the boiling waters. Men immersed coffeepots in the water to heat their coffee. There were other hot springs in the Black Rock Desert too, and if thirst-crazed cattle plunged into them, they were boiled alive until the flesh fell from their white tendons and bones.

Thornton attached a weight to a cord and lowered it into a lesser hot spring nearby. He played out two hundred feet without striking bottom. A Mrs. Lovelin accidentally plunged a foot into the hot water of the great spring. When her stocking was removed, her skin peeled off with it.

East of Sulphur a rough road today leads through the Kamma Mountains to Rabbit Hole Springs. It was on July 14, 1846, that the Applegate party split as they crossed the desert. Eight men struck off to the south searching for a way to the Humboldt River. Another seven men, including Lindsay Applegate, went east. Elsewhere in the West trailblazers often followed the tracks of buffalo or larger game, but in this waste, where fearful sandstorms blow up without warning, Lindsay Applegate's party came across nothing but a trail of a single rabbit. This they followed. The by now thirsting men followed the way the rabbit led until they came to a small puddle in the desert. They dug down into the stony ground to get at the source of the water and were able to obtain several gallons. When at dusk rabbits showed up for their evening's sip of water, they killed several for dinner.

According to John Applegate, today Rabbit Hole Springs has miniscule flakes of gold in it. If this were true during trail days, pioneers would scarcely have noticed, so intent were they in slaking their burning thirst in the tepid waters. Pioneers later opened up another spring nearby the Rabbit Hole so that by the time Bruff arrived at the site in 1849, he described the place as "a well or tank of water, and a crowd of thirsty men and animals surrounding it. A few yards to left of this another, similar hole, filled up with a dead ox, his hindquarters and legs only sticking out—aboveground. Dead oxen thick about here, and stench suffocating."

At all the hot springs and scant waterholes in the Black Rocks Desert, oxen died. At one waterhole, Bruff reported, "there was scarcely space for the wagons to reach the holes, for the ox-carcasses. Here and around the other springs, I counted eighty-two dead oxen, two dead horses, and one mule in an area of one tenth of a mile." Bruff contributed an exhausted mule to what he called a "depot of carcasses."

Beyond the Rabbit Hole, Lindsay Applegate found a country so forsaken that not even a coyote yelped at night. The men could not sleep because of thirst, and during the day mirages of beautiful blue waters lined with willows danced before their eyes. They sheltered beneath ledges of rock from the rays of the terrible sun. At last both Applegate parties reached the chalky waters of the Humboldt River. They knew they had succeeded in opening their trail through the wilderness from southern Oregon to the California Trail when they came upon a burned-out wagon train of hapless California-bound pioneers. Lindsay Applegate noted, "The line of our road was now complete. We had succeeded in finding a route across the desert and on to the Oregon settlements with camping places at suitable distances. We felt that our enterprise was already a success and that emigrants would be able to reach Oregon late in the season with far less danger of being snowed in."

That first summer of the Applegate Road 150 wagons started over it. In May, 1847, Levi Scott took twenty men back over the road to improve the worst spots, and another seventy wagons followed. By 1848 it had become a popular, if dangerous and difficult, route.

The point where the Applegate Road branched off from the California Trail is near Imlay. The Rye Patch Dam is a short distance below the site. Bats were flitting in and out of the little control house at the dam as Rick and I looked across the waters that have swallowed up Lassen's Meadows, where pioneer oxen once ate their fill on the banks of the Humboldt before starting over the low Antelope Mountains which border the river valley and hide from view the grim desert beyond.

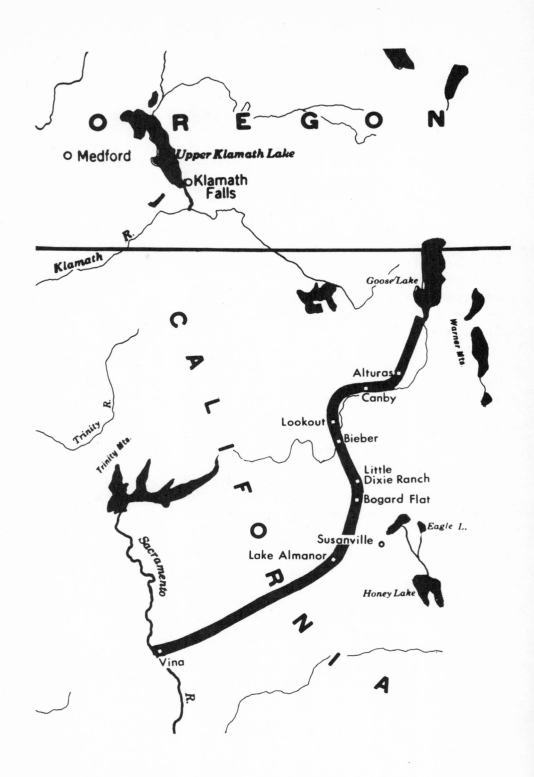

O R E G O N

o Medford

Upper Klamath Lake

oKlamath
Falls

Klamath R.

C A L I F O R N I A

Klamath

Goose Lake

Warner Mts.

Trinity R.

Trinity Mts.

Alturas

Canby

Lookout

Bieber

Little
Dixie Ranch

Bogard Flat

Eagle L.

Susanville o

Sacramento

Lake Almanor

Honey Lake

Vina

R.

15

Lassen Trail:
Northern Route to the Goldfields

●

Some embittered '49ers called it the Greenhorn's Cutoff, because nobody but a greenhorn would be crazy enough to take it. Others called it the Cape Horn Route because to trace its grueling miles of mountains and canyons was tantamount to going the long sea voyage around Cape Horn. It was also called the Death Route after the early fall blizzards of 1849 caught weakened travelers still in the mountains.

The Lassen Trail had its advantages. This northern route to the gold fields avoided the High Sierras and the deserts between the Carson and the Humboldt. Grass and water were plentiful along the trail, and much of the way the trail followed high ridges that, rugged and meandering as they might be, at least made unnecessary the murderous ascents and descents of other mountain cutoffs. Probably half the '49ers took the trail, but when word of their terrible hardships reached pioneers coming west in 1850, most of them avoided it.

One spring, heavy snows kept me from following the Lassen Trail through the high country of northern California, but finally in June of 1969 I set out with my family in our station wagon to trace its course from where it branched off the Applegate Road at Goose Lake to where it reached the Sacramento River at Vina. When my son Rick and I followed the Applegate Road late one summer, we found the portion around Goose Lake to be dusty, and dry but in June the same country turned out to be verdant with flowers and grass. Cool breezes soothed us as we got out of the car to look at the old ruts of the trail or to inspect a pioneer spring.

At the southern tip of Goose Lake in northeastern California, the Applegate Road turned northwestward toward Oregon, but the Lassen Trail struck out to the south. For the first few days travel on the trail was over easy terrain, but the Indians gave it the same unwelcome attention that they gave to the Applegate Trail. J. Goldsborough Bruff, who passed over the trail in 1849, came upon a fresh gravemarker which read:

> *Mr. Eastman—*
> *The deceased was killed by*
> *an Indian arrow;*
> *Octr. 4th. 1849.*

Mr. Eastman's friends had thrust the death arrow into the grave with a card attached to it. On the card was written, "This is the fatal arrow." Still another card on the headboard added, "The mules tied up in camp; man shot, and one mule stolen."

The Lassen Trail reached the headwaters of the Pit River a few miles west of today's town of Alturas, close to where Rattlesnake Creek flows into it. It kept to the southeast bank of the river to the vicinity of Canby. There close to the Canby Bridge it forded the river to the northwest shore. Descending the Pit River the trail crossed and recrossed the stream, which had taken its name from the pit houses in which the Indians lived along its banks. They dug holes in the banks, laid down crosspoles and covered them over with sod. Smoke from their cooking fires escaped through the rectangular door in the roof. Milt McGee, leading his pack train along the trail, fell into an abandoned pit dwelling, much to his annoyance. To pioneers the river just had to be called the Pit.

The Pit River Indians were a more active menace, too. In 1850 they stole twenty-seven mules from one train and stripped seven men of another of all their clothing. When the naked men rushed into the stream to escape, the Indians showered them with arrows. Six were killed, but the seventh got away when the Indians, hearing another white party firing at ducks, ran. The surviving man pulled himself out of the river and was rescued by the duck hunters who bound up his wounds.

Between Canby and Lookout the river roars into a canyon where wagons scraped along the rocky walls of the west bank. All night long in their camp in the canyon, sentries of the Davis County Train kept their vigil. In the morning as the pioneers broke camp, an Indian jumped out of the brush and shot an ox. He fled to safety and the train could do nothing but butcher the beast and divide the meat. Modoc National Forest Service roads and Stonecoal Valley Road took us to the trail side of the river. Here pioneers often had to chain the wheels of their wagons as they rolled down steep slopes and had to double-team up the ascents. It is no wonder that, until recent years, remains of wrecked wagons were common along this stretch of the trail.

What the pioneers called Round Valley is Big Valley to the ranchers who live in it today. The trail once meandered through this valley where we drove among meadows watered by ditches, where cattle munched on lush grass, and big cars parked in front of comfortable ranch houses. We spent the night in a motel in a village that grew up in pioneer days as Chalk Ford, so named because wagons crossed the river there on a ledge of chalk. A man named Bieber founded a trading post at the crossing, and the modern town is named for him.

It is below Bieber that the route along the Pit River became hard. A steep-walled canyon closed in on the river. Here Peter Lassen, leading the first party over the trail, ran into serious trouble. Uncle Peter, a bluff bachelor from Denmark, was a blacksmith and rancher who believed he could lead emigrants from the main California Trail to his own Spanish Land Grant holdings on the upper Sacramento. There they would settle down in a new town which he had founded in the fertile valley. On August 26, 1848, he started over the Applegate Road from the big bend of the Humboldt River in Nevada with a small party of ten to twelve wagons. He followed the established route to Goose Lake. There he turned the wagons into the trackless wilderness, confident that he could win through to his ranch where Deer Creek flowed into the Sacramento. Morale was high, and men spoke affectionately of "Uncle Pete," the emigrants' friend, who knew the mountains of northern California better than any living man. Then in the canyon of the Pit it quickly became apparent that Lassen was as confused as the greenest greenhorn in the party. Unable to descend the river farther, he led the emigrants into one dead-end canyon after another as he vainly sought for a way among the massive mountains. The men hacked their way through almost impenetrable forests. Finding that it was impossible to get their wagons through, they cut them down to carts. Some put packs on their oxen and left their wagons behind.

Lassen's party was dispirited and worn out when a surprising reinforcement came up the trail behind them. This was the train of 150 men and 50 ox-drawn wagons led by Peter H. Burnett, who later would become California's first governor. In September with the veteran Hudson's Bay Company trapper Thomas McKay as their guide, they had struck out over the Applegate Road from Oregon. News of the gold strike had reached them, and their wagons carried six months' supplies and even lumber to construct rockers in the rich mines the men were certain that they would open up in the Mother Lode. When they reached the Pit River, they were astounded to find a new road where McKay had expected only wilderness. Wondering who the mysterious road-builders were, the Burnett train thankfully followed the new road that led west and then south into a canyon and over hills. Finally they came up against an impassable mountain at the head of a valley.

"The slope would not be ascended except by some creatures that had either wings or claws," Burnett observed.

Plainly the road-builders had themselves become lost. The emigrants from Oregon retraced their route until they discovered where the earlier party, having doubled back on their tracks, had cut a precipitous trail up over a mountain. At a point southeast of the volcanic peak now named for Peter Lassen, they caught up with Lassen himself, and the combined parties found the strength and resolution to push on toward the still distant Sacramento.

The Lassen Trail split near the site of present-day Bieber. Bruff, still trekking westward, came to the point and noted in his journal:

We reached the end of Pit Valley here. The hills enclose it in gorges and canyons now for some distance, and we have our choice of ascending a very steep hill close by or crossing the stream, pass through a short narrow vale, and turn left, joining the other road, to proceed along through the mountains. I submitted the roads to the Company, pointing out the hill-road as the most rugged, and the shortest, while the ford road was the longest and smoothest probably a couple of miles difference. They desired to take the former one, so on we went on it.

One branch cut westward across the bend of the Pit and then southward across Beaver Creek to Poison Lake. The other, which not only Bruff but most other emigrants followed, stayed east of the river and ran south past Horse Creek into Little Dixie Valley. It passed Schroder Lake to Grays Valley and Lodgepole Siding on the Western Pacific Railroad, where it was joined by the other branch.

Modern roads took us quickly past Horse Creek into Little Valley, where the Little Dixie Ranch still keeps alive the old name. We drove quickly through country that was almost impassable to the pioneers. The Indians still proved to be troublesome in these mountain fastnesses.

At Bloody Spring. near the lower end of Spring Gulch, an Indian war party massacred a wagon train. In the wagons they found a sack of twenty-dollar gold pieces. Going to the edge of a canyon, they amused themselves by seeing who could throw the smooth-sailing coins the farthest. It was a cheerful sport, interrupted by soldiers from Fort Crook, which had been established in the Fall River Valley at present-day Fall River Mills to protect the trail. The soldiers killed a number of the coin-tossing bucks, and the rest faded into the forest.

We were unable to trace the trail from Bloody Spring Hill through Clark's Valley into Little Valley, but we easily found it behind the sawmill of the Indian Head Lumber Company. When we drove into the town of Little Valley, we stepped into Tiny's Tavern to have a cup of coffee of the kind that invites the legendary logger to stir it with his thumb. Ruby Slidewell, presiding with jovial good nature over the coffee-drinking loggers, advised us not to try to follow the Lassen Road, which is today a logging trail, because heavy rains had turned it into a quagmire.

The trail runs about seven miles to Schroder Lake and on through the Black Mountain Experimental Forest where the loggers told us the great trees noted by Bruff and other diarists were logged off long ago. It skirts Black Mountain and turns southeast toward Aspen Wells and then Dixie Springs. There Bruff discovered a cache of supplies that previous emigrants had buried by the trail. The Indians had broken into it and littered the ground with the bottles, pills, and powders of a medical kit. While Bruff's party was camped near Dixie Springs, Indians drove off sixteen oxen. The emigrants trailed the stolen oxen to a place where their captors had slaughtered and butchered them. Meat was hanging from the trees to dry.

We detoured around the drenched forests on paved roads and entered Grays Valley on California Highway 44. Three miles past Poison Lake we turned off the highway onto a road that led to old Lodgepole Station on Bogard Flat. The station has been abandoned, but the foundations of the buildings and a supply shed still used by the Western Pacific Railroad remain beside the tracks. Just northwest of the station the trail running southwest from Dixie Springs reaches the railroad. We could make it out first on one side of the tracks and then on the other.

The rangers at the Bogard Ranger Station in the Lassen National Forest were all away, but a ranger's wife gave us a forest service map and showed us the route of the old trail where it runs close to the main road and then southeast to touch the southwest tip of Feather Lake. Rejoining the railroad within less than a mile the trail follows beside it to Norvell

Flat. Here the heavy winter snows are whipped by winds into drifts of such depth that railroaders told us that oldtimers had to cut ledges into the snow to clear the tracks. One man at the bottom of the pit would shovel snow up onto a ledge where another man would shovel it up onto the surface. For twenty miles from Poison Lake through Bogard Flat and on to Norvell Flat, the Lassen Road is overlapped by the later Nobles Road, which comes from Susanville to the east.

Following the forest service map, we drove down the Old Lassen Trail itself where it runs across the flats east of Jennie Mountain. We were turned back at Robbers Creek because the water was much too high for us to cross at the ford. We could only drive around to the Westwood-Chester Highway, from which it is possible to drive back along the trail again toward the ford that we had found too deep. As we drove slowly along the trail to keep from demolishing our station wagon, we frightened a herd of deer that were peacefully browsing in the trail.

The trail once ran to the Big Springs, which now is surrounded by the cottages of the Big Springs resort on man-made Lake Almanor. Where wagon-train families camped along the Feather River, water-skiers now streak behind power boats. The Big Meadows, renowned in the journals kept by the pioneers, is drowned beneath the lake. Here men once hunted for deer, water fowl, and bear that they claimed tasted a little like pork.

From the Big Meadows the trail crossed the North Fork of the Feather River near the modern town of Prattville, which is on the south shore of Lake Almanor, and then ran west through what is still a magnificent country of forests and rushing streams. Such historic spots as Butt Creek, Soldier Meadows, and Deer Creek Pass are all easy to find along the trail. At Deer Creek Meadows until recent years a stretch of corduroy still survived for cars to jounce over just as had the early-day wagons.

Lassen led the first party from Deer Creek up onto the high ridge between Deer and Mill Creek, where still today a highway runs down to the Sacramento. Logging trucks thunder along the sixty-mile hogback where wagons rolled. This high country was known to the pioneers as Lassen's Pinery, because crews of his men were at work there cutting shingles and shakes for the buildings at his ranch on the Sacramento. Sometimes the crews helped the pioneers, gathered up their discarded gear and later brought it to them. Sometimes too, if some embittered travelers are to be believed, the crews stole from them, even taking the pitiful remains of their supplies.

The wagons rolled on past the Narrows where the hogback falls away on both sides until it seemed to the pioneers looking down from their teetering vehicles that they must fall off one side or another of the mountain. Suffering and tragedy rode with the pioneers, even in Lassen's Pinery. At a spot still called Bruff's Camp, a storm toppled a tree on the tent of the Alford family, crushing the father and a son to death. Another son and a young man traveling with the Alfords were trapped beneath a limb so enormous that nobody could move it. Bruff erected his tent over the trapped youths to protect them from the rain that turned to hail and then to snow. Men cut feverishly at the huge limb, but at nightfall the second son died, and at dawn his friend died, too. The pioneers dug a grave in a hailstorm and buried Willard, aged nineteen, and Lorenzo, aged fifteen, in the center with the father Orman, fifty-four, and their friend John Cameron, twenty-two, on either side. They fashioned a cross of rifle barrels to mark the tragic spot.

The storms swept the hogback without end during the winter of 1849. A mule loaded with supplies sent to Bruff sank in the mud at the bottom of Steep Hollow, and he found himself in the December blizzards without provisions, accompanied by a young man and a small boy who had been abandoned by his father.

A man called Lambkin had left the child because he could not keep up with his wild scramble down the trail to the warmth and safety of the Sacramento Valley. Bruff became attached to the plucky little fellow. When the kindly Roberts family came upon the man, the youth, and the boy straggling down the storm-blasted trail, they put the boy on a home-made sled and took him to their cabin. They had built the cabin on a hill to protect their possessions they were too weak to carry farther along the trail. Mother Roberts baked fresh bread and gave the travelers some.

That night everybody in the cabin and Bruff's tent became violently ill. Mother Roberts had mistakenly used caustic soda instead of saleratus to raise her bread. The marooned travelers hovered near death, but all recovered except for the small boy. On New Year's Day sorrowing for a child that had become his own, Bruff dug in the ground before his tent where the heat from the fire had melted the frozen soil. He buried the boy there and when he left the site erected an epitaph to "William, Infant son of Lambkin—an Unnatural Father. Died Jan. 1, 1850."

On April 4, Bruff and his dog started for Sacramento. He came to the dreaded Steep Hollow which, until the souvenir hunters of recent years reached it, was still littered with broken wagons. For food he peppered and salted a candle and ate it. His famished dog received the candlewick. Later he captured a bluebird which he mixed with cabbages, lettuce,

and radishes that had sprouted by the trail from seeds spilled by travelers of the previous year. He shared the welcome meal with his dog. Finally he came down the last rocky slope to the flat valley land of Lassen's Rancho Bosquejo on Deer Creek.

Benton City, the town that Peter Lassen planned at the end of the trail, has vanished. When we came down out of the hills to the valley, we stopped at Bob Lassen's Steak House at Vina, which long ago grew up on the old Lassen ranch, only to find that though his steaks are good he is not a descendant of Uncle Peter.

"There's not much left at Benton City," he said. "You can find the place because of all the holes dug by people looking for old bottles."

We drove to the old town site. Raspberries clumped along the path which led to the few foundations that remain. At the site there was a monument erected to Peter Lassen by the Masonic Lodge because he had brought the first Masonic charter to California.

It was the Gold Rush that ruined Benton City. Everybody hurried away to seek his fortune. Lassen lost possession of his vast ranch and himself went prospecting in the hills.

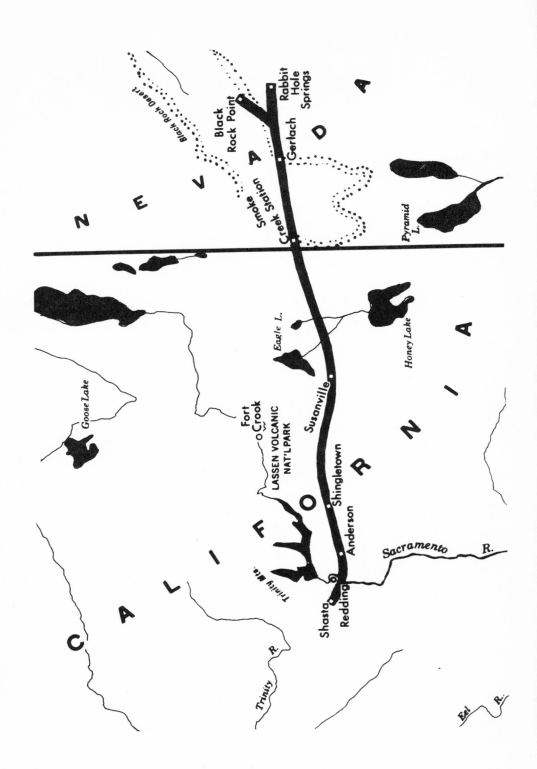

16

Nobles Road to
Old Shasta

●

Deer were grazing on the plashy meadows where Fort Reading once stood beside the Nobles Road in Shasta County, California. They paid no attention to the autos speeding by on the pavement that has long covered the wagon ruts, and they paid no heed to our family, either, as we studied the legend inscribed on a great rock. We learned that on May 26, 1852, the fort had been established by Co. E, 2nd Infantry, and that it had been evacuated in June, 1867. The soldiers marched off to garrison Fort Crook at Fall River Mills, from where it was expected they could protect both the Nobles Road and the more exposed Lassen Trail from Indians.

The stone that bears the legend was never put in the walls of the now vanished fort, but it was supposed to be. E. T. Thatcher was hauling it in an ox-drawn wagon along the Nobles Road in 1852, but as the wagon lurched up the steep bank of a creek, it tumbled off. The rock was too heavy to heave back into the wagon, so Thatcher left it where it fell. There it stayed until April, 1934, when it was lifted into a truck and brought to its original destination to serve as a marker for travelers who want to learn about the old days when the Nobles Road was the most important highway in northern California.

Shasta is now a ghost town preserved in a state historical monument on U.S. 299 west of Redding, but in those days it was the metropolis of the area. Many of the substantial old buildings of brick and stone still remain. On one of these a bronze plaque tells visitors that here, in the spring of 1852, William H. Nobles met with Shasta businessmen to seek

211

financial support. He wished to open up a new road over a route to the Humboldt River in Nevada, which he had just traced through the deserts and mountains. The businessmen listened eagerly to the young prospector for they realized that if the emigrants hurrying to California could be diverted over the new road to Shasta, their town and its economy would boom.

William Nobles, then thirty-five, had been born in 1816 in New York, the son of a minister. Trained as a machinist, he opened a blacksmith and wagon shop in St. Paul, Minnesota, where he built the first wagon ever made in the territory. He had emigrated west and met Peter Lassen, with whom he set out with some eighty other men to seek gold in the spring of 1851. The party reached Honey Lake Valley and then separated. Nobles prospected on eastward until to his surprise he came upon the Applegate Road at Black Rock Point in the Black Rock Desert of Nevada. He had stumbled on a new route to California which promised to be easier and more direct than any route yet discovered.

Realizing the importance of a new trail to the growing population of the upper Sacramento Valley, he hurried back to Honey Lake Valley and on west around the northern flank of Lassen Peak, then called Mount St. Joseph, through what was to be called Nobles Pass and down along Mill Creek to the McComber Mill, then an outpost of California civilization. He took the already existing road to the Sacramento River crossing at modern Anderson and continued on to Shasta, where a special meeting of business leaders was called to hear him.

The businessmen subscribed $2,000 and hired Nobles to return over his trail to the Humboldt River and there persuade emigrants on the California Trail to turn aside on the road to Shasta. Several men went with him to see that their money was well spent. They left Shasta on May 3, 1852, and returned on June 24, 1852, singing the merits of Nobles and his trail. As for Nobles, he went east to Illinois, where he triumphantly gathered up the girl he had married before he went west and took her to Minnesota. There he stumped for his new road so vociferously that the Minnesota legislature sent him to Washington. He made an impassioned speech before Congress about the advantages of the route.

When Nobles was in the East, emigrants moved over his trail in ever-increasing numbers. The horrible fate of the Donner Party frightened many pioneers away from the California Trail itself, and the hardships and suffering of the Lassen Trail promised little more.

A. P. Shull was the first to lead a part of twenty-six emigrants from the

Midwest over the trail. They left the Applegate Road at Black Rock Point, but later pioneers left it sooner at Rabbit Hole Springs to take a more direct route to the Hot Springs, the first springs on the Nobles Road. This not only proved shorter, but it kept wagon trains from running afoul of a predatory Paiute known as Black Rock Tom, who at night habitually sneaked down from the rock for which he was named to steal and murder where he could.

Nevada 49 closely follows the old trail along the northern fringes of the Black Rock Desert on its way to the vicinity of Gerlach, where the first water on the west side of the desert was to be found at Granite Creek. If approached on a paved road, Gerlach, named for Louis Gerlach on whose vast ranch it grew up, does not seem very prepossessing, but when you come at it as we did out of the desert, it is an oasis of civilization. Granite Springs is some three miles north of town. Here we found all that is left of a stone corral and fort which the U.S. Army built in 1866 to fend off the Indians from the trail.

As far as three men by the names of Curry, Creel, and Simmons were concerned, Fort Granite came too late. In April, 1865, they holed up in a sod house at Granite Springs, when Indians began firing at them from a stone corral some thirty feet away. A shot through a loophole killed Curry, but the others kept up a fusillade of lead. When the Indians ran out of ammunition, they substituted the screw ends of wagon bolts for bullets and kept on firing. Finally they raced to a storehouse adjoining the house and, sheltered from the defenders' fire, they tore out a wall. They set fire to the shake roof so that Creel and Simmons, not wanting to be burned alive, had no choice but to make a dash for it.

Simmons ran south along the trail toward Deep Hole Station, but he was shot down before he had gone far. Creel fared much worse. He fled east toward Hot Springs, but Indians on horseback easily captured him. They piled rocks on his arms, tossed on lumber from a handy pile, and burned him alive.

Not all the mayhem on the flats around Granite Springs was the work of Indians. Less than two months after Creel died such a grisly death, Charles Barnhart and William Rogan of a freight wagon party quarreled over a piece of rope. Barnhart pulled out his revolver and shot Rogan dead before some thirty civilians and ten soldiers. They immediately formed a kangaroo court and tried the murderer. The court sentenced Barnhart to one more hour of life to meditate upon his ways and to give them time to pull a pair of wagons together so that their tongues could be raised to form a gallows. When the condemned man was

213

placed beneath the typical wagon-train gallows with a rope around his neck, he was offered a last request.

"All of you get in front of me so that I can take a good look at you as I leave," he said.

The men obliged him and stared him in the face as he dangled. Both the victim and his murderer were then buried in the same grave.

Past the bold crags of Granite Mountain, the trail leads south toward Gerlach as far as the Great Boiling Springs, first discovered by John C. Fremont in 1844 and now in a park set aside by the Gerlach Lions' Club. Here the trail turns west again to Deep Hole Springs, which was surrounded in trail days by a meadow where oxen could munch their fill. The water was free of alkali and sweet to the taste, so a trader named Ladue Vary built a trading post of stone.

The building still shelters beneath tall trees. Here in 1862 the Indians burst in upon a man who had been left in charge while the trader went to Susanville for supplies. They tomahawked and scalped him and threw his body into the spring nearby. After that, the water never tasted quite right.

The post had not seen the last of the Indians either. Seven years later Indians swept down on Hiram Partridge, by then the trader, and Vesper Coburn, who worked for him. The men were collecting sagebrush for fuel

Nobles Road to Old Shasta

about two miles from the post. They ran for the station. Partridge was dropped by a shot. Another bullet broke Coburn's leg, but he raced on with his shattered bones stabbing through his flesh, until he too dropped and was given the *coup de grâce* by a screaming warrior.

Wall Springs, nine miles from Deep Hole, and nearby Buffalo Springs also have their tales of savage Indian attacks. Buffalo Springs, named by Indians for buffalo herds which once frequented the extensive meadows that surround it, was also the location of a pioneer salt works. Frank Murphy and George Lawrence set out evaporation vats as early as 1864, and the crumbling works can still be seen on the edge of the Smoke Creek Desert.

Desert roads that are treacherous to follow snake along the route of the old trail, which runs from Buffalo Meadows to Smoke Creek Canyon. Here, morning mist rose from the creek beside a camp where the celebrated Smoke Creek Station was built to house passengers who took the stage over the Nobles Road to the mining camps. Only a few soldiers' graves show that this also was the site of a rock fort. It was abandoned by the soldiers when they moved to Fort Granite after the cruel fate of Creel, Curry, and Simmons.

The trail climbs a ridge west of Smoke Creek past one of the Old West's many robber's roosts and runs past grassy Rush Creek Valley. Ruts are easy to find south of the modern road in this area, which is dominated by the notch in the hills known to this day as the Gunsight. Several of the now-deserted campsites along this section of the trail once boasted of inns to shelter stagecoach travelers and freighters.

The trail comes down into Honey Lake Valley, through which it follows the Susan River. The modern highway runs to Susanville, named by its founder, Isaac Roop, for his daughter. Roop, the postmaster at Shasta, moved to Honey Lake Valley when a fire burned out the post office. His log fort still stands on North Weatherlow Street, much as he built it in 1854 overlooking the pioneer campground. Today the campground is City Park.

The trail runs west along today's Main Street as far as Pine Street where it turns roughly north to the edge of town. It continues on along the approximate route of State Highway 44, over which we drove until we came to the region through which the Lassen and Nobles trails run together. Wagon trains rolling along the Nobles Road toward the Sacramento Valley met wagon trains rolling along the Lassen Trail coming in the opposite direction but also bound for Sacramento. This proved confusing to pioneers on both trails. On Novell Flat some pioneers following the

215

Nobles Road turned south on the Lassen Trail in order to avoid the heavy snows that began early in the fall in the high country now in the Mount Lassen National Park. This brought them into the Sacramento Valley south of Shasta and robbed the businessmen of that city of some of the profits they expected from the Nobles Road.

The old trail can be discovered where it runs beside Highway 44 as far as Poison Lake. Then it swings southward along Butte Creek. A modern woods road follows the creek, too, and some visitors drive to the Butte Lake campgrounds in Lassen Volcanic National Park over this road. From that point park service maps show the Nobles Emigrant Trail running past the Cinder Cone and Emigrant Lake to Badger Flat. To mark the trail through the forest, the first wagon trains bent the tips of trees. Some of those trees still can be seen today in the national park around Bathtub Lake.

No cars are permitted over the Nobles Trail between Butte Lake and Badger Flat, but it is popular with hikers. They hike as far as the Cinder Cone, which rises in black desolation from the piles of varicolored cinder and ash known as the Painted Dunes. In 1850-51, pioneers on the Lassen Trail saw weird flaring lights coming from the direction of Mount Lassen when they were as far as 160 miles away. Geologists believe that these lights came from Cinder Cone, which erupted shortly before the Nobles Road was cut through the forest in its vicinity.

Across Badger Flat and along Hat Creek we were able to drive on the Nobles Road. We picnicked beside the road among the pines and cedars. The Lassen Park Road itself obliterated part of the old trail, but it can be made out beyond Raker Peak where it skirts the Chaos Jumbles and climbs through Nobles Pass to the camp where the park employees live close by the main lodge at Manzanita Lake. A tablet at the north gate to the park marks the place where the trail crosses California 44 and 89 coming from the north and continues on to the point where California 44 leaves the park on its way west toward Redding.

From this high country of severe winter storms the trail drops down to Deer Flat along Highway 44. On Mill Creek it reaches the McComber Mill, from which it continues on past the present Grace Lake resort and into Shingletown over the Shingletown Manton Road. Still descending, it follows Highway 44 as far as Shingle Creek and finally passes along what is now Dersch Road. George Dersch and his family homesteaded along the road in 1861 where it forded Bear Creek. There, five years later, a band of Yana warriors killed his wife while the Dersch children hid in the orchard. This was one more grim incident on the Nobles Road.

Nobles Road to Old Shasta

The trail runs past old Fort Reading at Cow Creek and reaches the Sacramento River close to the Deschutes bridge east of Anderson. Here the Emigrant Ferry took the wagons across to the western side of the river, from which it was an easy journey over a smooth road to Shasta, the city the Nobles Road was supposed to make rich but which is now deserted.

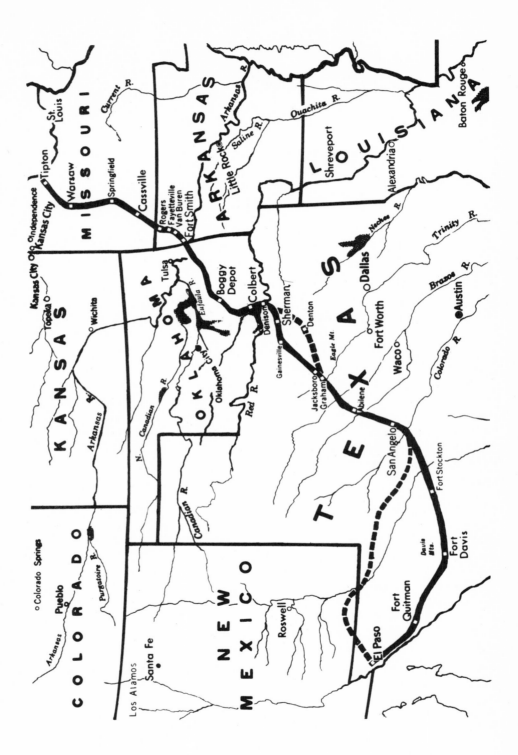

17

Butterfield Trail:
Nothing Must Stop the Mail

●

"Remember boys," said John Butterfield to his drivers, "nothing on God's earth must stop the United States mail."

Butterfield wore a flat-brimmed hat and a long yellow linen duster, tucked his pants into high boots, and was the very prototype of the Westerner in dress. He had been a stage driver for an Albany firm and had merged eastern stagelines into the infant American Express Company. When in 1857 Congress appropriated $600,000 to subsidize a semi-weekly overland mail service between St. Louis and San Francisco, Butterfield bid successfully for the six-year contract. The mail stages were to run

from St. Louis, Missouri, and from Memphis, Tennessee, converging at Little Rock, Arkansas; thence via Preston, Texas, or as nearly as may be found advisable, to the best point of crossing the Rio Grande above El Paso, and not far from Fort Fillmore; thence, along the new road being opened and constructed under the direction of the Secretary of the Interior, to Fort Yuma, California; thence, through the best passes and along the best valleys for staging, to San Francisco.

Butterfield first planned that his stages carry four passengers, forty pounds of baggage for each, and five to six hundred pounds of mail. Later stages carried six to nine passengers, with their knees locked together, inside with a few more seated on the roof. The post office subsidy was vital, but he expected to make his profits from packages, newspapers, and passengers.

Over a million dollars were invested in equipment and facilities. There were 700 horses stationed at corrals at every stop, repair shops at strategic points, and 750 managers, drivers, guards, and mechanics. The Abbot-Downing Company of Concord, New Hampshire, built the Concord stages designed by James Gould at the cost of $1,050 each. A coach came complete with leather boot, deck seat, brakes, lamps, and ornamental sides so magnificent that small boys cheered with delight as the vehicle came hurtling through town. Americans quickly took the beautiful coaches to their hearts, and within a year manufacturers were making baby buggies looking like them in miniature.

Mail and passengers were loaded onto Missouri Pacific trains at St. Louis for a 160-mile ride to Tipton. There at the end of the rails, the stage awaited. We found twentieth century Tipton to be a quiet town just off U.S. 50, some 35 miles west of Jefferson City, scarcely remembering its days of glory when it was at the start of the nearly 2,800-mile journey to San Francisco. From Tipton on September 15, 1858, the first stage set out for the West. The president of the Overland Stage Company and his son were aboard the inaugural stage and so was twenty-four-year old Waterman L. Ormsby, a correspondent of the *New York Tribune,* who planned to send his dispatches back to St. Louis with each eastbound coach they met.

The first coach went dashing away over the dusty roads leading southwest from Tipton toward Warsaw and Springfield. As the stage sped through towns, bands played, guns were fired, and men flung their hats in the air. At stage stops there were speeches, congratulatory handshaking, and barbecue dinners. Sometimes the stage rushed right past celebrations held in its honor, for hadn't Butterfield himself said, "Nothing on God's earth must stop the United States mail"?

Albert D. Richardson, journalist, took the Butterfield Coach from Missouri in 1859. During the first night the coach jolted as far as Warsaw, which is now near the head of the man-made Lake of the Ozarks. We found Warsaw to be a tidy vacation resort, given to water-skiing and fishing, but Richardson found it "a genuine southern town, surrounding a hollow square with court-houses, log houses, and stucco houses, with deep porticoes and shade trees; Negroes trudging with burdens upon their heads; deserted buildings; tumbling fences." He washed for dinner on the porch of his hotel.

South of Warsaw both modern Highway 83 and the Butterfield Trail run through a rocky and hilly region broken by rushing streams. Corn grows on hillsides and bottomlands. Springfield, then as now, was the

220

leading city of the Ozarks. Richardson was delighted with the town which "had pleasant, vine-trellised dwellings, and 2,500 people," but not so delighted with the hotel. "The low straggling hotel with high belfry," he wrote, "was on the rural Southern model: dining room full of flies, with a long paper-covered frame swinging to and fro over the table to keep them from the food; the bill of fare, bacon, corn bread and coffee; the rooms ill-furnished, towels missing, pitchers empty, and the bed and table linen seeming to have been dragged through the nearest pond and dried upon gridirons."

Through the Ozarks of Missouri and Arkansas the stage sped on to Cassville, then little and dilapidated but soon to become the temporary Confederate capital of Missouri when secessionist members of the Missouri General Assembly met there in 1861. On mountain roads the stages made one hundred miles in twenty-four hours, which impressed the speed-loving Americans of the day. Overtaking the local stages that plodded down the rutted roads through the mountains, the driver snapped his whip and shouted at his splendid horses and went flying by, spewing a great storm of mud behind him. Missourians spoke of the Overland Stage with pride and referred to the local stage with sorrow as "Under-land."

Each town on the road turned out to see the stages go by. There was Keetsville, which we could not locate at all, but was then, according to Richardson, "a dozen shanties which looked like a funeral procession in honor of Keets, whoever he may have been." The traveler could readily imagine the quality of its citizens upon learning that inhabitants of near-by towns called it "Chicken-Thief." The next town on the road was Scarce-O-Grease, and then the stage was across the state line into Arkansas.

Three days after it left Tipton, the first stage arrived at Callahan's Tavern, located in the northeast corner of what is now the city of Rogers, at 7 A.M. on September 18. Soon it was off again, rushing down what is now U.S. 71 to Fayetteville, which with its steepled churches presented a pretty picture to the passengers.

We found U.S. 71 through Winslow to be one of the most beautiful of all mountain drives, and so did stagecoach travelers. They also found it exciting. A traveler of 1858 reported: "I might say our road was steep, rugged, jagged, rough and mountainous—the wiry little animals tugged and pulled as if they would tear themselves to pieces, and our heavy wagon bounded along the crags as if it would be shaken to pieces every minute."

221

Settlers built their log cabins on the mountains near the stage road, and soon little towns grew up with such colorful names as Hog-Eye. Most of them are long since gone, but Winslow and Mountainburg still survive. Near Mountainburg we located the old townsite of Armada, and just south of it a board and stone home hidden in second-growth timber. We could make out the driveway leading from the old stage road up the side of the mountain.

At Van Buren old brick buildings still look down on Main Street, through which the Butterfield stages ran. Nestled beneath shady trees in the rich green valley of the Arkansas, Van Buren was counted among the most beautiful towns of the trail. There the stages were ferried across the river on a ferry of two-pole power, and then rolled five miles down the valley to Fort Smith.

Fort Smith, and not Little Rock, turned out to be the place where the stages from Memphis met the stages from Missouri. Erected in 1818, where the Poteau flowed into the Arkansas, to protect settlers from the Indians, Fort Smith grew into the most important trading post on the frontier of Indian Territory. Cherokees and Choctaws walked the streets of the town as valued customers. Some of the Indians kept Negro slaves, and these proved useful on trips to Fort Smith because they spoke English and could interpret for their masters. It was a lawless town. "There is no Sunday west of St. Louis and no God west of Fort Smith," was a frontier saying.

"The carrying of concealed weapons was common," wrote Albert Richardson, "and a citizen assured me that he had seen a clergyman in the pulpit on Sunday with the handle of a bowie knife protruding from his pocket."

Richardson also noted that worshipers were called to church, not by the ringing of bells, but by the tooting of horns. At least this proves that there were Sundays in Fort Smith, and God may even have been present, too.

In the lawless days after the Civil War, gangs of bandits roamed the border country. Sixty-five marshals, including Deputy Marshal Frank Dalton, died trying to pacify the area. The man who proved to be the greatest pacifier of them all was described as "white of hair and beard, with pink cheeks, and slightly rotund" with a "twinkle in his eye and a little contagious chuckle which always made children think of Santa Claus."

This benign old gentleman was Judge Isaac C. Parker, who may have had a twinkle in his eye but who sentenced 151 men to the gallows, more than any other judge in the nation's history. A replica of his gallows still stands close to his courtroom in the Fort Smith National Historic Site. On this "Old Government Suspender" on September 9, 1881, five murderers were hanged at one time. We read a sign at the site that the timetable to eternity ran: 9:50 at death machine; 10:32, death trap sprung; 10:50, pronounced dead; 10:54, bodies taken down. By 1896 such efficiency brought law and order to the Western District of Arkansas, but by then stagecoaches were a thing of the past.

At Fort Smith the Butterfield Trail entered the Indian Territory where, in muddy weather, the coach often was pulled by eight horses. When the stage floundered into a mudhole, the passengers got out and gave it a push. The horses wallowed up to their bellies in the mire, and the men sometimes sank in to their hips. To make up for lost time, the driver whipped his horses into a gallop once he was on a firm road.

"This was an experience," one traveler wrote describing a night ride. "One bounded, now on a hard seat, now against the roof, now against the side of the wagon."

If the road wasn't muddy, it was dusty. The horses' hooves kicked the dust in clouds into the interior of the coach where passengers sneezed and wheezed for breath. The coach passed by the hundred-acre farm of Governor Tandy Walker of the Choctaw nation and stopped at Skullyville, which derived its name from the Choctaw word for money, "iskuli." The tribe received its treaty "iskuli" or annuities there. The present-day town is on U.S. 271 southwest of Fort Smith. From Skullyville the Butterfield Trail struck across country on a diagonal course that has left few traces on the Oklahoma of today. On the second day the coaches reached Boggy Depot, Choctaw capital, which was a pair of trading posts and half a dozen houses.

At least at Boggy Depot, now the site of a state recreation area west of Tushka on U.S. 75, a man could buy a meal for about 50 cents and trade tobacco with the Indians for water to wash the dust and mud off his face. Some passengers, conditioned by newspapers and frontier pundits to believe that Indians were all blood-thirsty savages, were amazed at conditions in the Indian Territory.

"These once cruel and barbarous tribes were now governing themselves, educating their children, protecting life and property far better than adjacent Arkansas and Texas," wrote Richardson, "and rapidly assuming the habits of enlightened men."

The Butterfield Trail and U.S. 75 converge near Colbert, close to Denison Dam on the Red River which forms Lake Texoma. A few miles south the trail crossed the river into Texas. It ran south through Denison to Sherman, which was the first stage stop in Texas.

Passengers on the Overland Stage paid $200 for the trip from St. Louis to San Francisco and $150 from San Francisco to St. Louis, or 10 cents a mile for short distances. Meals were extra, and at Texas stops such as Sherman a man could buy a meal of beans, jerked beef, hoecake, onions, and coffee for a dollar. Catering to the coach passengers proved such a boon to Sherman business that the town doubled in size and built a new courthouse.

From Sherman the stages headed west on the old road that ran just to the north of U.S. 82. The site of the Gainesville stage station is where the new Interstate 35 intersects U.S. 82, about a mile north of Gainesville. Gainesville also grew with the movement of commerce along the Butter-field Trail, and aggressive towns just to the south became jealous. Denton and Decatur merchants complained and pleaded, and citizens improved roads and built new bridges until, in March, 1861, the route was changed to run through these two towns to Jacksboro, then called Lost Creek. It did the towns little good, for within months the Civil War broke out, and the entire trail was abandoned in favor of a route through the northern states to California.

The main trail led from Gainesville southwest across the West Branch of the Trinity River to Jacksboro. Richardson's stage found the river too swollen for fording.

"The little station was full," he wrote, "so we slept refreshingly upon corn-husks in the barn, or in the western vernacular the 'stable.' After breakfast we crossed the stream on foot by a slippery log, while drivers and conductor brought over heavy mail bags and trunks on the same precarious bridge. On the west bank another waiting coach was soon rolling us forward among mesquite groves."

At the end of the Civil War there was no peace on the Texas northern frontier. The plains Indians had taken advantage of the war to force settlers back east and south to Jacksboro, where families "forted up" for protection. In May, 1866, troops returned to pre–Civil War forts and built new ones. Fort Richardson, on the banks of Lost Creek at Jacksboro, was the farthest north, and from it troopers galloped out to oppose the raiding Comanches and Kiowas.

On May 16, 1871, General W. T. Sherman came over the trail to Fort Richardson. The very next day near Salt Creek a large force of Kiowas and Comanches attacked a wagon train, killed the wagon master, ten teamsters, and a night watchman. When General Sherman learned that the Indians who had attacked the train had been watching his own party cross Salt Creek and had only refrained from attacking because their medicine man had said the second party to pass would be more easily captured, he ordered Colonel Ranald MacKenzie, post commandant, to bring the Indians to terms. MacKenzie's far-ranging raiders struck deep into Indian country, destroying the Indians' supplies and horse herds until they no longer had the resources to attack the frontier.

We found the stone hospital building and frame officers' quarters still standing at Fort Richardson, but "Sudsville," across the creek from the fort, has vanished. Once this was the home of laundresses and married soldiers, to say nothing of gamblers, saloonkeepers, gunmen, and trail drivers.

From Jacksboro we drove along Texas 24, which runs north of the old road to Murphy's Station, which once stood near Graham. The earth in this part of Texas is black and fertile. It is also sticky when wet, and in wet weather stages made slow progress.

Fort Belknap, now a county park on Farm-to-Market Road 61, ten miles northwest of Graham, was a stage stop of importance, as well as the northern anchor of the antebellum line of forts which reached from the Red River to the Rio Grande. Several of the old buildings have been restored, and there is a fine historical museum in the onetime post commissary. From the fort it was six hundred miles to the Rio Grande. Here or in nearby posts horses were exchanged for Mexican mules, which were deemed better able to pull stages through the flat and dry country that lay ahead. Richardson reported in his journal:

Four stout men were required to hold them while the driver mounted to his seat. Once loosed, after kicking, plunging and rearing, they ran wildly for two miles upon the road. They can never be fully tamed. When first used, the drivers lash the coach to a tree before harnessing them. When ready for starting, the ropes are cut, and they sometimes run for a dozen miles. But on this smooth prairie they do not often overturn.

This was a wild country where guns settled scores.

"If you want to obtain distinction in this country, kill somebody," a post manager told Richardson.

Stages forded the Brazos, crossed what later was to become the cattle-drivers' Western Trail in the vicinity of Fort Griffin, and passed about twelve and a half miles west of Albany. Stages rattled past the old burned fort at Phantom Hill, cut across the route of Interstate 20 at Tye, west

225

of Abilene, and went on to Fort Chadbourne in Coke County. The trail crossed U.S. 87 at Carlsbad, north of San Angelo.

The famous Horsehead Crossing was about twenty miles upriver on the Pecos River from the present community of Girvin, which is on U.S. 67 west of San Angelo. From Girvin we drove up the Pecos on State Highway 11 to the vicinity of the crossing that was used by the Comanches riding south to steal horses from the Mexicans, by Mexicans traveling north in quest of salt, and by the Butterfield stages. The first stages had taken the Upper Road on the Pecos and followed it through the Guadalupe Mountains to Hueco Tanks and on to El Paso, but water on the route was scarce. Butterfield moved his route south to the Lower Road, which crossed the Pecos by ferry at Horsehead Crossing and ran to El Paso by way of Fort Davis.

We followed the Lower Road to a roadside park on U.S. 290, seven miles east of Fort Stockton. The old trail ran south of U.S. 290 to the Tunis Springs station. The state of Texas has moved the old station, stone by stone, from its original location to the roadside park where passing motorists can stop to see it. From the station it is a short drive into Fort Stockton, where we sluiced away the midsummer Texas heat with a dip in the municipal swimming pool. It is fed by Comanche Springs, first discovered by Cabeza de Vaca in 1534. Fort Stockton was an important post on the trail, and many of the buildings of adobe and hand-hewn limestone still stand. Officers row and an old guardhouse are on Williams Street between Fourth and Fifth. Not far away on the court-house square we found the Annie Riggs Hotel. Its wide veranda is as hospitable today as when stages set down passengers before it. Across the street is the Gray Mule Saloon, famed on the trail for its "red-eye."

The trans-Pecos country is the land of the ocotillo holding spidery arms toward the brazen sun, of prickly pear, yuccas, cedars, and greasewood. Cattle fatten on this arid range where the grass seems sparse. The trail ran to Fort Davis by way of Leon Springs and Barella Springs. We drove to Fort Davis, built of local stone and bricks made in St. Louis and brought to the site over the trail. The Overland Stage established a post at the fort, and Phocian R. Way described having "supper here in a hotel about six feet high and twelve feet long made out of mud. We then spread our blankets on the ground and slept soundly."

Fort Davis, the most important post on the Butterfield Trail, is the best-preserved fort in Texas. We stood on the parade ground surrounded by fifteen of the sixty-five original buildings. Houses in officers' row, two sets of troop barracks, a warehouse, and the post hospital are standing.

Motorists on US 180 come upon the ruins of the Old Pine Springs stage stop. The station was on the upper branch of the Butterfield Road in west Texas.

Texas Highway Department Photo

Other ruined buildings hulked like ghosts in the late afternoon. We were waiting for the sounds of a historic retreat to come echoing out of the past.

"The program you're about to hear was recorded at Fort Sill, Oklahoma," said Franklin Smith, superintendent of the Fort Davis National Historic Site. "The music was played by members of the 77th and 97th army bands, but junior high school band members were mixed in with the soldier musicians. The kids play their hearts out, and their contribution of spirit and sour notes is what gives the music its authenticity."

Smith, whose walrus mustache would do justice to a frontier cavalryman, kept glancing over his shoulder as he talked about the days when the U.S. Army was safeguarding stagecoaches and freight trains on the Butterfield Road.

"Those people who couldn't soldier, they turned into cooks; those who couldn't cook, they turned into musicians," he said.

It was one of those days in west Texas when the sky is part of the scenery. Sleeping Lion Mountain hunkered down close upon the fort. The shadows lengthened. Then the silence was split by the sound of massed buglers calling "Assembly." We couldn't see the troopers of long ago, but we could hear them running from the barracks and forming up their companies.

We heard the cries of "parade rest," and "sound off," and the band thumping invisibly the length of the troop line and back. We heard the boom of the sunset gun, and the band played "The Star Spangled Banner" in the original dirgelike scoring. When the troops passed in review we could hear the harness noises, the jingling of sabers, and the beat of hooves. The cannons, their trace chains rattling, rolled by on metal-rimmed wheels. Then the sounds of the past died away.

We strolled into the National Park Service Museum in the enlisted men's barracks to see such things as Jefferson-style boots, which fit either foot, broken plates, and whiskey bottles.

"The plates came from underneath a mess hall floor," said Superintendent Smith. "If a soldier broke a plate, he had to pay for it, so he usually just shoved it out of sight through a crack in the floor. Ninety to one hundred whiskey bottles came from beneath the sergeants' quarters."

We stayed that night at the adobe lodge in Davis Mountain State Park in Limpia Canyon. Before us in the dying sunlight was a vista of sharp-edged mountains and wind-hewn rock. Indoors as we settled down before a roaring fire in the fireplace, we half expected a knock at the door from a belated traveler arriving by coach over the Butterfield Trail.

It was in Limpia Canyon that the mail stage was attacked by Indians, who captured a bundle of illustrated newspapers. They opened the papers and looked at the pictures with fascination. They were still engrossed in the newspapers when avenging troops fell upon them. After that the Indians had a special belief in the power of the press. The newspapers were magic, and soldiers could tell just where to find their enemies if they were looking at the ensorcelling pictures.

The Indians struck at wagon trains and stagecoaches all along the road through west Texas. They robbed the mails and sometimes hung passengers by their heels with their heads a few inches from a slow fire so that they roasted their brains. They tied others to the wheels of the coach which they then set on fire.

George Giddings and his party were attacked when they thought themselves close enough to the fort to be safe:

As I was crossing the Escondido about nine miles from Fort Davis, our party was attacked. The Indians had no guns, but used bows and arrows exclusively. One of these missiles struck Parker Burnham in the neck. Jim Spears, the driver, placed the wounded man in the boot of the compartment in the rear of the coach. The six horses attached to the stage were then given their heads and ran all the way to Fort Davis, the Indians following close to the post. The coach was filled with arrows which they shot into it and which stuck to it. We kept up a steady fire from our revolvers at them, but I do not know how many, if any, we killed or wounded. One of our horses dropped dead, just as we pulled up at Fort Davis Post Office.

"The Indians are in virtual possession of the road," Lieutenant Edward L. Hartz noted from Fort Davis in 1857.

Richardson commented in his journal, "The Comanches regard our soldiers much as they would a company of children armed with popguns and penny whistles."

During the Civil War the stages and freight trains stopped running. When they resumed in 1865, the first to profit were the Apaches under Espejo. They held up the first westbound freight train where the Limpia narrowed down to Wild Rose Canyon through the Davis Mountains. A week later Espejo and his warriors stopped the first eastbound stage out of El Paso.

When the party showed fight, wily old Espejo shook out a flag of truce and offered a treaty. Two young Mexicans in the stage urged Mr. Davis, the party leader, not to agree, but they were ignored. An agreement was drawn up and signed, and Espejo rode away. The two Mexicans got down and started on foot in the opposite direction rather than trust their lives to the Apache's word. The stage started on. Within an hour Espejo swooped out of ambush, killed and scalped all aboard, and stole the stage and mules. The Mexicans walked 150 miles to Del Rio on the Rio Grande.

Barrel Springs was the next stop west of Fort Davis. Orville Brey, superintendent of Davis Mountain State Park, and Caleb Pirtle, an editor of *Southern Living*, guided us to the springs, which is on Texas Highway 166. We climbed up into the cliffs overlooking the old trail, where the Comanches had a lookout. Entire families lived in holes in the rock and watched the soldiers, the wagon trains, and the stages passing on the road. We found metates where the women ground corn and flint chips from arrows and spear points fashioned by men. Pictographs of handprints were on the ceilings of the holes in the rock. As we watched from the lookout on the mountain, a blue quail fluttered along the slope, and a mule deer picked its way among the cholla.

"The Indians sure had it all their way," mused Orville Brey, looking down on the vulnerable trail, and we had to agree.

From Barrel Springs the trail ran on to El Muerto and Van Horn Well, around which the town of Van Horn has grown up at the crossing of U.S. 80 and 90. Eagle Springs is next, and then at Fort Quitman the trail at last reached the Rio Grande. In nearby Quitman Canyon, Victorio's Apaches ambushed a stagecoach and killed the driver and a passenger, Union General James J. Byrne, who had received a leg wound at Gettysburg. The Apache bullet struck him in the thigh, reported Ranger Captain George W. Baylor, "within an inch of the wound he had received at Gettysburg. We buried him (a mixed crowd of Confederates, citizens and U.S. soldiers) and fired a couple of volleys over his grave." Soon after this, Victorio met his death from a Tarahumara sharpshooter's shot at Tres Castillos in Mexico, and his band was scattered. A handful of survivors, twelve warriors, four women and four children, stopped a stage in Quitman Canyon in January, 1881, and killed the occupants. This was the last Indian attack on the Butterfield Road in Texas.

The Butterfield Road ran up the Rio Grande Valley through the old Mexican villages of Socorro and Ysletta to El Paso, which Richardson reported was "a charming picture—a far-stretching valley, enriched with orchards, vineyards, and cornfields, through which the river traces a shining pathway. Across it appear the flat roofs and cathedral towers of the old Mexican El Paso."

230

Butterfield Trail: Nothing Must Stop the Mail

El Paso was the largest Overland Mail base on the trail, and from 1857 through 1861 the station and stables covered a block at the southeast corner of Overland and South El Paso streets. In San Jacinto Plaza, at the heart of the town, the Overland Trail crossed the Chihuahua Trail, which ran north to Santa Fe. Ben Dowell's saloon stood where the Hilton Hotel is now, and travelers on both trails stepped in for a convivial drink before setting out on the next leg of their journey.

The sounds of a historic retreat are heard across the parade ground of Fort Davis. Ruined buildings hulk like ghosts at the end of the day.
Texas Tourist Development Agency

231

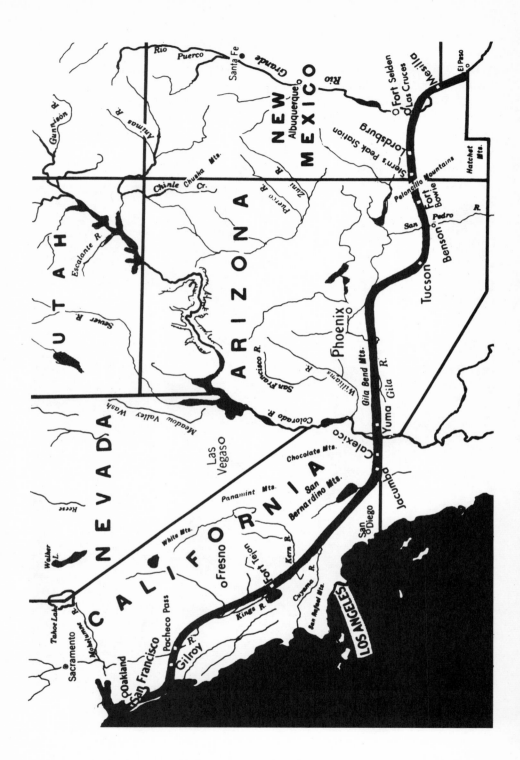

~18~

Butterfield Trail:
A Wolf Could Not Make His Living

●

Senator Thomas H. Benton described the territory between El Paso and California as so sandy, sterile, and desolate that "a wolf could not make his living."

The stages ran up the Rio Grande into New Mexico, keeping just to the east of Interstate 10 as far as Fort Fillmore where, true to the charge placed upon it by the Post Office Department, it swung west to Mesilla. Mesilla is a village founded by Mexicans who fled across the Rio Grande after the victory of the Americans in the Mexican War, only to have the Gadsden Purchase put them back in the United States. The town still centers on its dusty plaza and shows tourists its jail, from which Billy the Kid escaped. We lunched on crisp tostados and guacamole salad at La Posta, which was a stage stop. Not only Billy the Kid but such diverse men as Kit Carson and Pancho Villa sheltered from the Rio Grande heat within La Posta's three-foot adobe walls.

The trail turned west into the desert, running far to the north of Interstate 10. Before heading west we drove on north on U.S. 85, where eighteen miles past Las Cruces we found the stark adobe walls of Fort Selden. Many a stage on the Butterfield Trail made the same detour. Pursued by Apaches, they cut off the trail to find shelter at the fort. Legend has it that when Indians attacked the fort the paymaster, fearing for the $80,000 army payroll, buried it. He died in the attack, and nobody was able to find the treasure afterward. When we were at the fort, we could see the diggings of countless treasure hunters, who have done far more damage to the old ruin than have the elements.

233

Interstate 10 jogs northwest to intersect the Butterfield Trail at Lordsburg, now a cattle, farming, and mining town, but once a lonely station. The original trail continued on immediately to the north of Interstate 10 to the Arizona border, but when Shakespeare was founded in 1872 just two miles south of Lordsburg, the coaches detoured through it. It was presumed to be the most promising mining camp in all of southern New Mexico, but the ore failed to come up to expectations. Shakespeare was abandoned, and the coaches went back to the old route. Then unlike most ghost towns, Shakespeare came back to life. Diamonds were found where men had looked only for gold! Miners rushed back to Shakespeare and so did the stagecoaches, only to discover that the whole thing was a hoax. Somebody had salted the earth with uncut gems from Africa. Now only dilapidated houses and gambling halls remain from old Shakespeare, and the stagecoaches themselves have all gone.

Stein's Peak Station was the last stop in New Mexico. Fortified within walls of stone, the station crew fended off the Apaches and served meals and changed horses for the dangerous passage through Doubtful Canyon winding through the Peloncillo Range. The canyon was accurately named, for it was so narrow that rims almost scraped the walls. It was the haunt first of Apaches and then, later, bandits. Stages raced through the canyon at a dead run to avoid rocks which the Indians lobbed down from the top. If Indians were known to be in the vicinity, the drivers kept out of the canyon and took the rugged road over Stein's Peak Pass to the north.

The ruins of the station are a forlorn reminder of the old trail. Here too treasure hunters have been at work, pockmarking the desert with their spades. Their interest goes back to a bloody incident on the trail just a mile west of the station. It was April 4, 1861, and seven Texans were en route to California from San Antonio. Among them was John James Giddings, manager of the Texas division of the Butterfield Stage Lines. The wagon contained $28,000 in cash and $30,000 in gold. No sooner had the party ridden into Doubtful Canyon than bandits opened up with a fusillade and galloped to the attack. Depending upon which treasure hunter you talk to, Giddings is supposed to have buried the treasure either back at the station out of fear of bandits reported lurking in the canyon or under a rock near the wagon during the attack.

Later a passing wagon train came upon the charred wreck of the Butterfield wagon and five bodies. Giddings and another man were missing. Then a month later, an eastbound wagon train camped nearby. In the morning the freighters found the other two men dead in the rocks. A few gold coins were scattered nearby. They buried the dead. Since then treasure hunters have dug feverishly with the dim hope that somehow the bandits did not get the loot.

From Doubtful Canyon the trail headed for Apache Pass, also well named, for it belonged rock and crag to the Apaches. We took a road south from Bowie into the Dos Cabezas Mountains, through which Apache Pass is the only practical gap. The road through the shallow ravine today runs where the stages ran. The Butterfield Stage people were anything but cowardly, and they built a station at Apache Pass. In his book, *Arizona in the Fifties*, Captain James H. Tevis described the station. "A stone corral was built with portholes in every stall. Inside, on the southwest corner, were built, in 'L' shape, the kitchen and sleeping rooms. At the west end, on the inside of the corral, space about ten feet wide was apportioned for grain room and store room, and here were kept the firearms and ammunition." Captain Tevis wrote:

A mile beyond the station, the road followed a dangerous, narrow defile through the canyon, which was covered with a thick growth of walnut, ash, mulberry, and wild-cherry trees. It passed between two large rock points which stood up and almost hung over the road. The water had cut and worn its course through the canyon, leaving the rock standing bare on either side. At this turn White's train of emigrants was massacred while taking the trail to California. Cochise's father stood on top of the rock on the east side of the road, giving commands for the horrible murder.

The Indians would lie in ambush on the hills on either side of the pass, and with little difficulty wipe out stages or wagons. The bones of horses, mules, oxen, and men and the wreckage of burned-out wagons littered the dreary defile. A fort became a necessity if the trail was to be used at all, and Fort Bowie was founded just east of the pass in 1862. We stopped to see the ruins of the fort where Geronimo was brought after his capture, and then drove on west through country little changed since trail days to Dos Cabezas. In the 1850's this was Ewell Springs. The stage route passed along the outskirts of the sun-baked adobe village. We could still make out the ruins of the stage depot.

We found no more traces of the Butterfield Trail until we reached Pantano on Interstate 10 west of Benson. The old stage station of Cienega was in a box canyon near to town. It had all the appearances of providing safe shelter in time of need, but in reality it was operated by a bandit gang called the Benders for their drunken benders. Murders and robberies in the vicinity disturbed stage officials greatly, but they readily believed that the Apaches were responsible.

One day in 1872 three men in a buckboard tried to take $75,000 over the trail. Close to Cienega Station they were jumped by Indians. The three were killed, and the loot was buried nearby. The robberies and murders might have gone on indefinitely, except that one dark night in the fall of 1873 the Apaches swept down on the station and killed all the Benders. When a relief party reached the bloody scene, they found the Indian costumes the Benders had used in their raids. On a hill behind the station was a private cemetery. One shaft marked the graves of sixteen victims.

The next stretch of the road to the old Spanish pueblo of Tucson was scarcely safer than the previous two hundred miles. Coaches and wagons were attacked without warning by the ubiquitous Apaches. When fifty Indians came whooping and hollering out of the arroyos, at least one Butterfield coach escaped. The driver was shot by an arrow, but William Willis, the conductor, grabbed the reins and drove the horses at a gallop into Tucson.

J. Ross Browne, artist, who traveled on the trail in 1864, found Tucson "a city of mud boxes, dingy and dilapidated, cracked and baked into a composite of dust and filth; littered about with broken corrals, sheds, bake ovens, carcasses of dead animals and broken pottery; barren of verdure, parched, naked and grimly desolate in the glare of the southern sun."

This was the town. These, according to Browne, were the citizens: "traders, speculators, gamblers, horse thieves, murderers and vagrant politicians. If the world were searched over I suppose there could not be found so degraded a set of villains as then formed the principal society of Tucson."

The Old Pueblo may not have pleased J. Ross Browne, but it certainly did please William Willis, who pulled his coach up safely at the depot. We drove through today's clean and handsome city and started for Yuma on Interstate 10 and then Interstate 8. During the last part of its crossing of the desert, the old trail followed the Gila River, much as the prehistoric Indians had. J. Ross Browne was not delighted with Fort Yuma either:

Everything dries: wagons dry; men dry; chickens dry; there is no juice left in anything, living or dead, by the close of summer. Officers and soldiers are supposed to walk about creaking; mules, it is said, can only bray at midnight; and

236

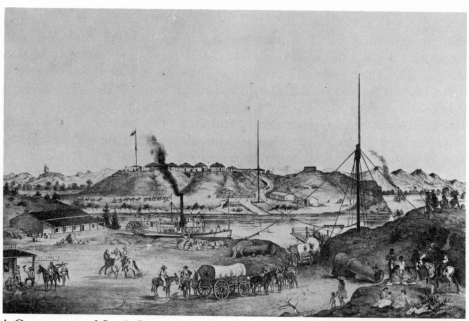

A German named Louis Jaeger operated the station at Fort Yuma and ferried stages and wagons across the Colorado to California.   *Courtesy Chicago Historical Society*

I have heard it hinted that the carcasses of cattle rattle inside their hides, and that snakes find a difficulty in bending their bodies, and horned frogs die of apoplexy. Chickens hatched at this season, old Fort Yumers say, come out of the shell ready cooked; bacon is eaten with a spoon; and butter must stand for an hour in the sun before the flies become dry enough for use.

A German named Louis Jaeger operated the station at Fort Yuma and ferried stages and wagons over the Colorado. On October 4, 1857, the inaugural stagecoach reached Yuma, and Waterman L. Ormsby sent a dispatch back east to the *New York Herald.* "About a mile below the fort is Arizona City, consisting of a few adobe houses. We crossed the river at this point on the ferry kept by Mr. Yager, who charges $5 for carrying an ordinary four-horse team. The boat is a sort of flat boat, and is propelled by the rapid current, being kept in its course by pulleys running on a rope stretched across the river." Jaeger was an enterprising businessman, and in 1859 he ran an advertisement in the *Weekly Arizonian* at Tubac. "Old Colorado Ferry Established in 1850, one mile below Fort Yuma, the only safe and reliable ferry on the Colorado. Ferriage at the lowest rates, and at all hours. A constant supply of groceries, Provisions and Mining Implements on hand for sale at low rates."

When the ferry reached the far shore passengers cheered, for it seemed

237

that the end of the long journey must now be at hand. After the first scorching hundred miles of California desert they were disabused of this notion. The stages labored through billows of sand even though the route twisted south into Mexico to avoid the worst dunes. The Butterfield Trail hugged the Mexican border, south of today's Interstate 8 and California 98 to Calexico and Mexicali in the Imperial Valley. East of Jacumba it crossed California 94 and headed into the desert wilderness now preserved in the Anza-Borrego Desert State Park. It passed by the Hot Springs to the old stage station, which still can be seen on Highway S2 south of San Felipe. The modern road follows it to the old J. J. Warner Ranch and Warner Springs. From the ranch the trail skirted Lake Henshaw to arrive at Mount Palomar, where it ran close to where the Palomar Mountain Observatory of the California Institute of Technology now studies the skies.

From Temecula to Corona and Chino, California 71 follows the old road except at Lake Elsinore, where the stages ran to the west of the lake and the modern road runs to the east. North of Chino the trail swung in an arc into Covina. The San Bernardino Freeway follows the trail into the heart of Los Angeles, where coaches pulled up with a clatter in front of the old Bella Union Hotel.

As far as the Mission San Fernando, the Butterfield stages took the Royal Road. In today's Encino, a nine-room house stands at 16756 Moorpark Street and appears much as it did when it was a Butterfield stagecoach stop. The Rancho Los Encinos was built with sturdy walls two feet thick by Don Vicente de la Osa in 1849. There he reared fourteen children and extended Spanish hospitality to all travelers. It seemed only fitting that the ranch house should become a way station for stage passengers.

Beyond Mission San Fernando the Butterfield stages climbed through Newhall Canyon along the route of today's Interstate 5 and continued on to Fort Tejon, now in a state historic park. The state of California has been busy reconstructing the old adobe buildings of the fort that once guarded miners and settlers and protected the stages laboring through Tejon Pass on the Overland Trail. In 1858 the Butterfield Overland Mail Station at Fort Tejon was one of the most important California posts.

The trail ran from Fort Tejon down the San Joaquin Valley. Here in the Golden West, travel still had its problems. For one thing, tobacco-chewing seat-mates were a bother, and so were women who took snuff and sneezed into the faces of their companions. Dr. Joseph C. Tucker of San Francisco described a night coach ride: "Three on a seat in an open mud wagon tearing along ten miles an hour through a wild country. Three in a row, actuated by the same instantaneous impulse, we would solemnly rise from our seats, bump our heads against the low roof, and, returning vigorously ram the again rising seat we had incontinently left."

The doctor did not think kindly of his seat-mate either.

"Upon waking you seldom failed to find him lying across you or snoring an apology in your ear."

At last the trail crossed the Coast Range through Pacheco Pass to the town of Gilroy. In Gilroy the Butterfield Overland Mail established a large office and stables. Passengers could shop in six stores and drink and play pool at J. Houck's Hotel. The stages meant new life to the town of six hundred, and children were excused from school to see the first stage come rolling in. Dogs and boys raced it from the edge of town to the depot. From Gilroy the stages took the Royal Road to San Francisco where, after a nearly 2,800-mile journey, they finally arrived.

As the first stage rolled through San Jose to San Francisco, the passengers were cheered by people in the streets as if they were adventurers from another planet. Waterman L. Ormsby wrote in his dispatch, "Soon we struck the pavements, and with a whip, crack, and bound shot through the streets to our destination. Swiftly we whirled up one street and down another, and round the corners, until finally we drew up at the stage office in front of the Plaza."

It was 7:30 A.M., twenty-three days, twenty-three hours and thirty minutes after the stage dashed out of Tipton, Missouri. The next night there was a mass meeting at the Music Hall in honor of the passengers. Said Waterman L. Ormsby, somewhat overcome by the wonder of modern overland transportation, "Had I not just come out over the route, I would be perfectly willing to go back."

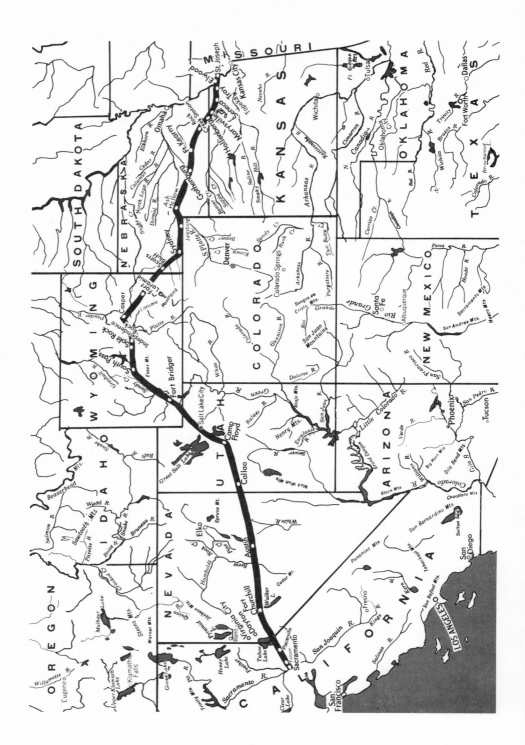

~19~

Pony Express Trail

●

Four hundred young men and boys, among them Bill Cody, aged fifteen, rode the 1,966 incredible miles of the Pony Express Trail between St. Joseph, Missouri, and Sacramento, California. The ideal age was twenty, but David Jay, who rode from Big Sandy Station to Marysville, was hired, although he was not yet fourteen years of age. The riders were picked for their nerve and light weight. They rode an average of seventy-five miles, changing mounts every ten or twelve miles, and in an emergency they sometimes rode up to two hundred miles without a break. Near Scotts Bluff, Nebraska, Mark Twain riding a stage westward encountered a Pony Express rider, and described him in *Roughing It*.

Away across the endless dead level of the prairie a black speck appears against the sky, and it is plain that it moves. Well, I should think so! In a second or two it becomes a horse and rider, rising and falling, rising and falling—sweeping toward us nearer and still nearer, and the flutter of hoofs comes faintly to the ear—another instant a whoop and a hurrah from our upper deck, a wave of the rider's hand, but no reply, and man and horse burst past our excited faces and go winging away like a belated fragment of a storm.

My son Rick, young Val Schaffner, and I parked our truck camper in front of the rebuilt brick building at 914 Penn Street in St. Joseph, Missouri, which was the eastern stables for the Pony Express. When it was built in 1858, it was called the Pike's Peak Stables, but ever since April 3, 1860, when the first Pony Express rider saddled up within

241

its walls, it has been known as the Pony Express Stables. Today the stables is a museum chock full of such things as the "XP" brand used to mark the horses, a picket pin used on the trail, and a fifty-two calibre Spencer seven-shot repeating carbine carried by a few riders. Most riders, counting upon the speed of their mounts to take them away from danger, carried neither gun nor knife, but it wasn't true that the riders all went weaponless. Nor was it true that all the riders carried a Bible, although Alexander Majors, one of the owners, who directed the operations, gave each a Bible and made him take an oath not to drink or swear while on duty.

The riders who terminated in St. Joseph were put up at the Patee House, at Twelfth and Penn, known as the finest hotel west of the Mississippi River. There they danced in the ballroom with the belles of the town, for Alexander Majors did not extend his strictures on his young men's conduct to include dancing. We strolled over to the Patee House, where we found Minnie Ziebold of the Pony Express Historical Association in the old Pony Express office. As we talked with her about restoration plans for the now decrepit hotel, the postman brought some mail into the office. He put down some letters near a scale once used to weigh mail for the Pony Express.

"First time I ever been inside here," he said, looking with wonder at the old things rounded up by the historical association to help recreate the days of the Pony Express. He looked at a picture of a rider galloping down the trail, carrying the U.S. mail through the Wild West, straightened his shoulders beneath his mailbag, and with a sigh strode off on his rounds.

We learned that the riders carried up to ten pounds of mail at the rate of $5 in gold for a half-ounce letter bound from St. Joseph to San Francisco. When a Government subsidy went into effect on July 1, 1861, the rate was reduced to $1 for a half ounce. As a rule the Pony Express carried the mail from terminus to terminus in ten days, but the fastest time on record was seven days and seventeen hours when riders rode furiously to bring President Lincoln's Inaugural Address to California.

The Pony Express met the Hannibal and St. Joseph train at the railroad station near Eighth and Olive streets. Because the smokestack of the steam engine *Missouri* flared out like Jenny Lind's hoopskirts, people called it a Jenny Lind. All across Missouri the Jenny Lind showered cinders and smoke upon the folks who came down to the railroad stations to see the historic train go rocking and wailing through town on its way to St. Joseph. The train was late in reaching St. Joseph, and it wasn't until 5:30 P.M. that a cannon shot reverberated from atop the loess bluff behind the Patee House to let the rider know that it was time to mount and ride. Late as it was, there was still time for Mayor M. Jeff Thompson to make a speech before a big crowd of townspeople and invited guests from the East.

"The mail must go," he orated. "Hurled by flesh and blood across two thousand miles of space—Fort Kearny, South Pass, Fort Bridger, Salt Lake City. Neither storms, fatigue, darkness or Indians, burning sands or snow must stop the precious bags. The mail must go!"

The cannon boomed, the mayor slapped the rump of the rider's bay mare, the crowd cheered, and the mail went racing off down the street to the steam ferry *Denver*, which took horse and rider across the Missouri River to the Kansas shore. Some say that Johnny Frye, young, handsome, and a favorite with the girls along the way, was the lad who rode off the ferry and into the Kansas dusk that day, but most historians believe it was Billy Richardson, an ex-sailor, who first carried the Pony Express mail from St. Jo.

On the same day another rider, Harry Roff, started from the west. The mail arrived in Sacramento on a steamer between 2:00 and 3:00 in the morning. As the dawn came up, the horse and rider galloped along the rough roads to Placerville. Roff covered the first 20 miles in 59 minutes, took 10 seconds to change his horse, and rode the next 14 miles at such a pace that he had completed his 34-mile relay in a total of 2 hours and 49 minutes. In the mochila, a leather sheet that fitted over the saddletree, rode letters and dispatches, news and information that on the eve of the Civil War bound California more securely to the Union. It is no wonder that not only sentimentalists but hardheaded historians have heard the hoofbeats of destiny in the thudding hoofs of the Pony Express.

The ferry across the Missouri from St. Joseph landed the Pony Express riders in Elwood, established in 1856 as an outfitting point for emigrants bound for Oregon and California. Construction of the first railroad west of the Missouri began at Elwood in 1859, and only twenty days after the first Pony Express rider came ashore from the Missouri River ferry a locomotive, *The Albany*, was ferried over and pulled up the bank by hand and set on the rails. From the start the Pony Express raced the iron horse and the telegraph, and only eighteen months after it began, the Pony Express ended, outdistanced first by wires and then later by rails. But Elwood was not to share in the wealth that rails brought to other pioneer cities. The Missouri washed the old town away, and Rick, Val, and I found little more than cattle shipping pens beside the railroad. Even a Pony Express monument that once stood beside U.S. 36 was washed away by the high waters of 1952.

Westward through Kansas the Pony Express Trail ran south of U.S. 36. It followed Peters Creek to the first relay station at Troy, which Sir Richard Burton reported in 1860 was "a few wretched shanties." Today the town is a prosperous county seat with a monument on the courthouse lawn to show where the relay station once stood. Johnny Frye may not have been the first Pony Express rider, but he is the one most remembered on the relay which ran through Troy. An old-timer sitting on a bench waiting for his daughter to finish shopping recognized us as out-of-towners and yarned about Johnny.

"He was a devil-may-care, good-looking young fellow, and the gals all set their caps for him. Once right near town here, a gal chased after him on a fresh horse. She got close enough to tear off a piece of his shirt so she could put it into a patchwork quilt she was making."

We started to move away, but he called us back.

"Yes, sir. Even the doughnut was invented by gals in love with Johnny. They took to baking him cookies, figuring that if they could fatten him up, he'd get too heavy for his job. Then maybe he'd marry one of them and settle down. But Johnny rode by so fast that they couldn't get their cookies into his hands. So they made big cookies with holes in 'em so that he could get a hold of 'em easy. Now we call 'em doughnuts."

Johnny carried the mail to his home station at Seneca, seventy-seven miles west of St. Jo, and that is where we drove next. A rider exchanged horses at relay stations, but at a home station, he handed his pouch to the next rider. He would rest and jaw with the station keeper and the hostlers until the mail coming in the opposite direction arrived. Then he'd gallop back along the trail to the next home station. The home station at Seneca was the Smith Hotel.

To get to Seneca, riders rode past modern-day Severance and on southwest to the once flourishing village of Kinnekuk near today's Horton. Kansas Highway 20 runs west from Horton much as the old trail did. In Seneca we learned that the Smith Hotel has migrated three blocks down Main Street from where it once stood at the corner of Fourth, and is now a private home. The building has been altered, but it still looks as hospitable as when it was known as the most comfortable inn on the entire trail.

West of Seneca the trail runs north of U.S. 36. There is nothing to see of it, although the site of the important Guittard's station is on a county road just north of Beatty. A farmhouse stands where the old station stood, and the barn that once sheltered Pony Express horses has been rebuilt. At Marysville the Pony Express crossed the Big Blue River. The Martin's Hotel of Pony Express days is gone, although the stable still exists. We twisted over the roads north of Marysville, where county roads intersect among cornfields, east of Hanover. There we came to the most complete Pony Express station still standing on its original location on the entire trail. The weather-beaten building, built as a ranch house by G. H. Hollenberg in 1857, once contained a general store and United States Post Office. Riders and the station staff slept upstairs. It is preserved by the state of Kansas and is proof of the state's appreciation of its heritage.

The Pony Express riders followed the Oregon Trail to the Platte River, and so did we. They rode on the turf mounded between the wagon ruts, for there they found it easy going, to such stations as Rock House and Rock Creek, where the old rock post office has been restored, and the Big Sandy Station. In 1864 the Indians wiped out a chain of former Pony Express stations along this route, and there is nothing left this side of Fort Kearny.

Fort Kearny marked the end of the eastern division of the trail. Westward along the Oregon Trail rode the young riders, stopping at stations long since vanished. The Midway Station still stands on the Lower 96 Ranch, three miles south of Gothenburg, its sturdy timbers showing the

Riders and the station staff slept upstairs at the Hollenberg Pony Express Station. The station still stands amid the cornfields east of Hanover, Kansas.
The Kansas State Historical Society, Topeka

marks of the frontier workman's adz. It was from Midway that rider Richard Cleve rode 160 miles through blizzards to the Kiowa station near present-day Hebron. He lost the trail in the blinding snow.

"I would get off the horse and look for the road," he said in a letter written in 1913, "find it and mount the horse, but in five yards I would lose it again. I tried it several times, but gave it up, so I dismounted and led the horse back and forth until daylight."

When the snow stopped, the thermometer plummeted to 35 to 40 below zero. The mail went through, but young Cleve spent 36 hours in the storm.

Gothenburg has another Pony Express station. It originally stood on the Upper 96 Ranch, four miles east of Fort McPherson and was built in 1854 as a fur-trading post. Later it was a bunkhouse and storage house on the ranch that was owned by C. A. Williams, who also owned the Lower 96 and the station there. Possibly reasoning that two of the few remaining Pony Express stations were too much for one family, Mrs. C. A. Williams gave the Sam Machets station on the Upper 96 to the town of Gothenburg in 1931. It was moved by the Gothenburg American Legion post to City Park in town, where it can be seen by motorists driving west along the Platte River Valley. Ordinarily a historical landmark as important as this Pony Express station has more meaning and value if left on its original site, but anybody who has visited it in City Park and seen how it brings alive the Pony Express story to the families who stop by cannot be anything but thankful to the Williams family which

246

has preserved two Pony Express stations, and the town of Gothenburg which makes one of them so easy for tourists to see.

The Pony Express riders rode on along the Oregon Trail to the California Crossing, where the emigrants crossed the South Platte and headed north to Ash Hollow. The Pony Express Trail continued on along the south bank of the river to Old Julesburg in Colorado. Here Jules Reni's trading post was a home station that broke every one of Alexander Majors' tenets. Old Jules's affection for whiskey and cards proved contagious. His affection for a gang of outlaws who threatened the safety of the U.S. Mail was something again, and the Pony Express route superintendent, Benjamin F. Ficklin, hired Joseph Alfred Slade, already a notorious gunman, to go to Julesburg and establish law and order.

Slade fired old Jules. Old Jules then shot Slade in the back with a double-barreled shotgun while he was riding down the trail, but failed to kill him. Pony Express men captured Jules and strung him up to hang, but the outlaws cut him down. When Slade recovered from his wound, he got together a posse of sorts and raided the outlaw hideout near Rocky Ridge. He captured Jules, tied him to a corral post, and shot him full of lead. Cutting off the dead man's ears, Slade nailed one to the post as a warning that the Pony Express was not to be trifled with, and dried the other for a watch fob.

Slade, who was supposed to have killed twenty-six men in his career, was not noted for his charm. Yet Mark Twain found him "so friendly and so gentle-spoken that I warmed to him in spite of his awful history." It was to him that young Buffalo Bill reported in the summer of 1860 to carry the mail west of Julesburg.

"Slade, although rough at times and always a dangerous character—having killed many a man—was always kind to me," wrote Bill in his autobiography. "During the two years I worked for him as pony-express-rider and stage-driver, he never spoke an angry word to me." Nobody knows that he ever spoke an angry word to Old Jules either.

Leaving Julesburg the riders followed the Overland Trail across the Platte and along Lodgepole Creek. West of today's Sidney, the riders crossed the Lodgepole and started north along the route surveyed by the topographical engineers in 1858 and named Jules Stretch for Old Jules. We took U.S. 385 north, although it runs east of the old trail. Wagons and stages cut around Courthouse Rock to the north, but the fleet Pony Express riders found a shortcut across Pumpkinseed Creek and to the southwest of the rock. Past Chimney Rock and Scotts Bluff the riders carried the mail. Nebraska Highway 92 follows the trail of their galloping horses.

The Pony Express riders took the Oregon Trail on westward into Wyoming. The first westbound Pony Express rider raced into Fort Laramie on April 6, 1860, just three days after the mail had left St. Joseph. Today only Old Bedlam, bachelor officers' quarters, the stone powder magazine and the sutler's store remain of the Fort Laramie buildings that were standing on that day.

We could find no traces of Pony Express stations along the Oregon Trail across Wyoming to South Pass. We particularly tried to find some indication of where the Split Rock Station stood on the south side of the Sweetwater beyond Devil's Gate, for the station figured in one of Buffalo Bill's adventures. Bill wrote in his autobiography:

As I was leaving Horse Creek one day a party of Indians "jumped me" in a sand ravine about a mile west of the station. They fired at me repeatedly, but missed their mark. I was mounted on a roan California horse—the fleetest steed I had, and laying flat on his back, I kept straight on for Sweetwater Bridge—eleven miles distant—instead of trying to turn back to Horse Creek. The Indians came on in hot pursuit, but my horse soon got away from them, and ran into the station two miles ahead of them. The stocktender had been killed there that morning, and all the stock had been driven off by the Indians, and as I was therefore unable to change horses, I continued on to Ploutz's Station—twelve miles further—thus making twenty-four miles straight run with one horse.

There is nothing left of Horse Creek Station, of the Sweetwater Station which stood near Independence Rock, and of what Bill calls "Ploutz's Station," which actually was Plant's Station, otherwise known as Split Rock.

The Pony Express riders forded the Sweetwater three times beyond Split Rock, and the Three Crossings became a terror in time of flood. They rode sometimes along the old Oregon Trail, sometimes to one side and sometimes to the other as they climbed over South Pass to Pacific Springs Station, where the blacksmith's shop and the barn still stand. From the springs the riders rode across a desolate waste, stopping at relay stations at such points as the Dry Sandy, Little Sandy, and Big Sandy for new mounts. They came at last to Fort Bridger. There we found the stables used by Pony Express horses still standing. On the west bank of the Big Muddy Creek there are also old fireplaces and the foundations of the first station west of Fort Bridger. Crossing into Utah,

248

the riders followed the Mormon Trail into Salt Lake City, largest city on the route between the eastern and western terminals.

Out of Salt Lake City the rider hurried away south past Traveler's Rest, Porter Rockwell's, and Joe Dugout's to Camp Floyd in Cedar Valley, where the station was in a still surviving inn in Fairfield. Cattle lowed and roosters crowed as we walked through the bucolic village to the inn, which is surrounded by old-fashioned hollyhocks. It is hard to imagine this quiet place as a town with seventeen saloons, gamblers, thieves, and women of poor repute all catering to the off-duty hours of the soldiers of Camp Floyd. The inn itself was an oasis of Mormon probity amid the riotous town. John Carson built the two-story adobe and frame hotel in 1858, and he allowed no liquor served in his place and permitted only square dancing. Alexander Majors could readily approve of this Pony Express station.

Captain James Hervey Simpson, the topographical engineer officer at Camp Floyd, laid out the Overland Stage route from Salt Lake to San Francisco over a shorter southern route, and it was over this Simpson Route that the Pony Express riders rode. Today a motorist can drive the old trail itself through a land where the sky is a vast timeless bowl and ranges of mountains reach up like islands from the desert floor. The sites of the old stations are marked so it is easy to stop where a station once stood and imagine the riders dashing up, standing erect in their saddles so that they could loosen the mochila and be ready to jump down and throw it around the saddletree of the next mount. There are the shouts, the hurried advice, and the rider is off again, the hooves of his horse drumming down the dusty road. There are some ruined walls remaining from the station at Simpson's Springs at the south end of the dry Bonneville Flats, and a family is living in the Bauchmanns Station. Willow Springs Station building is on a ranch near Callao. Otherwise the stations are gone, leaving only the road and the desert.

From Callao the road cuts north and west to Gold Hill. It runs through the Goshute Indian reservation close to Nevada Highway 2. We had to detour by way of U.S. 50 to the south to reach Ruby Valley. We were disappointed to learn that in 1960 the old stage station in the valley was moved to Elko, where we found it stranded beside the highway with an old stage and freight wagons.

The Pony Express Trail crossed the mountains over Hastings Pass, through which the modern road from Hobson to Simonsen now runs. It angled southwest to cut across U.S. 50 east of Austin. From this point the trail follows U.S. 50 towards Carson Sink. This is the stretch of the trail traversed by Pony Bob Haslam, one of the most famous of the riders. In 1860 he rode 120 miles in eight hours and ten minutes from Smith Creek to Fort Churchill to speed Abraham Lincoln's Inaugural Address toward California.

By the end of that year the Paiute Indians all but stopped the Pony Express. In December, Pony Bob reached Reed's Station on the Carson River, but found no change of horses waiting. He fed the horse he was riding and headed for Fort Churchill, fifteen miles down the trail. At Fort Churchill the next rider, being afraid of the Indians, refused to take the mochila. Haslam rode on as far as Smiths Creek, for a total ride of 190 miles. He rested and started back with the mail bound for the west. At Cold Springs he discovered the keeper killed by Indians, put spurs to his horse and rode on to the big adobe station at Sand Springs and safety. Pony Bob lived through many such relays to become later in life the manager of the Congress and Auditorium hotels in Chicago.

The Paiutes made the Nevada portion of the Pony Express Trail so dangerous that "the Carson Valley Expedition" was dispatched under the command of Captain Joseph Stewart. The soldiers fought the Indians near Pyramid Lake and then established a post on the Carson River, which was named Fort Churchill for General Sylvester Churchill, a Vermonter, who was the Army's inspector general. The post was close to Samuel Buckland's trading post, which was a stop on the Pony Express. Soon the riders were stopping instead at the fort where the stone building that housed the Pony Express station still stands.

From Fort Churchill the route ran southwestward along the Carson River to Dayton, a historic town on U.S. 50, where mail bound for the mining camp of Virginia City was separated. It was an easy run into Carson City and on southward to Genoa, founded as Mormon Station by Mormon settlers in 1851, but renamed for the birthplace of Christopher Columbus when streets were laid out and lots surveyed five years later. The museum in the re-created Mormon Station settlement displays a Pony Express Bible among its mementos of the trail.

Leaving Genoa, the riders climbed the trail into the Sierras. Nevada Highway 19 zigzags along part of the old road to the southern tip of Lake Tahoe. Hard by the casino that has made him rich, William E. Harrah has set up a statue of a Pony Express rider on his galloping horse. Especially at night with the neon lights from the hotels and clubs beside the lake splashing the heroic figure with garish colors, the statue seems out of place. Yet Harrah is right in seeking to remind his pleasure-bent visitors that once this overbuilt lakeshore was virgin timber and through the forest a lonely rider sped the mail.

From Friday's Station, also called Lake Side, the trail ran downhill to Yank's, on to Strawberry Station, and on from station to station down to Placerville. We followed the trail as best we could on U.S. 50. It was a fine summer day, and the traffic was moving fast among the mountains, where Pony Express riders often had to charge their mounts through thirty feet of snow. This would have been impossible, but the pack trains and horses and mules carrying supplies to the Nevada mining camps and precious metals out to Sacramento kept the passes open, except during the most severe storms.

A superhighway and the passing years have done away with any reminders of the trail except at Folsom, where the 15 Mile House Station was located in the Wells, Fargo and Co. Assay Office still standing in this old mining town. From Folsom it was not far to Sacramento. As Hamilton, the Pony Express rider, was riding past Sutter's Fort, he was met by a cavalcade of riders from the town. They hurrahed and raced their animals, stirring up enough dust to suffocate the man and horse they honored. Hamilton to all appearances considered the milling riders as just one more obstacle in the way of the mail, and he urged his horse through the crowd and rode straight to the Alta Telegraph Office in the Adams Building on Second Street between J and K.

Today the old building stands forlornly on a street that has been undergoing urban renewal for half a dozen years. Shabby men wander about from one cheap saloon to the next or sit in doorways and look out at the blurred world. A few fancy "restorations" have been made to serve as coffee houses or antique stores.

Then it was the center of a noisy reception, with bands playing, women and girls singing and crying, and dignitaries tossing their tophats in the air. They had something to cheer about. The mail had crossed the West in nine days and twenty-three hours. The side-wheeler *Antelope* was waiting at the nearby levee. The rider and his precious mail were escorted aboard, and the steamer, her paddlewheels churning, started down the Sacramento for San Francisco.

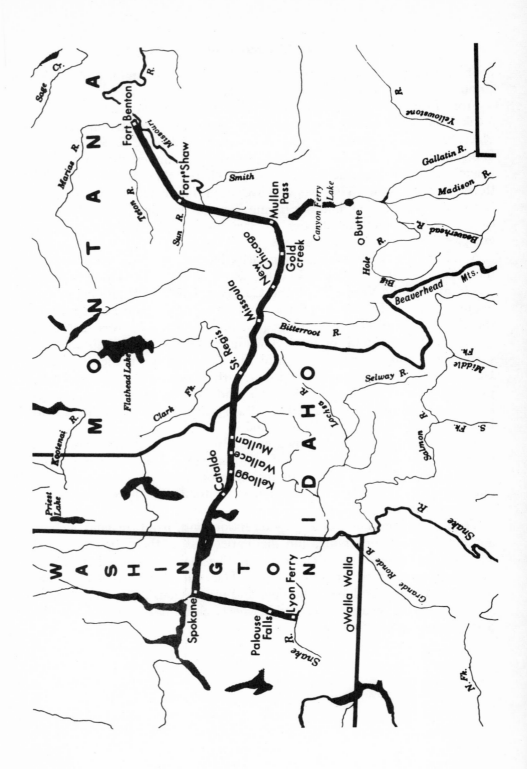

20

Mullan Road to the Gold Camps

●

Guests at the Grand Union Hotel in Fort Benton, Montana, used to look out their windows and watch herds of longhorns fording the Missouri River. Today the longhorns are gone, but the hotel, which opened for business on November 1, 1882, still stands. The dining room no longer serves meals, but travelers stay overnight in the boxy little rooms, which the pioneers considered luxurious.

Our family sat in the lobby and was tempted by the Old West ambience of the place to ask for rooms. Thoughts of our station wagon parked out in front crammed with a tent and the other paraphernalia of camping dissuaded us. We had come to Fort Benton to tent camp along the old Mullan Military Road, which was built from 1858 to 1863 from the old fort at the headwaters of navigation on the Missouri for 624 miles through the towering Bitterroots, across what is now the panhandle of Idaho and through present-day Spokane to Fort Walla Walla in Washington. Cut through the wilderness by the soldiers directed by Captain John Mullan of the Topographical Engineers, the road was intended to speed troops to trouble spots in the Indian wars. It became instead the road to the gold camps of Montana and an artery of commerce and settlement. We wanted to scout out where the old road ran, look for artifacts in deserted mining camps, fish, and explore what we knew to be some of the most spectacular country in the West. My wife Joan and our seventeen-year-old daughter Nancy were to do the cooking in camp; Jim, thirteen, and our young friend Guy Spinks, fourteen, and I were to put up the tent, tote water, and take care of any other camp chores.

Mark Twain said that "a good pilot could tap a keg of beer and sail his boat a mile on the suds."

To get a light draft mountain sternwheeler up to Fort Benton called for pilots skilled in navigating shallow waters, but at the height of river traffic there were seven hundred steamboats a year making the trip. There were a fair share of groundings on mudbanks and gravel bars and some disasters. The *Chippewa,* which in 1860 became the first boat to steam to Fort Benton, blew up in the following year. Thirsty deckhands tapped a whiskey keg. During the celebration they knocked over a candle, setting fire to the boat. When the flames reached barrels of gunpowder in the cargo, the boat exploded. This was scarcely a disaster for the Crow Indians, who discovered the wreck. Usually Indians had to content themselves with taking potshots at the passing boats, which sheathed their pilot houses with boiler plate, but the Crows were able to help themselves to bolts of calico, twists of tobacco, bundles of blankets, food, and beads. When a war party of Sioux happened along and tried to join the party, the Crows greedily fought them off.

Fort Benton was founded in 1846 by Alexander Culbertson of the American Fur Company to trade with the fierce Blackfeet. These Indians had the reputation of collecting more human hair every season than white trappers did beaver, but they did not turn out to be a match for the Fort Benton whiskey. To muddy Missouri water trappers added one quart alcohol, one pound of rank, black chewing tobacco, one handful red peppers, one bottle Jamaica ginger, and one quart black molasses. They mixed the concoction well and heated it until the strength was drawn from the tobacco and peppers. The fort opened with a house-warming at which one thousand Blackfeet were served this firewater, of which it could at least be said that no drinker ever lived long enough to become an alcoholic.

After 1860 the Gold Rush supplanted the fur trade in the life of the growing town, and trains of freight wagons set out from the steamer landings over the Mullan Road to the placer diggings of Montana. In 1867 up to a thousand head of oxen, hitched up and ready to pull out for the mines, were counted in the streets of the town at one time. Complete stamping mills came up the river and were loaded in five-ton wagons to be hauled over the road by straining teams of mules or oxen. To get his mules moving, a muleskinner literally stripped slashes off their hides with his whip.

"First you've got to get the mule's attention," he explained to bystanders, who objected to the flailing whip. Then a muleskinner seared the air with a stream of smoking epithets, and the train got under way. Bullwhackers were proud to compete with the muleskinners in profanity.

Today, where steamboats once lined the river front, we found Boy Scout troop 20 from Kalispell putting their canoes in the water for a trip down the Missouri. Nearby on the shore was a replica of a keel boat that early traders had used on the big muddy river. Only a few hundred yards farther along the river we came to the surviving block-house and foundation walls of old Fort Benton, serene in a shady park. Thanks to a model in a museum we were able to imagine what the fort must have looked like. The model was made out of tiny adobe bricks fashioned from actual adobe bricks taken from the original fort.

The Mullan Road started at the fort's sally port, but we discovered the first traces of it on the hills back of town. There Guy found a hinge of a wagon, and Jim found old glass, aged purple in the sun, as we followed the ruts on foot. The sun brought out the tang of the sage, and the wind puffed around us. The big sky of Montana arched high overhead. We drove to another stretch of the road over what Captain John Mullan described as an easy and almost level prairie with no running streams. We were delighted, as we hiked along the road, to come across a nest of killdeer where once oxen had plodded. Outlying installations of Maelstrom Air Force Base turned us aside once more, and we weren't able to find the old Mullan Road again until the banks of the Sun River. Cultivated fields stretch where the road passed by Twenty-eight Mile Spring, a wagon camp twenty-eight miles from Fort Benton, and Lake Benton to the Sun River Crossing.

In June of 1867 four companies of the 13th U.S. Infantry picked a site six miles above the Sun River Crossing to set up their post, which was first called Camp Reynolds and then Fort Shaw for General Robert Gould Shaw, of the 54th Massachusetts volunteers. The soldiers went to work with a will, and by Christmas they had erected half of the officers' quarters, half of the barracks, and part of the hospital around a four-hundred-foot parade ground. They made the walls bullet proof by placing 6x12x4-inch adobe bricks between boards for a total thickness of eighteen inches. The men dug clay from Adobe Creek a mile east of the fort and mixed it with wild hay to make the adobe. The old buildings remain, but today children go to school in them. The chapel is used for classes, and the mess hall was long used as the gym. School principal Wilford Poppie showed us through the buildings.

"We had to condemn the old adobe gym," he said. "We couldn't raise the roof, because the old walls wouldn't take it, so we built a concrete block gym around them. The floor is original."

The school custodian and a teacher live in General John Gibbon's house, which features a fireplace brought all the way from England to the frontier and a pine parquet floor. From the solid comfort of this house, General Gibbon set out in 1876 at the head of his troops to join General Terry and General Custer in the campaign that led to Custer's bloody last stand on the Little Big Horn.

We set up our tent beside the parade ground. As the women folk were cooking our meal, Mr. and Mrs. Poppie came riding up on a trail bike carrying an upside-down cake that she had baked for our dessert. The boys fished in a pool in the river where the soldiers used to fish, and later we went over to Ralph Parker's nearby dairy farm and sat in the kitchen and talked. Montanans are among the most hospitable of all Westerners, and as we pored over maps our farmer friend told us about the country through which the road runs. It is some of the best country in the state for hunting elk, deer, antelope, and lion.

"There are timber wolves and grizzly up in the mountains around Mullan Pass, but they won't bother you any," Ralph finished.

In the morning we had to face a wildlife crisis of our own. Two baby skunks had tumbled into the fort's abandoned cistern, and their whimpering had attracted the tenderhearted boys. How to get them out? Ralph took a look and said that the only humane thing would be to shoot them, and he went to get his gun. The boys' faces saddened. They noosed a loop at the end of a rope and fished with it in the cistern until at last they slipped the loop around a tiny skunk. Pulling it to the surface, they cut the rope well beyond puffing distance of the small creature's nervously lifted tail. They got the second baby out the same way, and the mother skunk, who watched the boys from beneath the old officers' quarters, easily slipped the nooses off her children.

Old freight wagons decay beside the Mullan Road at delapidated St. Peter's Mission in Montana.
Photo by Joan Dunlop

The Mullan Road is now a ranch road which took us between two buttes and past a Hutterite colony to abandoned St. Peter's Mission, where a double row of trees still leads up to fallen walls. Roses grow along a broken walkway. Three old freight wagons and extra wheels lay rotting near the old walls. We drove on to where our back road came out on U.S. 287. There the ruts of the Mullan Road run beside the pavement of the old highway.

Between the Dearborn River ford, which was just south of the present Dearborn River Bridge, and the Sun River, Captain Mullan's men had very little road-building to do, for the wagons could easily roll across the gently swelling plains. From Wolf Creek, where wagon trains camped the third night out of Fort Benton, the Mullan Road follows Little Prickly Pear Creek except where the creek gushes through a canyon. There Mullan's crews had to grade their track over the rocky hump of Medicine Rock Mountain. The trail climbs up Big Prickly Pear Creek to the railroad stop at Austin. From there our station wagon twisted and turned up the road to Mullan Pass, which Mullan himself was first to cross with a four-mule team pulling an army wagon.

"Captain Mullan, the kindest-hearted man that ever came West," a sign nailed to a tree announced. The sign was apt, for Mullan's kindness extended even to mules.

"Never maltreat them," he advised muleskinners, "but govern them as you would a woman with kindness, affection, and caresses and you will be repaid by their docility and easy management."

Judging by the expression on Joan's face, I wasn't sure that Mullan had made the right comparison. Captain Mullan also had additional words of advice to pioneers taking his road into the Northwest.

"If your wagon tires become loose on the road," he wrote in a guide for emigrants, "caulk with old gunnysacks or soak, or both. In loading wagons an allowance of four hundred pounds to the animal is enough on a long journey."

He suggested that emigrants take along a "jackscrew, extra tongue, and coupling pole; also, axle grease, a hatchet and nails, auger, rope, twine, and one or two chains for wheel-locking and two extra whippletrees."

The trip, he believed, should take wagons from forty-seven to fifty-five days, and pack strings around thirty-five days. The Federal Government spent $230,000 to build the road, but it appropriated no money to maintain it. Road repairs had to be made by local citizens, and the part of the road through the Bitterroots became almost impassable. In September, 1877, William Tecumseh Sherman, the captor of Atlanta, dispatched a military wagon train through the Bitterroots on the Mullan Road, even though he wrote to the Secretary of War, "It has become so obstructed by washes and fallen timbers that for years, it has not been travelled by wagons at all and reverted to the condition of a mere pack trail."

Mules even climbed trees, avowed Sherman, as his men hacked their way along the road to Fort Walla Walla.

That night we camped in the Helena National Forest on the Continental Divide, which runs through 5,902-foot high Mullan Pass. In the morning we awoke to a pristine world of mountain flowers, pines dripping with mist, and snowbanks on faraway slopes. From the pass the road took us down into the valley of the Little Blackfoot River, a tumultuous trout stream. U.S. 10 crosses and recrosses the stream as does the old Mullan Road, which we could make out cut into the sides of the hills.

On Gold Creek in 1852 a French half-breed named Benetsee found placer gold and set off the Montana gold rush. We drove up a side road from Gold Creek town to Pioneer, a deserted gold camp where prairie dogs and ground squirrels were playing around old tailings. We fished in a stream that flowed through the camp and searched the tumbledown houses for such keepsakes as an ox shoe, horseshoes, and the top of a sugar bowl.

We descended the Clark Fork River, which is known to geographers as the Clark fork of the Columbia. It has many local names, too: at its source it is called Silver Bow Creek, then Deer Lodge River, then Hellgate River, then the Missoula, and finally, before it merges with the Columbia, the Clark Fork.

Our next mining camp was New Chicago, named by miners convinced that their town would soon eclipse the "Back East" city in wealth and population. We stopped to talk to Harold Mitten, who quit hoeing in his kitchen garden to tell us about the old town, even though he was behind in his weeding because he had been out placer-mining in the hills. The town grew up around an inn on the Mullan Road, he said. Folks stopping at the inn found a gold scales on the front desk. The innkeeper was often away on a journey of his own, so when the guests checked out they weighed out enough gold dust to pay for their food and lodging and left it on the desk with the certainty that nobody else would take it. In a couple of years after its founding in 1872 New Chicago had two stores, two saloons, two blacksmith shops, a flour mill, and livery stable. The school opened in 1874 to accommodate pupils who ranged from "six years to six feet." Finally a Methodist Episcopal church was built. Its cornerstone contained an Epsom salts box, the *Doctrines and Discipline of the Methodist Episcopal Church*, a song-book of gospel hymns, four newspapers, a nickel, and a twist of Cotton Ball tobacco. I pointed out Mitten Peak in the background and asked Harold if he were related to Dennis Mitten for whom the peak was named.

"Not related at all," he said and struck at a weed with his hoe.

This was a pity, for Mr. and Mrs. Dennis Mitten were not only among the first pioneers in the valley but were real originals. When Chief Joseph and the Nez Perce went on the warpath, Mrs. Mitten bought a needle gun and a bottle of whiskey and fortified with both, marched up and down the one street of nearby Bear Gulch shouting military commands.

"Attention! Take aim! Fire!"

She'd fall on a knee at her own command, aim and shoot at the flags on the stockade fort. When she at last gave up her maneuvering and returned home to the Mitten Ranch, Dennis scolded her for not having dinner ready.

"Why do you have a gun anyway?" he demanded.

"To kill Indians with, of course."

"You couldn't kill an Indian. Now if I was an Indian, what would you do this minute?"

"I'd do this."

She pulled the trigger and shot him. Then she bound up the wound and nursed her husband back to health. Dennis later opened a saloon for workmen building the Northern Pacific through the canyon. When a laborer knocked him down in a quarrel, he ran and got his wife's needle gun.

"I'll shoot you and shoot you until I can knock you down!" he shouted, and chased through the brush shooting.

"You're overshooting him," Mrs. Mitten screamed. "You're overshooting, Dennis!"

It appeared the workman got away; but when a month later he was found dead on a sandbar with a bullet in his heart, Dennis was arrested and sentenced to Deer Lodge penitentiary. Things were quiet in the valley for a few years until he was released on parole. When Dennis came home, the saloonkeeper tossed a great drunken fete in his honor. It was snowing and very cold when the party broke up. The host handed each of the Mittens a bottle of whiskey, and perched on horses they started home. On the way Mrs. Mitten toppled from her horse in a drunken stupor. Too drunk himself to lift her back on the horse and unwilling to leave her to freeze, Dennis roped her to the horn of his saddle and dragged her home through the snow. She was dead on arrival, and Dennis went back to prison for murder. There was nothing to do but name a mountain for the couple.

With Harold Mitten's help we found the pioneer school, which is now used as a granary, a safe which had been blown apart in a robbery, and the office in which Captain Mullan planned road improvements on this section of the road. The Wells Fargo Trading Post and Saloon is now a residence. A housewife invited us in to see how the bar had been made into a kitchen. She dug in her garden where she said she often digs up pioneer relics. As we watched, she unearthed an old file, which she handed to Guy as a souvenir.

Ida Mae Royall was born in 1876, and we met her in a laundromat in Drummond, which is a few miles north of New Chicago. She remembered the wagons drawn by mules or oxen rolling by her girlhood home on the Mullan Road. Trim and keen, this old lady who had looked upon pioneer wagon trains was watching a TV show while the laundromat dryers thumped at her elbow.

From New Chicago we drove over the old road through picturesque ranches to Bear Mouth, once a pioneer trading center for the placer camps at Beartown, Garnet, and Coloma in the hills north of the valley. Only a few ruined buildings remain. Below Bear Mouth the Mullan Road ran close to Clark Fork. At what is now Milltown, Mullan bridged the Blackfoot River close to where the modern highway bridge crosses.

Here where the Blackfoot and the Clark Fork come together Mullan established Cantonment Wright to winter his men in 1861-1862. The Indians extended their own brand of hospitality to the road-builders by stampeding some fifty head of beef cattle and work oxen. Still other animals died by January from lack of forage. These problems did not keep Mullan from establishing work camps along the road to the west of his main camp so that he could resume work as soon as possible in the spring.

It was cold. One man tried to pass between Cantonment Wright and a work camp. Overtaken by the night, he built a fire to warm his feet. His moccasins which had become wet during the day were frozen to his feet, and he could not get them off. Terrified, he returned through the woods to Cantonment Wright where he soaked his feet in a tub of warm water to thaw them out. Not only his moccasins but the flesh of his feet came off clear to the bone. The surgeon saved his life by amputating his legs above the knees. The spring floods dealt unkindly with the suffering men too. Eight bridges were washed out, and the big bridge across the Blackfoot was swung askew.

The canyon narrows along U.S. 10 into Hell Gate, so called by trappers, who found it littered with human bones. From the earliest days an Indian trail led through the canyon. Raiding Blackfeet ambushed party after party of Nez Perce and Flathead coming along the trail. One look at the heaps of skulls and bones was enough to make an Indian cry out, "I-sul," in horror. From this expression comes the name Missoula, given to what is now the largest city of Hell Gate. Mullan's road builders brought their road down through the grim canyon.

In August, 1860, Frank L. Worden and C. P. Higgins loaded a pack train with merchandise in Walla Walla and headed east over the Mullan Road to Hell Gate Ronde, where they intended to establish a post to trade with the Indians. They cut logs for a 16-by-18-foot cabin, and in so doing launched the brief career of Hell Gate, one of the Old West's liveliest towns, three miles from today's city of Missoula. Narcisse Sanpar, a Frenchman, went to work building the store, which was roofed over with poles covered with sod. With the rush to the gold fields, trade became brisk. Gold dust brought $18 an ounce at the store. Worden and Higgins sold flour at $30 a hundred pounds; potatoes, $6 a bushel; yeast powders at $1.50 a box. Whiskey was much in demand, and the traders could count on each horse in a train to bring in four gallons. Each shipment went a long way, for they mixed one part whiskey with 10 parts water, and added tobacco and cayenne for taste, color, and potency.

Soon the first court was held in Bolt's saloon close to the Worden and Higgins store. Tin Cup Joe brought charges against Baron O'Keefe, a rancher, who killed his horse when he found it nibbling at his haystack.

Frank Wood, the prosecuting attorney, harangued the jury about good citizenship until O'Keefe demanded, "Who are you? What kind of a court is this anyhow?" O'Keefe then turned on the judge. "Say, Old Brooks, who in hell made you judge? You are an old fraud. You are no judge; you are a squaw man. You have two squaws now. Your business is to populate the country with half breeds."

O'Keefe lunged toward the judge, and in the uproar, judge, jurors, constable, and prosecuting attorney all dashed out of the saloon to safety. When quiet returned, they sneaked back in and awarded $40 damages to Tin Cup Joe. Nobody ever collected from O'Keefe.

Hell Gate also celebrated the first white marriage in Montana. George White married Mrs. Mineinger in March, 1862. The townsfolks celebrated with a dinner, featuring chickens stolen from a nearby farm. When the bride got ready to cut the cake, it was discovered that a man named Blake had taken it. There was nothing to do but to get drunk. During its five years of existence nine men died with their boots on in Hell Gate. Since three of them, all members of a bandit gang, were hanged from a pole fastened to a log corral in the lower part of town at one time, the record was not too bad. An additional bandit was seized the next day on the O'Keefe ranch and also hanged.

In the fall of 1864 Worden and Higgins built a gristmill and sawmill four miles upstream on the Clark Fork. Later they moved the store to the site, which became Missoula. Hell Gate crumbled. We found only a few moldering structures. Kids playing basketball showed us the remains of the old store. There is nothing much left of the O'Keefe Ranch either, although the cottonwoods still stand as the pioneer planted them. The ranch had passed out of the hands of the family, but James Garner, who plays TV's "Maverick," bought it and restored it to the O'Keefe heirs.

We were unable to find any traces of the Mullan Road in Hell Gate Ronde, which is one of the most beautiful valleys of Montana, or it would be except for a paper pulp mill which belched great clouds of noxious smoke over the landscape as we drove toward it. A young cowboy on a horse, aided by a little girl also on a horse and two boys on bikes, was driving a herd of cattle down the road ahead of us as we approached the mill.

At St. Regis we deserted U.S. 10 to take the hardtop Mullan Road over the Camel's Hump. The road returns to U.S. 10 east of De Borgia. There, two miles east of town on U.S. 10, is Mullan Point, where Mullan and his men sheltered in their Cantonment Jordan during the severe winter of 1859-60. On November 1 snow fell, and within five days the snow was eighteen inches deep. On November 8 the temperature dropped below zero. The men built a dozen cabins. They were still at work on the storehouse and office on December 5 when the temperature dropped to 42 below zero. Animals died of exposure and exhaustion, the mailman came and went on snowshoes, and Mullan completed maps and made his field notes. Dr. Lewis Taylor, the surgeon, noted that the men's salt meat diet would bring scurvy before the winter was over. He was right. There were twenty-five cases, and Mullan sent men through the wilderness to the Pend d'Oreille Mission to obtain vegetables from the priests.

On Christmas morning the men bucked waist-high drifts to bring in white pine boughs to deck their cabins. They hunted elk and deer along the river, and for dinner there were roasts and chops simmered in field ovens. One day in the bitter cold a hunter set out and lost his way in the timber. For four days he was without food or blankets. When he returned to base, his frozen feet had to be amputated to save his life.

Early in March, Mullan and his men began work on the Bitterroot Ferry, fifteen miles away. When the snow melted in May, they began to work on the road. One hundred and fifteen men labored for six weeks to cut grades for wagons over Big Mountain. They blasted with black powder, and one worker lost the sight of an eye in a premature explosion.

U.S. 10 follows the Mullan Road up the St. Regis River through a deep forest where the tragic fire of August, 1910, destroyed many pioneer homes, burned railroad trestles and six billion board feet of timber, and took eighty-seven lives. Dead trees killed in the holocaust still stick up gray and bristly upon the mountaintops as proof of how long it takes nature to repair the damage of a fire. There are traces of the old road to be seen along the highway, but the next major landmark is at Cataldo, Idaho. The Mullan Road crossed the rugged Bitterroots over St. Regis Pass, which is now very difficult to reach, except on foot, and it has been obliterated through such mining towns as Mullan, Wallace, Osburn, Kellogg, and Smeltetville.

As we drove over a newly completed section of I-90, beyond Smelterville, we saw a noble-columned building crowning a hill. It turned out to be the Mission of the Sacred Heart at Cataldo, built by black-robed Jesuits in 1853. We stopped to see the mission, which Indians erected with hand-carved tools and wooden nails. In the back of the altar the handprints of the redskins who built the mission, Idaho's oldest building, can be seen. Mullan camped at the mission during the construction of the Mullan Military Road in this area.

On July 4, 1861, Mullan and his road builders finished their grading as far as a canyon west of the mission which ever since has been known as Fourth of July Canyon. The men fired their rifles and set off explosions to celebrate the holiday. Frightened by the racket, the Indians fled through the forest to the mission to tell the priests that the white road builders had gone mad and were shooting one another. During the festivities somebody carved "M.R., Fourth of July 1861" on an enormous white pine that generations of travelers have gazed upon. Then on November 20, 1962, a windstorm lashed the forest and snapped off the historic tree. The blazing remains on the stump that the storm left standing. Rangers have capped the stump with metal and surrounded it with an iron fence.

In the back of the altar of the Mission of the Sacred Heart at Cataldo, Idaho, are the handprints of the Indians who built it in 1853.
Idaho Department of Commerce and Development

Nobody can follow the old Mullan Road past Lake Coeur d'Alene without being moved by the beauty of this renowned mountain lake. At first Mullan built his road south of the lake, but the spring floods soon convinced him that he had better locate it along the lake's north shore. He did so in 1861. We followed along the north shore from where a boat takes sightseers from the city docks of Coeur d'Alene down the lake and up the St. Joe River to Heyburn State Park, where the first road may be found at several places.

It is only a short drive from Lake Coeur d'Alene to Spokane, busy metropolis of eastern Washington. Pine-green hills crowd down upon a city, which has grown up where the Mullan Road crossed the Spokane River at Antoine Plante's flatboat ferry. When Antoine Plante, half French, half Flathead Indian, established his ferry in 1851, Spokane was nothing but a waterfall and a sandbar. Today the capital of the rich "Inland Empire" sprawls on both sides of the river. We found the trail leading down to the old ferry crossing in Pasadena Park. On the far side of the river there is nothing left of the trail itself, but it ran along Sprague Avenue, passed close by the Edgecliff Sanitarium and crossed Twenty-ninth Street in the Glenrose District on its way to Moran Prairie. On U.S. 195 south of Spokane we stopped to see the monument where the Mullan Road crosses the highway. There are other markers to be seen indicating where the road went south through what are now the farms and ranches of eastern Washington. It is a country of scablands, canyons, and small lakes.

264

We camped on the shores of a small lake. All night the wind soughed among the trees. In the morning we drove on across a vast land where wind devils danced and dust flew in the car windows. The Mullan Road ran right through Benge and down what is now the road from Benge to Washtucna. About five miles south of Benge we came to one of the most interesting of the landmarks on the Mullan Road. In 1864 George Lucas built a way station of stone and thatch beside the Mullan Road. The stone corral and stone fence still survive beside the road.

The Mullan Road passes about three miles east of Washtucna and starts across a tableland on the west side of the Palouse River. Mullan, exploring the river for a route to push his road, came to the Falls of the Palouse in 1859.

"The water presses there through rock cliffs not exceeding ten feet in width and forming a cascade of over one hundred feet, reaches the bottom in a pond-like rock excavation," noted Mullan. To his discredit as an engineer, he underestimated the height of the falls by ninety-eight feet. The Mullan Road swings wide around the rugged Palouse canyon, which is now a state park. We stopped to see the falls, but by afternoon we were at Lyons Ferry where the Palouse flows into the Snake. Since 1859, when Edward L. Massey put the first ferry in the water, there has been a ferry operating at this point on the Mullan Road. During most of the better than a century that the ferry has gone back and forth across the Snake, the Lyon family has been the owners. According to Captain Mullan's guide for travelers using his road, the ferry charged four dollars for wagons and fifty cents for each man. We found the cable-operated ferry ready to take our car across the river, just as in early days it had taken wagons across. Nearby engineers were building a huge steel and concrete bridge to take the place of the old ferry. The ferry operator plainly was against progress.

"Are you one of the grubby engineers from the bridge?" he demanded of young Guy.

A state park to preserve this historic site is to be established so that motorists using the new bridge may learn about the days when the Mullan Military Road was busy with traffic. Then it was still a laborious four-day wagon trip from the Snake River to Fort Walla Walla, but it was only a few hours drive for us. That night we camped in a park at Walla Walla. This is all that is left of the fort from which Captain Mullan set forth with pick and shovel and horse-drawn slip scrapers to build the road that was to become the artery of commerce and settlement between the headwaters of navigation on the Missouri and the Columbia.

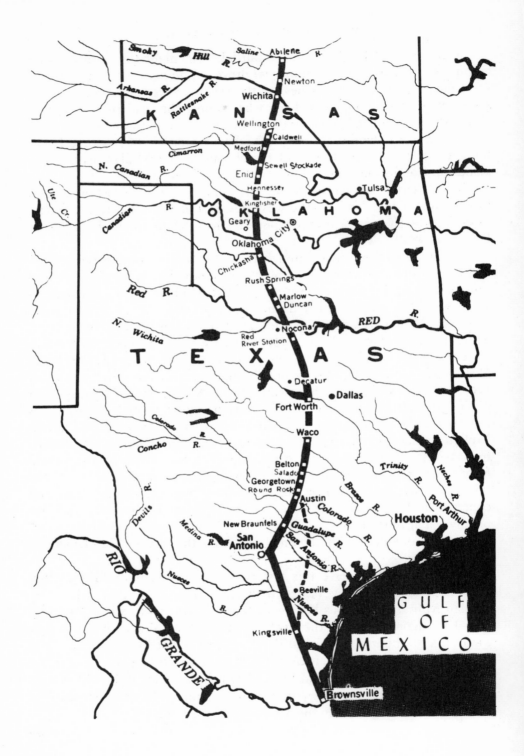

21

Chisholm Trail

●

> *I woke up one morning on the old Chisholm Trail,*
> *Rope in my hand and cow by the tail.*
> *Coma ti yi youpy, youpy ya, youpy ya,*
> *Coma ti yi youpy, youpy ya.*

Texas cowboys did not have good voices. They were hoarse from holler-ing at cattle and sleeping in the damp. They sang sad love songs, minstrel songs, and Methodist hymns, although the words they put to the tunes would have seared the ears of a preacher. They sang in the "Cowboy's Lament" of how a cowpoke was shot down in a gambling fight, and they sang of death beneath western stars in "Oh, Bury Me Not on the Lone Prairie," which was written on the banks of the Red River during a trail drive to Kansas. They sang to the cattle to keep them quiet as they rode their "night mares" along the perimeter of the herd. As long as men in camp could hear them singing, they knew that all was well, so it soothed them too.

> *Come along, boys, and listen to my tale;*
> *I'll tell you of my troubles on the old Chisholm Trail.*
> *Coma ti yi youpy, youpy ya, youpy ya,*
> *Coma ti yi youpy, youpy ya.*

There were troubles to tell about. The Chisholm Trail ran a wild and uproarious course from the coastal plains of Texas to railhead first at Abilene, then Newton, Wichita, and last of all Caldwell in Kansas. It was a trail of many surprises and dangers—of prairie fires, of thunderstorms

267

and hail large enough to kill cattle, and of cyclones, unseasonal blizzards, of rustlers and meat-hungry Indians, of angry farmers and hostile sheriffs, and above all, of stampedes.

One herd stampeded eighteen times on its way from Texas to Abilene. All it took was the cough of a horse, the snap of a branch beneath a boot, a hungry coyote sneaking up to the chuck wagon, a clap of thunder, a sudden burst of rain or once simply a shred of tobacco blown by a breeze from a cowpuncher's loosely rolled cigarette into a steer's eye, and the whole herd was up on its feet.

"One jump to their feet and the second jump to hell," a cowboy said, for it was hell with the herd plunging crazily into the night, frightened out of their bovine wits by the roar of their own galloping hoofs, blue and white static crackling on their plunging horns from the friction of their bodies, heedless of everything but terror. They ran until they fell exhausted or plunged over the brink of a ravine. One dark night in Texas, 2,700 crazed beasts stampeded over the sides of what ever since has been called Stampede Gulley and ended up a colossal tangle of bloody carcasses.

The only way to stop a stampede was to get ahead of the leaders and turn them until the herd ran in a circle, milling ever slower and slower until at last the fear was spent. But a cowboy racing the herd in the dark could be swept from the saddle to death beneath the frenzied hooves by a low-hanging tree limb, or thrown if his horse snapped a leg in a prairie hole. Let him go down and the herd swept over him. After all, stampeding cattle could smash a chuckwagon to bits and tear up a tree trunk as thick as a man. Teddy Blue Abbott, who rode up the trail with one of Print Olive's herds, used to tell what happened to one cowboy who got in the way of a stampede. Helen Huntington Smith quotes Teddy in her book *We Pointed Them North:*

We were camped close to the Blue River one night, near a big prairie dog town. And that night it come up an awful storm. It took all of us to hold the cattle and we didn't hold them, and when morning came there was one man missing. We went back to look for him, and we found him among the prairie dog holes, beside his horse. The horse's ribs was scraped bare of hide, and all the rest of horse and man was mashed into the ground as flat as a pancake. The only thing you could recognize was the handle of his six-shooter.

Most of the danger to a cowpoke came from the dark. Charlie Siringo wrote in his *A Texas Cowboy* that once when he was trailing cattle north to Kansas, his boss decided to equip his men with lanterns. Charlie wrote:

Mr. Stephens thought he would try a new scheme that trip up the trail, so he bought a lot of new bulls-eye lanterns to be used around the herd on dark stormy nights, so that each man could tell just where the other was stationed by the reflection of his light. This night in question being very dark and stormy, Stephens thought he would christen his new lamps. He gave me one, although I protested against such nonsense. About 10 o'clock some one suddenly flashed his bulls-eye towards the herd, and off they went, as though shot out of a gun.

It was several days before the cowboys could round the cattle up again.

Some Texans claim that the Chisholm Trail was named for Thornton Chisholm, DeWitt County rancher, who sent 1,800 Texas longhorns over the trail from Cardwell Flats, two miles east of today's Cuero, on April 1, 1866, but most historians believe that it was Jesse Chisholm who gave his name to the greatest of the cattle trails. Jesse was never a cowman, he never drove cattle over the trail, and he never saw the Texas stretches of it. He was an Indian trader, half Cherokee, and a man that the Indians said spoke "with a straight tongue."

In the spring of 1865 Jesse loaded up his wagons with trade goods at his post near present Wichita, Kansas, and headed southward to the Cimarron River, then southwest to the Washita River. In May, 1861, Black Beaver, a Delaware scout, had led the federal garrisons of Forts Cobb, Washita, and Arbuckle northward to safety at the start of the Civil War.

Eleven companies of troops and 150 women and children had left a plain trail on the prairie that Chisholm now followed. After that he used the trail regularly with wagonloads of trade goods. He often ransomed white captives from the Indians, and he also took these over his trail to safety. In July, 1867, Buffalo Bill Matthewson brought two boys whom he had rescued from the Comanches down Jesse's trail to Fort Arbuckle, where he turned them over to the post commander for return to their homes in Texas. Bill was surprised to meet Texas cowboys driving a herd of longhorns north and guided them over the trail as far as the North Canadian River, from where it was easy to follow Chisholm's wagon tracks.

At the end of the Civil War at least five million longhorns roamed wild on the Texas grasslands, and increased by over a million a year. Thousands were slaughtered for their hides and tallow, since there was no way to get the beef to market while at the same time cattle prices soared in the northern states. Joseph G. McCoy, an Illinois farmer turned Chicago cattle dealer, found the way.

In 1867, Abilene, Kansas, was twelve log cabins roofed with sod. There was so little traffic on the only street that a prairie dog town existed in the middle of it. Then McCoy came to town. He made a deal with the Hannibal and St. Joseph Railroad, bought land and built shipping pens, a frame hotel for cowboys, a livery stable, and a bank. He sent handbills to Texas, and dispatched a stockman riding south along Jesse Chisholm's trail to spread the word that he was ready with hard cash to buy cattle.

In the handbills Texans read that the Chisholm Trail was the trail for them. "It is more direct," McCoy had written. "It has more prairie, less timber, more small streams and fewer large ones, altogether better grass and fewer flies—no civilized Indian tax or wild Indian disturbances—than any other route yet driven over." These were sweeping claims for a man who had never been over a western trail in his life, but ranchers read them and set their hands to rounding up the wild cattle for the first trail drives that over the next thirteen years were to add up to the greatest migration of domestic animals in the world's history.

The best place to begin a journey over the route of the Chisholm Trail is at Brownsville on the Rio Grande border of Mexico. There the drovers bought or rustled Mexican cattle and rounded up the wild herds of the brush country and set out past the King Ranch to San Antonio. We drove U.S. 77 north from Brownsville over the vast plain, which seems little changed from trail days. One branch of the trail led past Beeville, through DeWitt County, home of the Texas Chisholms, and on to Gonzales and

The greatest migration of domestic animals in history took place over the Chisholm Trail, from the ranges of Texas to the railheads of Kansas.
Nebraska State Historical Society

Lockhart to Austin. Another branch led to San Antonio where herds from the west were collected.

In San Antonio cooks bought their supplies while the hands enjoyed the pleasures of the town's saloons and gambling halls. San Antonio was anything but effete in those days, but its citizens complained about the cowboys' behavior. They could understand the drinking, the gambling, the wenching, but when cowboys fastened one end of a rope to their pony's bridle and carried the other inside instead of neatly tying the pony to the hitching post outside, they objected. The rope in the store was something to trip over, and the practice had to cease.

Thornton Chisholm's drovers may have taken cattle over the Chisholm Trail in 1866, but they had to take them clear to St. Joseph, Missouri, to find a market. It was a Californian, Colonel O. W. Wheeler, who first took cattle over the trail from Texas to Abilene and to the new pens of Joseph McCoy. In August of 1867 he arrived in San Antonio, rich with Gold Rush money, which he had made by selling mining supplies and by buying steers in southern California and driving them north to the gold fields where they sold for high prices. Now he proposed to buy 2,400 steers and drive them north to Kansas and west to California. The herd was collected outside San Antonio and started north through the heat of late summer. Right on its tracks went several other herds collected by

271

Texans who, desperately seeking markets for their cattle, were willing to drive them to California or to hell if need be.

In the years that followed fourteen million cattle were driven over the Chisholm Trail, but there is little on the face of the earth to show that such a vast multitude of beasts ever passed this way. The Chisholm Trail was also later used by stages and freight wagons, and in a few places their ruts were pointed out to us as the old trail. Only one place in Oklahoma could we see where the elements, the growth of grass, and the plows of man have not destroyed all signs of the cattle.

The trail ran along the grasslands just east of the rugged Balcones Escarpment, which divides the picturesque hill country from the black-earthed plains. This is the route of Interstate 35 and U.S. 81 today, so we drove these roads across Texas. Where the trail passed the old German settlement of New Braunfels, we stopped off to lunch at Kermit Krause's restaurant. Trail drivers scarcely went hungry in New Braunfels, and we found Kermit Krause serving roast beef stew at 45 cents a bowl, and beef sandwiches at 15 cents if you go to the bar, twenty cents if you have the sandwich brought to your table. Krause is the great-grandson of Franz Coreth, an Austrian nobleman who came to the town in the 1850's and almost starved, and he has no intention whatsoever of going hungry or letting any of his guests go hungry, either. Most of his dishes would please a cowhand, but he also serves such things as tartar steak with caviar on rye bread. At the table, folks got to talking about the Chisholm Trail, and they urged us to go to Fisher's Store where drovers purchased supplies on the way.

"It's the only post office in the U.S. that sells beer," we were told. "In the 1870's an inspector came along and told old man Fisher that he could either quit selling beer or give up the post office. Fisher said he'd stick to the beer so the inspector had a beer on the house and went away and forgot about it."

The herds from south Texas came together at Austin, where they were driven through the Colorado River at a ford close to the modern bridge on U.S. 183 that skirts the state capital to the east. Once I drove Interstate 35 from Austin to Dallas to catch a plane. It rained steadily, and the highway seemed to run on interminably and monotonously through the immensity of Texas. This is what most people experience on Interstate 35. Yet just off the highway are old trail towns as fascinating as any communities in America. There is Round Rock, named for a huge rock in the floor of Brushy Creek where the cowboys forded their cattle. The St. Charles Hotel, built in 1850, gave a night's rest in bed to cattlemen whose drovers could be counted on to keep the herds quiet in their absence. There the outlaw Sam Bass and his gang, grown tired of robbing stage-coaches on the trail, tried their hands at bank robbery. An informer had tipped off the Texas Rangers, and on July 18, 1878, Bass was shot down in a gun battle. He died a few days later and is buried in Round Rock Cemetery.

The Chisholm Trail passed by Georgetown, where cotton grows luxuri-antly on the black, waxy soils, and Salado, where the guest register in what drovers knew as the Shady Villa Inn includes those of such diverse guests as Robert E. Lee, Ulysses S. Grant and Jesse James. We dined at the old hotel, which today is called the Stagecoach Inn. It was out in front of the inn on the eve of the Civil War that old Sam Houston, piqued at his fellow Texans for trying to take Texas out of the nation into which he had struggled so hard less than two decades before to bring it, stood up before an audience of rednecks and spoke for the Union.

"But General Sam," cried a frontiersman, "we could lick them Yan-kees with cornstalks."

"But," fired the old man back, "those Yankees won't agree to fight with cornstalks."

Across the street from the inn is the excellent Central Texas Area Museum, where we learned much about the old trail and the country through which it ran. Salado has many pioneer houses dating to trail days, including the Baines house, the home of Lyndon Baines Johnson's grandfather.

Belton, the next town down the trail, is colorful too. The first store-keeper in the town sold his wares right from his wagon, and the first saloon is supposed to have been a whiskey barrel and a tin cup. It was the home of the Sanctificationists, a pioneer band of women who de-serted their husbands' beds because their religion told them that sex was wrong, and of a sheriff who stopped drovers and demanded an illegal fee before he would let them pass down the trail. The sheriff stopped Eaton Cranfill's herds. Cranfill had no cash and persuaded the sheriff to accept a steer. When the sheriff agreed, Cranfill's son Jim roped a huge steer and tied him to a tree for the sheriff. He used a rope which he had weakened with his pocketknife. Before the Cranfills reached the Leon River, the steer was back in the herd. The Leon is now impounded in the Belton Reservoir.

The Chisholm Trail veered considerably west of U.S. 81 north of Bel-ton. We turned west on Texas Highway 36 to the little village of White-hall, where two boys showed us a pair of oak trees that bear the scorches of drovers' fires. Folks at Whitehall claim that the place was a favorite camping place on the Chisholm Trail. Here the trail boss would wave his hat about his head in a tired circle and then in the direction for the two men riding on each side of the herd to point the lead steers to their bed ground. He directed them to a spot where the grass was succulent, or, if it were a hot night, to a rise where the breeze would be cool. No timber should be close, for Indians or rustlers might lurk in it, and a nearby ravine might prove a cattle trap in case of a stampede.

The first of the three or four watches took over. The wrangler roped and dragged dry branches to the chuck wagon or gathered cow chips and sunflower stalks for the cook fire. He helped cooky unload the wagon and after dinner wash the dishes too. Everyone wanted to be on the good side of the man whose sourdough biscuits were proof of his skill, and whose coffee was called six-shooter coffee because it was deemed so strong that it would float a pistol. The men ate their fill of beans, called Pecos strawberries, potatoes, onions, steak, and often boggytop dessert, which was stewed fruit with a biscuit covering. Whiskey was forbidden in most trail outfits, so a man fortified himself against the night with a second cup of the potent coffee, made by boiling grounds for half an hour. If a stranger happened along he was invited to "light, unsaddle, and eat," for Texas ranch hospitality rode the trails with Texans.

Some cowboys read in the evening by the light of a hard-twist string stuck into a cup of tallow. Some read the stars, to which they gave their own trail names—The Diamond, Ellenrods, Job's Coffin, the Seven Stars, Midnight Triangle, and the Big Dipper. They told the hours of the night by the Dipper from the position of the stars in it. Jesse James Benton, who took to the trail as a boy of twelve, was taught a cowboy prayer:

> *Now I lay me down to sleep,*
> *While over me the gray-backs creep.*
> *If I die before I wake,*
> *I pray the Lord my soul to take.*

It the camp were a muddy one, cowboys lay down to sleep in a triangle, so that each man's head was on another's ankles. As the night hours slipped by, tired men on watch took chewing tobacco from their pouches, mixed it with saliva, and rubbed it on their eyelids to keep awake. Cattle might get up, lowing, then lie down again, or they might leap up and plunge away, bringing the herd to its feet in a stampede. The herd men rode around the cattle in opposite directions, stopping to talk when they

274

met. If a storm threatened or if the cattle were restless, all hands were put on guard. Let a cowpoke complain, and the boss would remark, "You can sleep all next winter."

On the prairies west of Waco, herds from the Matagorda Bay Country joined the main trail. The Brazos River seemed always in flood, and herds usually bedded down on the banks before crossing. They forded the river at Kimball Bend upriver from Waco where the river was less turbulent, but even so, the cattle often had to swim with only the tips of their noses and their great horns showing. When crossing a river, cowboys urged the cattle in. Once they reached a swimming depth, they usually headed for the opposite bank unless they were scared by driftwood or too fast a current. Then they might mill in what cowboys called a merry-go-round, until they either drowned or cowboys rode headlong among them and got them started for the far bank again. Let a rider be unhorsed among the struggling cattle, and he was in dire danger of beating hooves and tossing horns. Weighted down by his heavy boots, he grabbed the tail of a horse or steer to be pulled to shore. The chuckwagon was floated across the stream with or without benefit of a raft.

A day started with the cook's call of "Grub pile!" Men saddled up, and the drive began. First went the chuckwagon to find a good place to set up for the noon meal. Then came a young boy or a Mexican driving the horse herd. Then came the cattle. Nine or so men drifted the herd. Two riders on each side pointed the lead steers. Behind them the swing riders pressed on the flanks. Farther back came the tail riders keeping the lame and the balky cattle with the herd. At the tail of the herd, the dust, heat, and smell were the greatest, and a man had the best chance to learn new cusswords.

About noon the cattle began to graze, and the cook and boss located the noon camp about half a mile from the herd. Soon the flap-board on the chuckwagon was down and a cold lunch was being served. Men talked until the cattle lay down and began to chew their cuds. Then it was time to get moving again. Herds made six to ten miles in the morning, and perhaps more in the afternoon. Toward night the cattle got fractious. At the smell of water, they bellowed and quickened their pace to a fast shuffle. Arriving at a stream, the strong lead steers rushed in up to their flanks, drank, and wallowed. Rear cattle forced them farther out, sometimes into dangerous mud or quicksand or into deep water and a stiff current.

A trail cowboy was young, with hard muscles and steady nerves. He was handy with a lariat and the six-shooter, and he rode as few men before or since have ridden. His felt hat, broad-brimmed against the sun, his red bandanna pulled tight about his mouth to strain the dust from the air, and his chaps of goat or calfskin to keep the brush from tearing through his pants which in the early days of the Chisholm Trail were mostly Confederate grays—all were as practical as they were colorful. Colonel Bill Sterling of the Texas Rangers avers that the fancy boots worn by modern-day Texans are a recent addition.

"When those old boys went up the Chisholm Trail," he says, "they wore shoes, or, if they were lucky, they had a pair of old Confederate cavalry boots. German bootmakers came in during the '70s and developed the high-heeled cowboy boots. Those heels kept you from slipping right through the stirrups."

At Fort Worth the drovers bought spare saddles, new six-shooters, ropes, and grub. By early trail days Fort Worth was a frontier village with a store and a saloon built around an abandoned Mexican War camp, which was on a bluff on the south side of the confluence of the two branches of the Trinity River. The Chisholm Trail crossed the Trinity below the junction of the Clear Fork and the West Fork.

Today Fort Worth is as proud of its museums as it is of being the place "where the West begins." We were visiting Heritage Hall on downtown Main Street when we got in a conversation with a retired rancher. He was showing his grandson through the museum that tells the story of Fort Worth from its founding until the arrival of the first railroad in 1876.

"The Chisholm Trail brought a fortune in gold to Texas when we needed it most," he said, "but it spoiled the country."

"Why you can't even find the trail anymore, Grandpa," said the boy, "so how did it spoil the country?"

"Cattle coming down the trail ate the beans of mesquite trees. Their droppings spread the seeds farther north, and then still farther north. Once this was all rich grass—great for buffalo, wonderful black soil good for cotton—but the cattle spread the mesquite clear into Oklahoma. The trees started along the Chisholm Trail and fanned out, and they've spoiled the countryside."

Today the Trinity is a narrow ribbon of water between tree-lined banks, but it still flows over a broad plain as proof that it is not as tame as it appeared to us in early November. The Chisholm Trail ran north and a little west to follow approximately along the line dividing Wise and Denton counties. It passed well east of Decatur, which is on U.S. 81. This was the land of the Rev. George Webb Slaughter, rancher and circuit rider, who rode the Chisholm Trail preaching to cowboys with a six-shooter tucked in his belt in case of an Indian attack. The Rev. Mr. Slaughter, whose ranch was in hilly Palo Pinto County, was a very successful rancher, and his herds moved down the Chisholm Trail to market with the others.

This was also prairie country with long grass and easy streams to cross. Cowboys found the life easy in this generous country. Riding the herds at night, they sang their sad songs and watched the shooting stars come flashing down, and around the campfires they swapped yarns and scraped their fiddles. To a small boy growing up in Denton County the lean cowpunchers and the trail were irresistible. As young Jesse Benton lay in his bed at night he could hear the lonesome cowboy songs, drifting across the range. They sent chills up and down his back. As he got a bit older, his brother and he hunted for calves left in the wake of the herds. Calves dropped by cows on the trail were usually too weak to travel. The boys picked them up in a wagon and brought them back to their barn to raise.

"Most of them fellers was just young kids, two or three or four years older'n me," he recollected years later.

He was only twelve when he slipped out of the house one night and moseyed up to a campfire. The men accepted the boy, and in the morning he rode down the Chisholm Trail. He soon was initiated into the life of river crossings, dusty trails, heavy biscuits called stomach cheaters, and of a terrifying stampede with the steers rampaging, their horns popping and banging together. As the herd moved, the cowboys picked up stray cattle. They sat around at the noon stop figuring with a stick in the dirt how to mark out somebody's brand. Usually a herd had its own trail brand because there were cows from a number of ranches included in it. When much later in life Jesse Benton thought about it all, he did so with a mixture of nostalgia and wonder.

"Soaking wet from top to bottom, your boots plumb full of water and your toes squishing in it, and why us boys liked to be cowboys and could stand it, I can't say. I reckon it were the excitement," he wrote.

The trail came down off the prairies into the broken country along the Red River. Just below the mouth of the Fleetwood Branch Texas Rangers had established the Red River Station. The place is east of U.S. 81, so we had to drive to Nocona and then north on Texas 103 to reach the site. The station, now called Spanish Fort, was one store and one saloon in trail days, but it was the jumping off place for the drive across the Indian Territory.

277

At Red River Station inspectors checked brands on the cattle and often asked for a bribe. Once two men scrutinized thirteen herds and found two unbranded cows. They told the trail boss that he must pay $50. A quick signal to his men, and the inspectors were seized and their arms tied. The cowboys tossed them into the chuckwagon and carted them chuck-a-bump along the trail as far as Pond Creek. There they were set free to trudge back to the station.

The Red River was hazardous with quicksand and rushing currents. Its reputation sent many a shiver of apprehension up the backs of green hands as they approached it for the first time. Once a veteran trail driver named Tommy Newton rode ahead of the herd to scout the crossing. He found the river low, its sandbars dry in the sun. This didn't keep him from going back to his outfit and telling the rooky drivers that the river was on a hell-raising, boiling rampage.

"When we hit the bank, there'll be no time for taking off clothes and six-shooters," he cried. "You had better shuck now and put your stuff in the wagon. I'll go ahead with the wagon and cross it on a ferry boat above that bend."

The cowboys stripped except for their hats, undershirts, and drawers. While they grazed the cattle an hour longer to prepare them for the ordeal, Tommy drove ahead in the wagon. On the far bank of the river, he sent the cook on two or three miles ahead to make camp and ducked down out of sight to watch the fun. Soon the herd came rushing over the hill to the water with the almost naked men riding furiously about, keeping them in a manageable mass. When the cowboys saw the shallow waters and the serene currents, they swore darkly. J. Frank Dobie, who records the event in his *A Vaquero of the Brush Country*, reports that there were many sunburns in camp that night, but he doesn't tell what happened to Tommy Newton.

Some of the cowboys who drove the herds north were boys indeed, but there were few women and little children with the outfits. George Cluck, whose ranch was on Brushy Creek in Williamson County, did things his own way. He brought along Mrs. Cluck, and their three children, aged seven, five and two. She was also expecting another baby. A spyglass and a shotgun at her side, she rode in a hack pulled by two ponies. At the Red River, the hands floated the hack across by fastening cottonwood logs to its sides. Riders carried the children across, and Mrs. Cluck rode over mounted behind her husband.

In Indian Territory a band of rustlers stopped the outfit. There were sixteen cowboys, outnumbered, mostly young and scared, and there was Mrs. Cluck.

"If any one of you boys doesn't want to fight, come here and drive the hack and give me your gun," she barked.

"You won't get any of our cattle," shouted Cluck, who well knew his wife's mettle. "We have sixteen fighters as good as ever crossed the Red River. They were raised on rattlesnakes and wildcats and they're all crack shots."

The rustler leader looked at the men with a smile, but when he caught the woman's steely glare, he wheeled his horse and spurred off across the hills, his men behind him.

The Clucks were lucky. Other outfits had to pay a toll of beeves to rustlers, who often threw stones at the cattle to start a stampede. Sometimes horse thieves joined an outfit to learn the routine. Once in the Indian Territory it was a simple matter to desert with a good part of the horse herd.

The Indians also demanded beeves as a toll for crossing their territory, and started a stampede if steers weren't cut out of the herd and presented to them. A Comanche brave could shoot an arrow clear through a steer. When the animal dropped, they ate the flesh raw to satisfy their craving for meat.

Not all encounters with the Indians went badly. Once an old Kiowa chief and his warriors halted an outfit and demanded six beeves.

"I'll give you two, but not six," replied the trail boss.

"Two not enough. You give me six or I'll come with my young braves tonight and stampede your cattle."

"Well, when you come tonight, be sure to bring a spade."

"Why spade?"

"Well, the cook broke the handle of our spade yesterday. When you come to stampede the cattle, I aim to kill you. Unless you bring a spade, we can't bury you."

The chief decided that two cattle were sufficient.

Across Oklahoma U.S. 81 closely follows the Chisholm Trail. The trail snaked up from the river past Fleetwood Store and bent around a big woods of blackjack oak called Blue Grove. The old Reid Store and the Suggs Camp Grounds on the trail were east of today's Sugden. A dirt road leading east from Addington runs across the rolling prairie past Monument Hill, a flat-top mesa covered with reddish sandstone boulders that the cowboys heaped into two piles three hundred feet apart. With their knives and spurs, the men scratched their initials and brands on the rocks. The trail passed to the west of Monument Hill.

The Old Duncan Store was on the trail east of today's oil town of Duncan. Beyond Duncan the trail swings more to the west so that at Marlow it coincides closely with the pavement of U.S. 81. Marlow is named for the Marlow brothers, who lived in a dugout on the brushy banks of Wildhorse Creek. In the middle of the night they often crept from their dugout to raid the herds. They drove the longhorns to a stretch of timber, a dozen miles east of the trail, about where the Chisholm Trail Lake is today. In a day or two they drove the cattle back to the outfit, saying they had found them straying on the prairie or had rescued them from rustlers. They were given handsome rewards as public benefactors. Then one outfit caught them rustling their cattle and handed them a rustler's bitter end.

A little farther north the popular trail camping ground at Rush Springs is now in the Municipal Park of the town of Rush Springs. The spring still bubbles. East of Chickasha is the Rock Crossing of the Washita. Along the river the grass grew rank and luxuriant, and the cattle lingered in the meadows until the cowboys, whooping and hollering, drove them on north along the trail.

From Chickasha, Oklahoma 92, following each turn of the Chisholm Trail, runs north through Amber to Tuttle, site of the Silver Creek trading post. There is no way to drive on north to the Bond Crossing of the Canadian River, respected by trail drivers for its sweeping current. At the river the trail divided. The west branch, which was favored by stagecoaches and many of the herds, ran northwest through El Reno and north along today's U.S. 81 to Dover. The east branch reached Dover by way of present-day Yukon.

On the banks of the North Canadian River Jesse Chisholm built a home for his family at Council Grove. Indians came there often to trade and take counsel with Jesse. It was during a council that Jesse ate liberally of bear's grease that had been melted in a brass kettle. Whether it was through poisoning picked up from the brass or ptomaine is uncertain, but Jesse fell ill and died. The date was March 4, 1868, and Jesse never knew that the great cattle trail that ran where his trading wagons had led would be named for him. His friends held a wake at his grave. They drank a barrel of whiskey and fired thunderous salutes with their guns. Today Jesse's grave is close to the river about six miles north of Geary.

By 1889, at the time of the Land Run, the track of the Chisholm Trail near Kingfisher was overgrown with grass. Men rushing in wagons and buggies to take up homesteads plunged into the trail without warning. It was so deep that vehicles were wrecked and horses' legs broken.

Dover, just beyond the Cimarron Crossing, was the site of Red Fork Ranch where freighters changed teams. It was on a hot August day in 1866 that Colonel Wheeler swam his herd across the Cimarron River and came upon Jesse Chisholm's wagon road. He turned his lead steers into the road, expecting it to peter out after only a few miles. To his surprise it ran on mile after mile, clear out of Indian Territory into Kansas and finally to an Indian village on the Arkansas River, called Wichita.

Hennessey, also on U.S. 81, is a town proud to be named for a freighter on the Chisholm Trail.

"It was right out here at Bullfoot Springs that Pat Hennessey met his end," explained a housewife. "He was a freighter—had a two-wagon outfit—and he was heading down the trail to Fort Sill with a load of oats for the cavalry. In those days freighters took the Chisholm Trail to Dover and the trail which branched off from there direct to Fort Sill. Got right outside town here when the Indians attacked. Pat got killed and his wagons got burned. There was a stage station here too, but it got burned the day that Pat got killed."

Pat's grave is a block off the highway in Hennessey.

From Dover to Enid the trail and the highway are one, but at Enid the trail angles off northeastward through what is now Kremlin to the crossing of the Salt Fork of the Arkansas at Pond Creek. In the early 1870's a man named Sewell built a stockade about a mile south of today's Jefferson. The Osage Indians had become troublesome. War between the tribes had almost ceased, and scalps to accompany a warrior to the Happy Hunting Ground (as was the Osage custom) were in short supply. A premium was placed on the blonde pates of Texas cowboys, and drovers died so that their hair could accompany a brave to his grave. A Negro's scalp was not considered as worthy of the honor, and some outfits hired black cowboys because they were less likely to be killed. The Osage war trail crossed the Salt Fork near the Chisholm Trail, and cowboys in the area thought a great deal of their scalps. Often they sheltered in Sewell's Stockade.

The trail ran east of Medford and passed out of the Indian Territory to Caldwell, the first town in Kansas and the last of the cow towns at the end of the Chisholm Trail. Abilene, the first terminus of the Chisholm Trail, yielded to Newton, farther south in the summer of 1871 when the Atchison, Topeka, and Santa Fe tracks got that far. Wichita took Newton's place in the spring of 1872 when a spur was built there from Newton, and the rails in turn made Caldwell trail's end in 1880.

Caldwell was as riproaring as its predecessors until John Henry Brown became marshal. He quieted things down to such an extent that appreciative citizens gave him a gold-mounted Winchester. Today Caldwell is perhaps too quiet, for unlike the other Kansas cow towns, it never regained its prosperity when the cattle herds ceased to come.

In the days before Caldwell became trail's end, cowboys drove the herds northeast past today's Wellington to Wichita, now the state's largest city. In 1872 Wichita and Ellsworth were the great cattle shipping points. Yet only a few years before, Wichita had been a village of Indian huts on the banks of the Arkansas, where Jesse Chisholm established his trading post. When the boom hit Wichita, carpenters couldn't keep up with the demands for houses, stores, saloons, and hotels. When the jerrybuilt hotels filled up, the cowboys slept in the Blue Front store which had a supply of blankets and buffalo robes.

John Beard, known as Wichita Red Beard, opened a dance hall and saloon beside Rowdy Joe's saloon. With his shotgun tucked between his knees, he watched the dancers. On the last day of the shipping season, he held a huge drunken bash. In the course of it he marched next door to Rowdy Joe's and took a pot shot at Annie Franklin, one of Joe's belles. Bill Anderson fired a shotgun blast in retribution, and Wichita's Boot Hill had a new citizen. It was a brawling town, which today's Wichita tries to bring back with its Cow Town collection of old buildings. Girl Scouts showed us through Cow Town. We drank sarsaparilla in an old saloon as the girls told us innocuous little details about life in a town that was far from innocuous.

Newton is farther north on U.S. 81. In 1871 when the Santa Fe Railroad reached the area, the town sprang up around stockyards and cattle chutes. Twenty-seven saloons, eight gambling halls, and a redlight district called Hide Park because the girls showed so much of their hide distinguished the town by the end of the first season. By mid-August there were two thousand cowboys and cattle buyers in town, and the click of chips, the bawling of singers, and the blare of brass bands never stopped.

Kansas 15 leads on north to Abilene, the original town at the payday and whiskey end of the Chisholm Trail. Wheeler, driving his first herd of cattle north, stopped on the prairies south of Abilene because he received bad news. Cheyennes and Apaches were on the warpath to the west, making his plan to drive the herd overland to California precarious. Cholera was riding the western trails. Should he winter on the plains of

Wichita's Cow Town is an authentic restoration of the riproaring
end of the trail for drovers and their herds from Texas.
Ozark Frontier Trail Photo

Kansas, slaughter the cattle, or attempt to drive them back south to
Texas? He was puzzling over his dilemma when two horsemen galloped
over the prairie from the north. They handed him handbills, proudly
announcing "Joseph G. McCoy, Cattle Dealer, Abilene." Wheeler
pointed his lead steers toward Abilene, and the Texas outfits behind him
on the trail followed where he led.

Abilene had sprung up beside the railroad tracks. There were cabins, a
drovers' hotel, a new cattle depot with barns, pens, and loading chutes, a
ten-ton scale to weigh the cattle, and a man named Joseph G. McCoy in a
shack office with gold coins ready to do business. When on September 5,
1867, the first trainload of twenty cattle cars rolled out of Abilene bound
for Chicago's stockyards, Wheeler's steers were among them. The Chisholm Trail was complete.

Yet only thirteen years later a cowboy could not drive his cattle north
of Caldwell without encountering barbed wire and angry farmers with
guns leveled in his direction. The days of the Chisholm Trail were
brought to an end by barbed wire and quarantine laws. The cowboys in
the last years of the trail mournfully added a pair of concluding verses
to their ballad:

> Good-by, old trail boss, I wish you no harm.
> I'm quittin' this business to go on the farm.
> I'll sell my old saddle and buy me a plow;
> And never, no, never will I rope another cow.
> Coma ti yi youpy, youpy ya, youpy ya,
> Coma ti yi youpy, youpy ya.

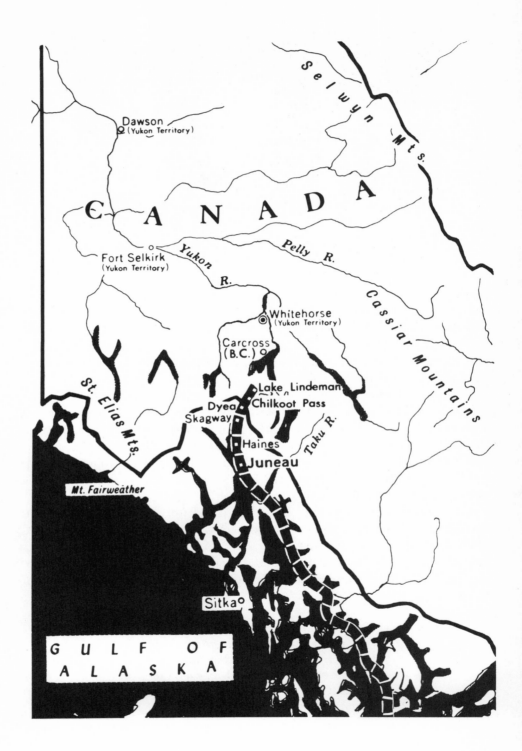

22

Chilkoot Trail

●

Hikers are warned not to camp at the summit of Alaska's Chilkoot Pass, because even in July unseasonal blizzards can howl down from the surrounding peaks. My five Boy Scouts, a troop committeeman, Bob Spinks, and I were exhausted after the last five miles' hard scrabble up the tumble of house-sized rocks that caps the pass, and we had no heart to go farther. It was past midnight but in the "Land of the Midnight Sun" we could still make out the faint trace of the Chilkoot Trail of the Gold Rush of '98 which we were following from the ghost town of Dyea on Taiya Inlet to Lake Lindeman on the Canadian side of the mountains.

Just over the summit we found a natural refuge sheltered by rocks from the wind. The summer sun stabbing fitfully through the persistent fogs that cloak the pass had melted the snow and revealed a carpet of lichen upon which we stretched out our ground covers and our sleeping bags. We spread aluminized space blankets over us to keep the night moisture out and our body heat in. Tired but elated because we were a day ahead of schedule, we fell asleep quickly.

In only a few hours I awoke to an overwhelming nausea. Slipping from my sleeping bag, I hurried up into the rocks away from the camp until the attack had spent itself. When I returned to my bag, I shook with a violent chill. Waves of nausea rode over me, followed by an even more severe fit of shivering. This was no mere touch of camp stomach. We were using dehydrated foods because of their light weight, and the scouts were clean and careful in their cooking. There seemed little chance for contamination. Yet I felt certain that I was suffering from food poisoning. All night I expected Bob or one of the scouts to become sick, but no one did. Whatever was wrong with me was mine alone. For three days I was not going to be able to keep down either food or water, and it would be seven days before my stomach, raw from retching, would retain solids.

When a scoutmaster teaches his boys such scouting skills as first aid, how to use a map and compass, or mountain hiking, he scarcely thinks that they may have to use them to rescue him, but before I was to get safely out of the wilderness, the scouts sleeping peacefully at my side were going to have to call on all their training and ingenuity. Each one of them was to take a long stride toward manhood. I was to learn what it must have been like during the days of the gold stampede to be sick and weary on the Chilkoot Trail.

In 1898 Canadian Mounties counted more than 60,000 stampeders crossing the summit of Chilkoot Pass, but today only a few hardy hikers make it over the trail in a year. When I decided to hike the Chilkoot Trail, the patrol leaders council, which runs our boy-led troop in Arlington Heights, a Chicago suburb, voted to send a patrol of our strongest mountain hikers with me. The junior high school age boys, Bob Spinks, and I planned to live in the open out of the packs on our backs, to hike where the Gold Rushers had gone, relive their dramatic history, and find artifacts.

It was July before we completed our training and our preparations. We traveled by rail coach from Chicago to Prince Rupert, British Columbia, where we took the Alaska Ferry for 490 miles up the inside passage to Skagway. On the boat we stowed our packs along one wall of the passenger lounge, ate our meals at the snack counter, slept in sleeping bags on the floor, and as long as daylight lasted roamed the decks. The boys darted to port to watch the gray bulk of a whale surface and blow or a fishing vessel chug past, and darted to starboard to watch porpoises play or a small iceberg drift by. The mists swirled over the waters, first hiding and then revealing the mountains and forests that reach down to the narrow passages through which the ferry, its radar cycling cautiously, made its way.

It was through these waters in July of 1897 that the dowdy little steamship *Excelsior* sailed on its way to San Francisco. Aboard were a score of miners loaded down with bags of gold, a thousand pounds in all worth from $500,000 to $750,000. When Tom Lippy, a YMCA physical education instructor from Seattle turned prospector, staggered down the gangplank with a suitcase holding more than two hundred pounds of nuggets and dust from the Klondike worth $54,400 the crowds on the dock went wild.

Press wires hummed the news of the Klondike strike across the nation. The reports told of a second, even richer gold ship heading for Seattle. The next day when the steamship *Portland* slipped up to Schwabacher's Dock in that city, five thousands people were waiting. Even so, the crowd could scarcely believe the story that there was a ton of gold aboard the ship. When it turned out that there was not one ton, but two, gold rush fever swept over the city.

Gold fever! Gold! Nils Anderson, a penniless lumberjack, had borrowed $300 to go north to look for gold. Now he came ashore with $112,500 worth of gold. Another Scandinavian hurried from the boat to the express office carrying a canvas sack.

"I tank I have twenty thousand five hundred dollars," he told the clerk.

The clerk weighed the gold on the scales and advised him that he was wrong. He had $42,000.

Up north of Seattle in Anacortes, the wife of Seattle bookseller William Stanley was waiting his return from the north. She took in washing and picked blackberries to keep alive. Her husband came down the gangplank toting $90,000 in god.

Within three hours of the docking of the *Portland* Seattle's waterfront was jammed with would-be prospectors all seeking passage north. This was just the first wave of the stampede that was to draw men from all over North America and from across the sea. The last great gold rush was under way.

Seattle was the favorite port of embarkation for the north. Men crowded aboard any old tub that would float and slept jammed together on the decks as the craft crept up the Inside Passage to Dyea, where the Chilkoot Trail began, or to Skagway, at the start of the White Pass Trail. The offshore islands screened the passage from the Pacific storms or most of the ancient ships never would have made the voyage safely. Even so, ships went aground in the fog and broke up. Some capsized as they tried to cross less sheltered straits, and some simply disappeared without a trace. This in waters where our seagoing ferryboat sailed with only the tremor of its engines to betray our movement.

Past great rivers of ice reaching down to deep fjords we sailed to Skagway. Dyea, roistering city of tents and shacks housing 20,000 men, is dead, and today's boats dock at its old rival Skagway, where in an evening rainstorm we went ashore. A round-faced young man loaded us into a mini-bus, and we twisted over a roller-coaster road to where Dyea once was.

The tideflats at Dyea were deserted and lonely again as they were when John J. Healy, a onetime Montana sheriff, came ashore to establish a trading post. To this post in March, 1887, an Indian brought a half frozen prospector named George Williams on a sled. They came from the Yukon on the trail that led over the Chilkoot Pass. In the pass a blizzard struck. Their sled dogs died in the cold, and they only survived by digging a cave in the snow with their hands and huddling in it. Frostbite blackened their faces, fingers, and feet. Their only food was mouthfuls of dry flour. When this ran out, the Indian took Williams on his back and lurched down the trail to Sheep Camp, where a few prospectors were waiting for the spring to start the trek over the pass. The prospectors revived Williams with hot soup. Then the Indian borrowed a sled and took him down the icy slopes to Dyea.

Williams lived for two days and then died. When the men in the store wanted to know why the dead man had crossed the pass in the winter, the Indian dug his hand into a sack of beans on the counter.

"Gold!" he cried. "All same like this."

He flung a handful of beans on the floor. Gold fever! Gold!

After Williams' cruel experience, few men, gold-hungry as they might be, were willing to attempt the Chilkoot Trail in the winter. When in the winter of 1893 four miners from the Yukon tried to cross the pass, one died, and another was crippled for life. They abandoned $14,000 in gold dust in their weakened condition because it was too heavy to carry over the trail. But then came the frenzy of 1898, and by the thousands men started up over the snowbound pass.

Before the Klondikers, as they romantically liked to be called, could climb the trail, they had to first land their supplies and gear. There were no docks, and belongings were brought ashore from the ships on scows. Old and spavined horses were swung over the side in slings and dropped into the water to swim ashore. Bales of hay and lumber were floated ashore. There on the flats by the inlet were piled stacks of food and blankets, casks marked medicine but which contained whiskey, picks, shovels, and all the paraphernalia that the Klondikers rightly or wrongly believed that they would need.

On most ships the passengers elected a beach commander to supervise the unloading. They drew lots to decide whose things went ashore first. Until all the cargo was ashore, nobody was supposed to take his things from the beach. But when the tidal bore began to rush up the inlet, men wrestled their belongings to higher ground, forgetting their companions whose goods still bobbed up and down in the scows. Teamsters charged $20 an hour when the tide was running out and $50 when the tide was coming in. Beach commanders waved their six-shooters to keep order, but there was no order. When all was ashore, the scows themselves were broken up, and their lumber used to fashion more ramshackle gambling houses, saloons, and hotels along the muddy track that was called Trail Street. In such tumbledown restaurants as Delmonico's, a man could get a meal of bacon, beans, bread, coffee, and dried fruit, which the Gold Rushers called petrified fruit, for $1.50. For another 50 cents he could buy a drink.

In Dyea at the foot of the snowy mountains the Gold Rushers gathered. There was the Seattle barber who had rushed away leaving a customer half shaven in his chair; there were doctors who had deserted their patients, ministers their congregations, and a party of gamblers who had held a meeting in a Chicago saloon and decided to gamble their very lives on striking it rich in the gold fields. There was a newsboy who climbed the pass with old newspapers to sell, another man with grindstones to sharpen picks, and another with 10,000 bottles of mosquito lotion. There was Charlie Meadows, who carried a portable bar to dispense whiskey at 25 cents a peg. From time to time he shot the spots off a playing card at 30 feet with his pistol, a trick he'd learned in the Buffalo Bill Wild West show. There also was Frank Novak, who had murdered a man back home in Iowa and cremated his corpse so that he could pass it off as his own in an effort to collect insurance money. Hot on his trail came C. C. Perrin of Thiel's Detective Service in Chicago. There were thieves and villains and many honest men fevered with gold. They all, sooner or later, started up over the trail.

Today roses ramble about a solitary decrepit house that is all that remains of Dyea. We hiked past it in the rain and on up the trail where we hoped to find shelter in a deserted lumber camp that was marked on our maps. With our hooded ponchos thrown over our heads and packs, we looked like gnomes stalking through the gloom. At first the trail wound along the banks of the Taiya River through a dense forest of Kenai birches and lodgepole pines. Huge ferns brushed against us. Mosquitoes buzzed, and a plague of large toads hopped across our path. The river was overflowing with the run-off from melting snow and ice in the pass above us, and in places the chilling water gurgled calf-deep over the trail itself. We sloshed through the mud, scrambled over rocks, and teetered over frothing tributaries on logs. At first the boys talked and joked as they went, but when the trail started to make the first steep climb of two thousand feet in a mile, they fell silent.

Our blond-thatched senior patrol leader, fourteen-year-old Guy Spinks, led the patrol. Lithe and sure-footed, Guy clambered over the slippery rocks, pausing every hundred feet or so to glance back at the others to be sure that they were climbing safely. Usually a scoutmaster tags along at the end of a scout group on the trail, but because we were in potentially dangerous country, I followed behind Guy so as to give him any urgent advice that might be necessary. After me came Johnny Hoffnagle, fourteen, our map and compass man, and my son, Jim, thirteen, both wiry hikers, Mark Rinella, fourteen, as dark-haired as Guy is light, and as cheerful and poised stepping from rock to rock to cross a rushing mountain stream as he would be leaning on a girl's locker at school. Then there was good-humored Dale Riechers, also thirteen, deliberate in everything from tying a shoelace to climbing over a rock slide, and Bob Spinks, a man of steadfast good nature.

Without warning Guy pitched forward onto his hands and knees in a swirl of water. Doodlebuglike beneath his heavy pack, he could not get to his feet until I looped my arms around his waist and gave him a violent tug. The rain turned to a torrent, then a drizzle. When at last about 1:30 A.M. we reached the logging camp, it was a torrent again. We stretched out our ground covers and sleeping bags in the dusty dilapidation of a ruined cabin and what had been a sauna. Rain dripped through the sagging roofs, but our space blankets kept us dry.

Somehow the Klondikers managed to pack seventy-five to one hundred pounds of gear up the trail over which we had hiked. Even horses made the climb. Small logs thrown down to corduroy the muddiest places so that the horses could pass still gave us sure footing. In between were mud wallows in which horses became mired. Old Ben Card, remembering his trip over the trail as a youth, recalled coming upon a horse sunk in the mud up to his neck. There was nothing to do but end the animal's misery with a bullet from his thirty-eight.

In the morning we set off after a hastily cooked breakfast through a downpour which turned to mist and at last to dim sunlight. We hiked along first an old logging road and then a footpath, well marked and easy to follow. In places we walked on more rotting corduroy.

It was only two miles to Finnegan's Point, named for Pat Finnegan and his two muscular sons, who built a corduroy bridge over the river and charged two dollars per horse for its use. When the Klondikers brushed the Finnegans aside and used the bridge without paying a toll, Pat and his sons opened a bar. A blacksmith set up a shop, and while a man waited for his horse to be shod, he could sample Finnegan's whiskey. A brace of Seattle sisters pitched a tent and offered beans and bacon, bread and butter, dried peaches and coffee for 75 cents.

After Finnegan's Point, Gold Rushers agreed that hell began. The branches of spruce, hemlock, and cottonwood clawed at the packers as they clambered over prodigious piles of boulders or wallowed in a quagmire at the bottom of Dyea Canyon. This redoubtable cut in the mountain is only about fifty feet wide, and packers alternately had to share its bottom with the river and climb precipitous slopes along the canyon wall.

As we moved up the canyon, hanging glaciers and snowfields loomed in the pass above us, and the streams we crossed on logs or on rough bridges maintained by the state of Alaska ran gray-green with glacial silt. We cooked our noon meal at what was left of Canyon City, once an important camping spot with a dozen houses. No buildings are left, but the site is cluttered with rusted tin cans, broken glass and china.

We followed the trail on up the east bank of the river to where it emerged from the gloom of the canyon at Pleasant Camp. By that night we were within smoke-smelling distance of the comfortable cabin kept up by the state at Sheep Camp. Floodwaters had washed out the last

In the winter of 1898 gold-rushers labored antlike up the 1200 steps cut in the snow and ice of the Scales, close to the summit of Chilkoot Pass.
Courtesy of Guy Spinks

few bridges below Sheep Camp, and we were slowed by the need to scout out safe log and rock crossings at each mountain torrent we came upon. Above Sheep Camp there never have been bridges, so we knew as we approached the cabin that we were getting a foretaste of what the next few days' hikes had in store. The cabin was also the last on the trail.

Two young couples from Juneau, Alaska, were already at Sheep Camp. They had set out on the trail two days before and had been turned back by an impenetrable fog in the pass. A snow and rock slide had smashed past them out of the mist, and they had retreated to Sheep Camp. One of the men showed us the tear in his pants where a flying rock had bruised him.

"The rivers on the Canadian side of the pass are all in flood," one man told us. "We're going back to Skagway, and we don't think you can get through either."

The Alaskans stared in wonder at the boys, tired but methodically going about their camp chores. Jim and John built the fire in a days-of-'98 stove while Mark and Dale prepared the food for cooking once the fire was ready. Afterward Jim and John would clean the cook kit. It was Guy's task not only to lead the hike but to set up the camp, bring water, and dig what sanitary facilities were needed. Bob and I, remembering Baden-Powell's admonition that "scouting is for boys," almost always kept our hands off the jobs to be done. The boys, because of their skill, spirit, and energy, were a happy contrast to the Klondikers who in the days of '98 had waited at Sheep Camp for conditions to improve at the summit enough to let them get over.

Beside the frothing waters of the river hunters camped before the Gold Rush days and searched the fog-shrouded peaks for mountain sheep. The summit of Chilkoot Pass is only four miles away but it is still another 3,500 feet up. In the winter of 1897-98 the Klondikers gathered at Sheep Camp and looked apprehensively up the mountain where a vast hanging glacier and dangerous snowfields waited. Thomas Moore in his manuscript, "Grubstake," reports that in 1898 his companions and he found "quite a camp of 20 or 30 buildings made of logs or rough boards."

Among the buildings was the Seattle Hotel, which Ben Card's parents had fashioned out of a twelve by fourteen tent stretched over a framework of logs. Later in life he told Professor Dow V. Baxter of the University of Michigan:

We covered the ground with poles and when we got time to whipsaw some lumber, we floored them over. At seventeen, I got me a horse: did some packing and kept our restaurant going by buying food from licked stampeders. Before leaving the hotel of a morning, I'd take a hundred, maybe two hundred dollars from our valise. Then I'd keep an eye open for the not-too-hard-to-find, discouraged and often sick newcomer who wanted to sell his outfit before turning his back on the north.

The day would begin early. Dad would roll out of bed about three in the morning, get the fire going and the mush water on. Then Mother would get up and start breakfast. When Dad flipped the tent flaps back, Sheep Camp knew that our restaurant was open for business.

Our rooming accommodation consisted of bunks three tiers high. Each bunk was provided with straw and one blanket. We charged a dollar for each bunk. When these were filled, latecomers would pay a dollar, furnish their own blanket and sleep on the floor—but out of the weather.

One night a man arrived late at the Seattle Hotel.

"Our Seattle Hotel bunks were filled," Ben Card remembered, "and all floor space was taken by paying stampeders. Man—there wasn't any room to walk. Then a preacher showed up; he said he was a preacher and he said he was sick. Mother's heartstrings were tugged, so finally she told him to crawl in my bunk. When I crawled out the next morning, Man— I wasn't fit to pack. Mother diagnosed my ailment and Holy Smokes! It was lice!"

" 'You got us clean people lousy. Get out, you lousy preacher,' cried Mother Card, 'and make sure you don't come back.' "

Mother Card kept a loaded thirty-eight in her bed as protection against other kinds of undesirable visitors.

The town was a hodgepodge of humanity. Maoris from New Zealand erected wattle huts, and a Boston doctor set up his patented aluminum shelter. The wattle huts proved serviceable, but a crust of ice formed on the ceiling of the doctor's shelter and melted whenever he lit a fire. Starving horses, deserted by their owners, wandered through the town. They crashed into tents in the winter dark and stumbled over the guy-lines. Angered Klondikers rounded the hapless animals up and shot them. The bodies were soon hidden by the snow that fell day and night, and sometimes for weeks at a time. A newcomer to Sheep Camp drove his tent pole seven feet through the snow before he could find ground. In the spring he found that the "ground" was a dead horse.

While most of the men on the trail were looking for gold, there were others who were looking for the man who had found gold. Soapy Smith, king of Skagway's gangs, sent con men up the trail. There were also gamblers such as Wilson Mizner, who later became a Broadway play-wright and the owner of the Hollywood Derby.

At Sheep Camp theft was the darkest crime of all. On February 15, 1898, three men, Wellington, Dean, and Hansen, went on trial before a miners' court in a tent saloon for stealing a sled. Dean was freed because he had only recently joined the others, but Wellington was found guilty. At the sentence he broke away from the men holding him, slashed a hole through the tent wall with his knife, and ran off down the trail firing his pistol over his shoulder at his pursuers. When his pursuers closed in on him, he shot himself in the face and fell dead into the arms of Mizner's brother Addison, who in the 1920s became the favorite architect of the land boom in faraway Florida.

The miners returned to the tent and sentenced Hansen to fifty lashes. Stripped to the waist and tied to a post, he was whipped unmercifully with a knotted thong that raised purple welts on his back with each blow.

"More!" cried half the crowd.

"Enough!" cried the other half.

At the fifteenth blow, the Mizners cut him loose. He was given a meal to eat and sent hiking off down the trail, calmly smoking his pipe and wearing a sign on his back on which a miner had scribbled "Thief!" The camp saw him out of sight and then dug a grave for Wellington. As the hapless man was dropped into the snow, a miner who had been a minister at home pointed a moral, "He that maketh haste to be rich shall not be unpunished." Then all present hastened off on their pursuit of gold.

Sheep Camp was as far as the horses could go, for the trail above that point was so rugged and steep that a man could scarcely make it. To keep miners from starving in the frozen Yukon, the Canadian government required that each Klondiker bring sixteen hundred pounds of supplies with him when he crossed the border at the summit. This meant an almost interminable series of back packs for each man up to the summit and then back to his cache at Sheep Camp for another load.

Most Klondikers toted their own packs, but many hired Chilkoot Indian porters. At first the Chilkoots charged twelve cents a pound to carry loads over the pass to the upper end of Lake Lindeman. Periodically they struck on the trail for higher wages until they were receiving 38 cents a pound with higher charges for such things as lumber, stoves, trunks, and even pianos, which were actually carted over the trail to the dance halls of the Yukon. At last the Indians were earning $1 a pound for the crossing.

The Chilkoots, with their mustaches and Mongolian faces, had long controlled the pass into the interior. For a generation they kept both other Indians and whites from using the pass, but when a U.S. gunboat sailed into Dyea Inlet and fired blanks from a Gatling gun in the direction of Chief Hole-in-the-Face, who was threatening some twenty miners on the shore, the Chilkoots decided to open their pass to traffic—at a price.

On a diet of dried salmon, the Indians could pack two hundred pounds at a time. Even their women and children could carry what they called a "white man's burden" of seventy-five pounds, and the Chilkoots earned more money out of the Gold Rush than most of the miners did. They would have earned even more except that they were strict Presbyterians and refused to pack on Sundays. The Indians demanded their pay in silver, too, after one man paid off his porters with Confederate bills.

Sheep Camp was the last place that wood was available on the trail, and in the morning we cooked a good breakfast before we got under way. The morning sparkled with sunlight, and we felt confident we could make the summit. After our friends of the night started back down the trail toward the coast, we moved out of camp. Along the trail we found blueberries growing profusely and spotted rusted pots and pans discarded long ago by the heavily burdened Gold Rushers. We stopped to rest at Stone House, a mile above Sheep Camp. According to William Haskell it was "so called because nature seems to have arranged the rocks here with more symmetry than usual, which is saying very little." There beneath an overhanging boulder was one of the two rest stops that miners could safely make along the trail above Sheep Camp.

Once a huge glacier glowered over the pass above Stone House. Harry de Windt, the British explorer who crossed the pass in the mid-1890s, noted that "a child's touch would send it crashing into the valley below." During the summer of 1897 rains and melting ice built a lake in the heart of the glacier. Then in September autumn winds tore a half-acre chunk of ice loose so that a twenty-foot wall of water was loosed on the pass. It smashed forty tents at Stone House, and flung the great boulder a quarter of a mile down the pass. It also wiped out a gambling casino at the spot and rushed away with Arizona Charlie Meadow's portable bar and all his liquor supply. Amazingly, only three men died in the flood.

Not far above Stone House we crossed the first big snowfield. The boys stopped to pack snowballs, but as snowfield followed snowfield, some hundred feet thick, they forgot about snowballs and paid sharp attention to their senior patrol leader, who was leading them on the safest

295

Boy Scouts of Troop 333, Arlington Heights, Illinois, and the author backpack over the rocky trail on their way to the summit.

Photo by Robert Spinks

course. Guy carefully avoided the edges of snowbanks or rocks sticking up through the surface, because he knew that in those places the crust would be soft and that a hiker could break through the surface and fall dozens of feet to serious injury or death. He picked a safe way through jumbled piles of broken boulders called talus and over the dangerous rolling gravel called scree. He made certain that no hiker climbed beneath or behind the hiker ahead of him.

We paused to prepare a quick, energy-producing lunch at the Scales, from which an almost insurmountable steep slope of scree led to the summit. In the winter of 1898 Gold Rushers labored antlike up the 1,200 steps cut in the snow and ice on this slope. To many it proved to be a literal stairway to heaven, for they died on it of exhaustion and exposure. Thomas Moore described the icy staircase climbing up the pass until it vanished in a blinding snowstorm at the top:

It was one steady string of men climbing up these steps from morning until night. No sooner would one man's foot leave a step than it would be taken by that of the man behind him. The trail was wide enough for only one man, and a rope, tied to stakes frozen in the snow, ran from bottom to top, by means of which the men could help themselves up. Two men made it their business to keep the steps cut and the rope in place. They did their work at night, receiving their pay for it in donations from the packers.

296

Every twenty or thirty feet, a small square place was shoveled out to the left with seats made of the snow, where the weary packer could step out of line and rest. This was the dreaded final ascent to the pass where men, tortured by dysentery and stomach cramps, had to pack even the dogs and sleds that they hoped to use on the far side of the pass through the ice and snow. Blizzards and gales screamed for days. It took a man at least six hours to climb a thousand feet beneath his pack with his teeth clenched against the winds and snow. The climb was made even more bitter because an aerial tram started at the Scales and ran to the summit. Electricity whisked loads of equipment and supplies over the heads of the suffering men, but only the affluent among the Klondikers could pay for this service. It is not surprising that many would-be prospectors looked at the final ascent and gave up. They sold their supplies for 10 cents on the dollar and returned to the coast.

In the winter of 1898 a storm raged for two months in the pass. It snowed without a break for two weeks. On Saturday, April 12, six feet of new snow fell. Over the trail hung a great beetling brow of snow and ice. Indian packers withdrew to Dyea, and the more prudent among the Klondikers stopped at Sheep Camp. Others, fevered with gold, pressed on up the trail taking advantage of a brief lull in the furious storm.

"All of a sudden," said a Klondiker, "I heard a loud report and instantly began to feel myself moving down the hill and, looking round, saw many others suddenly fall down, some with their feet in the air, their heads buried out of sight in the snow."

The great avalanche swept everything before it. Thirty feet of snow covered ten acres and entombed hundreds of men. A thousand men hurried down from the summit and up from Sheep Camp to dig them out. Small airholes marked where a human being was buried. They could hear muffled cries from some who were suffocating. One man lost in the avalanche first prayed and then cussed until he died.

Joppe, who ran a tent restaurant at the Scales, was among those buried. When he was dug from the snow, he appeared dead. His sweetheart, Vernie Woodward, wrapped herself around him and sobbed. She rubbed his cold arms and legs, breathed into his lungs, cried and prayed. After three hours, others tried to drag the hysterical girl away, but she stayed with her lover until, to the astonishment of everybody, Joppe opened his eyes and gently spoke her name.

Sixty-four died. They were found frozen in the snow in the positions of walking or running, just as the avalanche had caught them, for once

297

they were in its grip they could not move. Soapy Smith appointed himself coroner and stripped each corpse of valuables. Then the bodies were loaded on sleds and taken down the trail and buried in an alpine draw to one side.

Even as religious services were held for the men who had died on the mountain, the antlike march of Klondikers resumed up the slope to the summit. The dead were forgotten until the spring. When the snow melted, the bodies floated in water until men less fevered with gold than others took them down to Dyea, where they now lie buried in the Slide Cemetery.

July temperatures at the summit of the Chilkoot Trail rarely drop below freezing except at night, and it was in the 50's as we climbed up the last precipitous stretch of scree to the summit. Clouds of mist began to swirl in, and we were anxious to make it to the top before the fog closed in again. High snowcaps shouldered about the pass, which is about one hundred yards wide. Then we were at the top, and the boys shouted in their triumph. From the summit the trail was all downhill into Canada. We knew it was unmarked, but we expected no trouble.

In the winter of 1898 conditions at the summit were very different. Klondikers who won their way to the top piled their goods in the snow and hurried down to the Scales for another load. Knowing that more snow would fall before they returned, they stuck long poles into the middle of their belongings to mark the place. Snow reached depths of seventy feet in the pass, and the poles notwithstanding, many gold seekers lost their stores until the spring thaw.

At the summit the Klondikers had to check through the Canadian customs. Polite mounties ran rods into bales of hay to make sure that whiskey was not concealed within and checked each man's supplies to be sure that he had the sixteen hundred pounds of food that the Canadian Government believed would keep him from starvation in the frigid Yukon. The Mounties wrapped in their buffalo coats also succored the sick and hungry. Close by the Mounties stood Detective Perrin, still looking for Frank Novak, who managed to slip past him. Later on the pursuer and the pursued were only a few miles from each other on Lake Lindeman and Lake Bennett, building boats to continue their chase north to the gold fields. Detective Perrin finally caught up with Novak on the Klondike and arrested him without a struggle.

There was no firewood on the trail between Sheep Camp and Crater Lake, so entrepreneurs hauled it to the summit where it brought a price of $1 a pound. At the summit a doughnut and a cup of coffee went for

$2.50, and to most men marooned in the periodic storms this seemed cheap at that.

A sentry with a Maxim gun and the Union Jack whipping in the storms made it clear to even the most unruly gold seekers that the Queen's law was a real presence at the summit. One of the chores the Mounty on night sentry duty had was to shovel away the snow so that it would not suffocate the men at sleep in their shack. With six feet of snow falling in a single night, this duty was not an easy one. The Mounties stuck to their post throughout the storm that howled through the pass for two months, but another storm became so severe that they had to retreat to Crater Lake, which nestles in an old volcanic hollow five miles below the summit. There they pitched their tents on the lake surface. When the ice melted beneath them, they pulled their sleds inside and slept on top of them out of the wet. As the storm slackened, they returned to the summit.

All told, the Canadians collected some $150,000 in customs duties at the summit. The problem then was how to get the money safely out over the trail. Inspector Zachary Taylor Wood, a descendant of U.S. President Zachary Taylor, was given the assignment. Fearing Soapy Smith's gang, he pretended to be a Mountie transferring to another post and loaded his kit bags with gold and banknotes. It took several men to help him carry his bags down the trail to Dyea. There he rented a small boat to take him to Skagway. As the Mountie and his bags of cash and gold sailed over the inlet, a gang of men in another boat attempted to ram him. He held them off by gunpoint. At Skagway, Soapy Smith and a party of armed men awaited him on the docks.

"Why not hang around and visit Skagway for a while?" Soapy asked urbanely as his men fingered their triggers.

Inspector Wood seemed to have little choice, but just then the British steamer *Tartar* edged in close to shore. Sailors with loaded rifles lined its rail. The Mountie politely declined Soapy's invitation and left with his bags aboard the *Tartar*.

The men who cowered in the blizzards at the Summit were often sick with dysentery and from eating poor food. It was at the summit that I also became ill. In the morning I got out of my sleeping bag with the others, but my stomach writhed as I watched the boys cooking breakfast over a spirit stove. I scrunched down in the rocks and hoped that I would feel better. The boys found their usual off-hand ways of showing sympathy and went about their chores. They remained cheerful. When a high-flying hummingbird, attracted by Dale's orange jacket, flitted about him, they twitted him about his "flower power" over birds. A black bear ambled across a snowfield just below our camp and stared with amazement at us. He went into some rocks and then returned to take a second incredulous look.

Then we were off down the mountain, through snowfields and jumbles of scree and talus. The trail was easy to follow to our first destination, blue Crater Lake, below us. Several times I had to pull out of the march, my stomach heaving nothing but bile. The boys waited with sober faces. I was still strong, and we made good time despite the halts. Along the lake the scouts found discarded saws, axheads, gold pans, and even a pair of matching spoons. By noon I was finding it increasingly difficult to keep up with my hardy youngsters, and I was glad when Guy sent a couple of boys ahead to set up a noon camp in the first sheltered place.

We lounged on the soft cushion of tundra plants in the lee of a hill while the boys cooked lunch. Mark, who had slipped into the water while crossing a glacial stream during the morning's hike, came to me with a blister caused by his wet, rubbing sock, and another boy came to me for an aspirin. Another boy asked me to rub his back where his heavy pack had been chafing. Lying in the lee of the hill it was easy to feel better and to do small things for my usually very independent scouts who had, for a brief spell, become dependent.

My stomach still could not tolerate food or water, and when we took to the trail again, it began its painful useless writhing. We crawled over several miles of huge rocks and slipped down snowfields only to find more rocks. I began to get light-headed. When I no longer could keep my mind on whether Guy was leading the boys over the safest and best way, I asked Bob to become acting scoutmaster and concentrated on getting myself to our next camp.

Each climb grew harder than the one before. It seemed odd that we had to go up so much when the trail should be taking us down. In some places as I climbed, I found Guy's strong young hand reaching down to help me. His face was taut, but his blue eyes were reassuring. I could not help but smile. If I put my weight against his boy's strength, I would drag him from the hard rock of manhood onto which he had climbed.

The boys skillfully traced the trail that disappeared and reappeared in the rocks and among the snowfields and the ice run-offs. We forced our way through deep thickets as we got down below the tree line and came to a place where the old trail divided. One branch climbed high on a mountain ridge where it runs for two miles to a point overlooking Deep

Lake. The lower one followed the tim of a canyon through which Deep River flows. The boys decided against the high trail because of the initial difficult climb that they feared I could not make. They also spotted a series of rock cairns that led along the lower one.

It began to rain as we set out along the lower trail. I was dizzy, and I stumbled often. The rock cairns ceased. The trail vanished. We came to a side canyon that blocked our advance. We could only scrabble up treacherous slopes to get around the canyon. The storm worsened by evening, and the boys had to admit that they had lost the trail. Their decision to take the lower trail had proved costly, for very few hikers have taken it since 1898, and it is very hard to follow.

"We'll probably find the crazy kooks who put up those cairns dead on the trail," grumbled John.

"You know, John," I lectured him despite my lethargy, "that all a cairn means is that a party has gone this way and is finding it easy going. If they run into trouble, they're scarcely going to go back and take down all the cairns they've piled up."

We continued our hike and found the three-weeks-old camp left by the cairn-builders. It was a poor campsite, but we paused there while Guy and Mark pushed on ahead to find a level place where trees and rocks afforded some shelter against the billowing clouds of rain. I slumped by the trail until Guy came back and taking my pack marched off with it. Jim guided me at a slower pace to the camp. When we got there, I found my sleeping bag already stretched out snug and dry beneath a sheltering space blanket, and after a spell of retching, I got into it and fell into a stupor.

The rain drizzled to an end, and a fog rolled down from the mountains upon us. We started off at a slow pace. I stumbled and fell. So did John and Jim, whose shorter legs could not readily make it up to footholds that the longer-legged boys ahead of them found easy. Then we found the trail again. John searched our maps and discovered that since we had gone in the right direction even when we lost the trail, we were now only a few miles from Lake Lindeman, where an abandoned trapper's cabin stood. Lake Lindeman also was the end of the historic trail. There the Gold Rushers took to rafts or sleds in the winter to continue on their way down through a chain of lakes to the Yukon.

Once again Guy and Mark forged ahead to scout for the cabin, but in the swirling fog they went right by it. By the time they doubled back, the other boys, Bob, and I had already arrived at the hut. The boys stretched out my sleeping bag on a filthy bunk, and I climbed into it.

It was something close to heaven to have arrived at this tumbledown cabin, abandoned more than fifty years before by a trapper. It was staunch shelter against the wind that now drove the returning rain against the log walls. The stove worked, and the boys soon had a fire going and were drying out their clothes and gear. The stovepipe got so hot it threatened to set the roof on fire, and smoke eddied about the room.

Mark climbed up on the roof to stretch out a red space blanket as a distress signal for any vagrant plane and anchored it in place with a moose skull. I dozed off and on. The boys slept in shifts. I could hear them talking in soft voices, making plans. When I stirred, they brought me hot lemonade, which my stomach would not tolerate, and showed me Gold Rush artifacts that they had found. The cabin stood where once a tent city spread beside the lake. Gold Rushers camped by the lake shore, cut trees, whipsawed lumber, and built clumsy boats and rafts. All told, Klondikers built an astounding seven thousand boats of one kind or another. At the spring thaw they took to the water, still following the lure of gold.

"We have a plan to get you out of here, Mr. D.," said Guy.

"It'll be time enough to talk about it if I'm not better in the morning," I replied.

I felt better in the morning, but I was so weak I could scarcely walk.

A cabin built by a trapper fifty years ago sheltered the author and his Scouts when he was taken ill while hiking the rugged Trail of '98.
Photo by Robert Spinks

When I lurched from my bunk, all the boys were watching. It was obvious that I would not be able to walk out of the wilderness for some days to come.

"All right, Guy," I said. "What is your plan?"

"We've got to get you to a hospital," he said. "Johnny has worked it out on the map that if we cut due south of here around Lake Lindeman, we can go around a mountain spur and come out on the White Pass and Yukon Railroad. There's a river in the way, but we can cross it. I'll stay with you because I have the best first aid training, and Johnny will lead the others because he is our best map and compass man. The guys'll flag down a train and get help. We're right on the lake so a float plane can fly in and take you out."

I agreed. Bob set off with the scouts. I was thankful that he was with them, for his steadfastness would see them through. Guy, rummaging on a dusty shelf, found some ancient tea bags. He brewed some tea, and this was the first thing my stomach kept down. I slept much, but whenever I awoke I found Guy sitting nearby, his eyes always on me ready to bring more tea, sometimes to show me an old bottle or a tin cup that he had found. I had led a boy into the mountains, but he was now a young man.

The other boys ran into heavy going from the start. Dense brush, flooded valley lands, and a roaring river that could only be crossed by wading slowed their progress. So did a misplaced mountain. A great peak loomed where our maps indicated no mountain should be. The boys had to circle around its shoulder following compass bearings. They climbed up and down ravines, forded swollen rivers, and sloshed through the muskeg. At last ahead of them they heard the unmistakable noise of a train grinding up a steep grade. They soon saw the train, but another swollen stream separated them from the railroad, and they could not get to the tracks in time to attract the engineer's attention.

The next train was a westbound passenger train loaded with tourists who, with their cars snugged down on flatcars, were riding from Whitehorse, Yukon Territory, on the Alaska Highway, through the dramatic mountain wilderness over the White Pass to Skagway, where they would take the Alaska Ferry back south. The White Pass and Yukon Railroad, which ended travel over the Chilkoot Trail when it was completed through White Pass in 1899, has become one of Alaska's most spectacular tourist attractions, and thousands of travelers go over it every year to view the wilderness of mountains and canyons that separate the Yukon from the coast.

The boys shouted and waved, and the train screeched to a stop. Then the boys were climbing up into the cars while tourists snapped their pictures. As soon as the railroad people heard the boys' story, they went into action. A bush pilot was sent winging out of Whitehorse to pick up Guy and me. When he buzzed our cabin, Guy ran down to the lake to guide the plane to the beach.

"We'll leave some dehydrated food on the shelves for the next hikers who need it," said Guy. "We'll leave all the powdered eggs."

Remembering how wretched the eggs had tasted, I shared his grin. Guy and the pilot helped me to the plane, and soon we were in the air, winging over huge snowcapped mountains and blue lakes set amid sweeps of unbroken forest. The land slipping beneath us is as wild today as it was when the Klondikers hurried through it on their way to the gold fields.

Roy Minter of the White Pass and Yukon Railroad was waiting with his car at the boat landing where the plane tied up at Whitehorse, and soon we were at the hospital. As a nurse was giving me the first of many shots, I looked out of the window beside my comfortable bed and saw a beautiful fox, his brush trailing behind him, trot daintily from the forest across the hospital lawn. The wilderness that has all but swallowed up yesterday's trails of the hardship and suffering of the Gold Rush juxtaposed to a modern town beside the Yukon and my own newfound ease struck home to me. Then the fox was gone, and I fell asleep in a soft bed, which is something that our Gold Rush predecessors on the trail never would have found along the Yukon, as they went on down the river toward the still distant Klondike, still led on by the dream of great wealth.

Bibliography

●

Manuscripts, Letters, Pamphlets, and Documents

Amesbury, Robert. "Nobles' Emigrant Trail." Susanville, Cal., 1967.

Bannon, John Francis. "History Below the Jet Trails." American Airlines Booklet No. 2, Historical Series.

Blake, R. B., and Crockett, George L. "Nacogdoches." Nacogdoches, Tex., 1960.

Burgess, Howard, and Orchard, Vance. "One Hundredth Anniversary Lyons Ferry Commemoration Day." Lyons Ferry Centennial Committee, 1960.

"California's Historical Monuments." Compiled from a series of articles in P. G. and E. Progress. San Francisco, 1965.

"California Trail in Idaho, The." Reference Series No. 52, Idaho Historical Society.

"Chimney Rock." United States Department of the Interior, National Park Service, Washington, D. C.

Fletcher, R. H. "Montana Historical Markers." Montana State Highway Commission.

"Fort Laramie's Historic Buildings." Fort Laramie Historical Association, Fort Laramie, Wyo.

Frear, Samuel T. "Jesse Applegate, an Appraisal of an Uncommon Pioneer." A thesis presented to the Department of History and the Graduate School of the University of Oregon. June, 1961.

Gilstrap, W. H. "Dedication of Monument Marking End of the Oregon Trail." Washington State Historical Society Publications 1907-1914, Vol. 2. Olympia, Wash., 1915.

Halverson, Katherine, and Barnhart, William. "Fort Fetterman." Archives and Historical Department, Cheyenne, Wyo., June 1966.

Hill, Ivy Hooper Blood. "The Flint Creek Valley, Montana." July, 1962.

"Historical Sign Program in the State of Idaho, The." Idaho Department of Highways, 1966.

"History of Fort Shaw." Fort Shaw, Mont.

"In these golden tracks . . . ." Idaho Historical Society, Boise, Idaho, 1959.

Krueger, Carl G. "Route of the Mullan Road over the Bitterroot Divide." Coeur d'Alène, Idaho, 1964.

Kruse, Anne Applegate. *The Halo Trail*, Drain, Oreg., 1954.

———. *Yoncalla Home of the Eagles*. Drain, Oreg., 1950.

Ladd, Richard S. *Maps Showing Explorers' Routes, Trails and Early Roads in the United States: An Annotated List of Maps in the Map Collections of the Library of Congress*. Washington, D.C., 1962.

Latz, J. R. "The Chilkoot Trail Today—Dyea to Bennett." Ottawa, Ont., 1963.

Leggett, Herbert B. "Early History of Wine Production in California." Wine Institute, San Francisco, 1941.

"Los Padres National Forest," United States Department of Agriculture Forest Service, Washington, D.C., 1939.

Meacham, Walter. "Applegate Trail." Oregon Council, American Pioneer Trails Association, Salem, Oreg., 1947.

Moore, Thomas. "Grubstake." MS in Provincial Archives, Victoria, B.C.

"Mullan Road in Idaho." Reference Series No. 287, Idaho Historical Society, Boise, Idaho, Dec., 1964.

Nardini, Louis Raphael. "No Man's Land," New Orleans, 1961.

Nichols, Claude W., Jr. "The South Road: Its Development and Significance." A thesis presented to the Department of History and the Graduate School of the University of Oregon, June, 1953.

"Oregon Trail in Idaho, The." Reference Series No. 50. Idaho Historical Society. Boise, Idaho.

Overbaker, Joel F. "A Souvenir History of Fort Benton, Montana." Fort Benton, Mont. n.d.

———. "Centenary History of Fort Benton, Montana 1846-1946." Fort Benton, Mont., 1946.

Paden, Irene D. "Pioneer Trails of the West." Traveler Publishing Co. San Francisco, 1962.

"Route of the Oregon Trail." Oregon State Highway Department.

"Route of the Oregon Trail in Idaho." Idaho Department of Highways, Boise, Idaho, 1963.

Salmon, Cutler. Letter written at French Camp, California, Oct. 30, 1853. From the collection of Elwyn Arnold.

"Santa Fe Trail." The Santa Fe Trail Highway Association, Shawnee, Kansas.

"Scotts Bluff." United States Department of the Interior, National Park Service, Washington, D.C., 1966.

Shuffler, R. Henderson. "Old Ten-Ox Crossing." MS, Texana Program, University of Texas, Austin.

Bibliography

"Stone Fort, The." Stephen F. Austin State University, Nacogdoches, Texas.

Swartzlow, Ruby Jelensen. "Lassen—His Life and Legacy." Mineral, Cal., 1964.

"Texas Historical Markers." Compiled by the Texas Historical Foundation in cooperation with the Texas State Historical Survey Committee.

Tilford, F. "Sketch of Meadow Lake Townships." From *Bean's History and Directory of Nevada County* in the Bancroft Library.

Utley, Robert M. "Fort Davis." National Park Service Historical Handbook Series No. 38, Washington, D.C., 1965.

Wilkinson, Norman B. 'The Conestoga Wagon." Historic Pennsylvania Leaflet No. 5. Historical and Museum Commission, Harrisburg, 1962.

Periodicals

"A Glimpse of the Wyoming Gold Rush in the Early 1870's." *The Westerners Brand Book.* Chicago Corral, Vol. 22, No. 10 (December, 1965).

Applegate, Jesse. "A Day with the Cow Column in 1843." *Oregon Historical Society Quarterly*, Vol. 1, No. 4 (December, 1900).

Applegate, Lindsay. "Notes and Reminiscences of Laying out and Establishing the Old Emigrant Road into Southern Oregon in the Year 1846." *Oregon Historical Society Quarterly*, Vol. 22, No. 1 (March 1921).

Anderson, Harry H. "From Milwaukee to the California Gold Fields." *The Westerners Brand Book.* Chicago Corral, Vol. 26, No. 8 (October, 1969).

Bacon, Thorn. " 'Bet-a-Million' Gates." *The Kiwanis Magazine* (January, 1969).

Baxter, Dow W. "The Chilkoot Trail Then and Now." *The Beaver* (Summer, 1964).

Bell, W. Bruce. "The Old Chisholm Trail." *The Kiwanis Magazine* (October, 1960).

Crockett, Capt. Robert. "Across the Rockies in Fifty-Two." *Southwest Virginia Enterprise* (February 5, 1929).

Donovan, H. George. "Ghost Towns and Camps of Arizona." *The Westerners Brand Book.* Chicago Corral, Vol. 20, No. 8 (October, 1963).

Dunn, Milton. "History of Natchitoches." *Louisiana Historical Quarterly*, Vol. 3 (January, 1920).

Ege, Robert J. "Major Eugene M. Baker's Expedition." *The Westerners Brand Book.* Chicago Corral, Vol. 25, No. 10 (December, 1968).

"El Camino Real." *Southern Living* (April, 1968).

Gorby, John S. "After Serra on California's Royal Road." *Touring Topics* (August, 1931).

Grove, Fred. "Fort Gibson." *Oklahoma Today*, Vol. 15, No. 3 (Summer, 1965).

Hardin, J. Fair. "Fort Jesup—Fort Selden—Camp Sabine—Camp Salubrity." *The Louisiana Historical Quarterly*, Vol. 16, No. 1 (January, 1933); Vol. 16, No. 2 (April, 1933).

Hardin, Martin D. "Up the Missouri and over the Mullan Road," ed. by John E. Parsons. *The Westerners New York Posse Brand Book*, Vol. 5, No. 2 (1958).

Harrington, John. "Along California's Royal Road," Part III. *Westways* (March, April, May, and June, 1938).

Houghton, S. G. "The Truckee River Story." *Nevada*, Vol. 26, No. 1 (Spring, 1966).

Hunt, John Clark."The Oregon Trail—Then and Now." *American History Illustrated* (August, 1968).

———. "Stampede to the Yukon." *American History Illustrated* (January, 1969).

James, Harry C. "Forty Years Ago from 30,000 Feet Up." *Desert Magazine* (June, 1960).

Larrison, Earl J. "The Desert of Owyhee." *Desert Magazine* (August, 1960).

Lawry, Mabel. "Fort Lancaster." *Texas Parks and Wildlife*, Vol. 26, No. 12 (December, 1968).

Leadabrand, Russ. "In the Path of the Padres." *Westways*, Vol. 58, No. 10 (October, 1966).

McKee, Irving. "Early California Wine Growers." *California* (September, 1947).

Morris, Charles W. E. "Tar Pits Yield Relics of the Past." *Christian Science Monitor* (July 1, 1968).

"Oregon Ho!" *Kiwanis Magazine* (February, 1966).

Prucha, Francis Paul. "The Army Forts of the West, 1826-1845." *The Westerners Brand Book*. Chicago Corral, Vol. 24, No. 3 (May, 1967).

Russell, Don. "Their Name Is on the Waters." *Inland* (Autumn, 1965).

Ruth, Kent. "Heartland of Soonerland." *Oklahoma Today*, Vol. 14, No. 2 (Spring, 1964).

Sargent, Alice Applegate. "A Sketch of the Rogue River Valley and Southern Oregon History." *Quarterly of the Oregon Historical Society*, Vol. 22, No. 1 (March, 1921).

"Scotts Bluff Re-Photographed." *Sunday Omaha World-Herald Magazine of the Midlands* (October 16, 1966).

Smith, Waddell F. "Waddell F. Smith on the Pony Express." *The Westerners Brand Book*. Chicago Corral, Vol. 22, No. 11 (January, 1966).

"Stage Lines." *Butterfield Express*, Vol. 4, No. 3 (January, 1966).

Stone, Buena Cobb. "Southern Route into Oregon; Notes and New Map." *Oregon Historical Quarterly*, Vol. 47 (June, 1948).

"The Chisholm Trail." *Oklahoma Today*, Vol. 20, No. 1 (Winter, 1969).

Thruelsen, Richard. "Tucson." *The Saturday Evening Post* (October 6, 1951).

Trego, Peggy. "Historic Humboldt River Trail." *Desert Magazine* (August, 1960).

Van Orman, Richard. "A Room for the Night." *The Westerners Brand Book*. Chicago Corral, Vol. 23, No. 12 (February, 1967).

Bibliography

Wilson, Bruce A. "The Mullan Trail." *Ritzville, Washington Journal* (May 10, 1956).

Winther, Oscar Osburn. "Early Commercial Importance of the Mullan Road." *Oregon Historical Quarterly*, Vol. 46 (March, 1945).

———. "Jo Lane and, Incidentally, the Rogue River Indians." *The Westerners Brand Book*. Chicago Corral, Vol. 25, No. 8 (October, 1968).

Books

Abbott, E. C., and Smith, Helena H. *We Pointed Them North: Recollections of a Cowpuncher*. New York, 1939.

Adams, E. *To and Fro, Up and Down in Southern California, Oregon, and Washington Territory*. Chicago, 1888.

Adams, Ramon F. *Come & Get It: The Story of the Old Cowboy Cook*. Norman, Okla., 1952.

———. *Cowboy Lingo*. Boston, 1936.

———. comp. and ed. *The Best of the American Cowboy*. Norman, Okla., 1957.

Anderson, Sylvia F., and Korg, Jacob, eds. *Westward to Oregon*. Boston, 1958.

Arkansas American Guide Series. New York, 1941.

Atwood, A. *The Conquerors: Historical Sketches of the American Settlement of the Oregon Country*. Tacoma, Wash., 1907.

Bancroft, Hubert H. *California Pastoral*. San Francisco, 1888.

Bandelier, Fanny. *Journey of Cabeza de Vaca in 1528/1536*. Chicago, 1964.

Bari, Veleska. *The Course of Empire*. New York, 1931.

Barrows, William. *Oregon: The Struggle for Possession*. Boston, 1884.

Bay, Stuart. *The Cry Was Gold*. Culpeper, Va., 1963.

Beadle, J. *The Undeveloped West; or Five Years in the Territories*. Philadelphia, 1873.

Benton, Jesse James. *Cow by the Tail*. Boston, 1943.

Berton, Pierre. *The Klondike Fever: The Life and Death of the Last Great Gold Rush*. New York, 1958.

Bigelow, J. *Memoir of the Life and Public Services of John Charles Fremont*. New York, 1856.

Block, Eugene B. *Great Stagecoach Robbers of the West*. Garden City, N.Y., 1962.

Bowles, S. *Across the Continent*. New York, 1866.

Bradley, G. *Story of the Santa Fe*. Boston, 1920.

Branch, E. Douglas. *The Cowboy and His Interpreters*. New York, 1926.

———.*Westward: The Romance of the American Frontier*. New York, 1930.

Brown, Dee, and Schmidt, Martin. *Trail Driving Days*. New York, 1952.

Browne, John Ross. *Adventures in the Apache Country*. Chicago, 1964.

Bryant, Edwin. *What I Saw in California: Being the Journal of a Tour, by the Emigrant Route and South Pass of the Rocky Mountains, Across the Continent of North America, the Great Desert Basin, and Through California in the Years 1846, 1847.* New York, 1848.

Buel, J. *Heroes of the Plains.* Philadelphia, 1891.

Burdett, Charles. *Life of Kit Carson: The Great Western Hunter and Guide.* Philadelphia, 1869.

Burton, Richard. *The Look of the West 1860* Lincoln, Neb., 1963.

Carle, Edwin. *The Royal Highway.* Indianapolis, 1949.

Carter, Hodding, with Betty W. Carter. *Doomed Road of Empire.* New York, 1963.

Chisholm, Alexander. *The Old Chisholm Trail.* Salt Lake City, 1964.

Chisholm, Fanny G. *The Four State Chisholm Trail.* San Antonio, 1966.

Christiansen, Paige W., and Kottlawski, Frank E. *Mosaic of New Mexico's Scenery, Rocks, and History.* Socorro, N.M., 1967.

Cody, William F. *The Adventures of Buffalo Bill.* New York, 1923.

Coleman, Louis C., Rieman, Lea, and Payette, B. C. *Captain John Mullan: His Life.* Montreal, 1968.

Conkling, Margaret B., and Roscoe P. *The Butterfield Overland Mail 1857-1869.* Glendale, Cal.

Coons, Frederica B. *The Trail to Oregon.* Portland, Oreg., 1964.

Cox, W. *Luke Short and His Era.* New York, 1961.

Coyner, D. *The Lost Trappers.* New York, 1847.

Crockett, Davy. *Davy Crockett's Own Story: As Written by himself.* New York, 1955.

Croy, Homer. *He Hanged Them High.* New York, 1952.

Davis, Button. *The Truth about Geronimo.* New Haven, Conn., 1963.

Davis, Jean, comp. *Shallow Diggin's.* Caldwell, Idaho, 1962.

De Voto, Bernard. *Year of Decision: Eighteen-Forty-Six.* Boston, 1943.

Dobie, J. Frank. *A Vaquero of the Brush Country.* Dallas, 1929.

Egan, William M., ed. *Pioneering the West, 1846 to 1878. Major Howard Egan's Diary.* Richmond, 1917.

Ehrenberger, Herman. *With Milam and Fannin: Adventures of a German Boy in the Texas Revolution.* Trans. by Charlotte Churchill; ed. by Henry Smith. Dallas, 1935.

El Comancho. *The Old-Timer's Tale.* Chicago, 1929.

Emory, W. H. *Notes of a Military Reconnaissance from Fort Leavenworth, in Missouri, to San Diego, in California.* Washington, 1848.

Estergreen, M. Morgan. *Kit Carson, a Portrait in Courage.* Norman, Okla., 1962.

Farnham, Thomas J. *Travel in the Great Western Prairies, the Anahuac and the Rocky Mountains, and in the Oregon Territory.* New York, 1843.

Bibliography

Faulkner, Virginia, comp. and ed. *Roundup: A Nebraska Reader*. Lincoln, Neb., 1957.

Field, Matthew C. *Matt Field on the Santa Fe Trail*. Norman, Okla., 1960.

Fitzpatrick, Lilian L. *Nebraska Place-Names*. Lincoln, Neb., 1960.

Fortier, Alcee. *A History of Louisiana*. New York, 1904.

Friedman, Ralph. *Oregon for the Curious*. Portland, 1965.

Gard, Wayne. *The Chisholm Trail*. Norman, Okla., 1954.

Gillis, William R. *Gold Rush Days with Mark Twain*. New York, 1930.

Gregg, Josiah. *Commerce of the Prairies*. Norman, Okla., 1954.

———. ed. by M. G. Fulton. *Diary and Letters of Josiah Gregg*. Norman, Okla., 1958.

Hammond, Dorothy, and Henricks, George. *The Dodge City Story*. Indianapolis, 1964.

Hancock, Samuel. *The Narrative of Samuel Hancock*. New York, 1927.

Hastings, Lansford W. *The Emigrants' Guide to Oregon and California*. Cincinnati, 1845.

Hebard, Grace Raymond. *The Pathbreakers from River to Ocean*. Chicago, 1912.

Horgan, Paul. *Great River: The Rio Grande in North American History*. 2 vols. New York, 1954.

Howe, Octavius Thorndike. *Argonauts of '49*. Cambridge, Mass., 1923.

Hughes, John T. *Doniphan's Expedition, Containing an Account of the Conquest of New Mexico; Gen. Kearny's Overland Expedition to California*. Chicago, 1962.

Hulbert, Archer Butler. *Forty-Niners: The Chronicle of the California Trail*. Boston, 1949.

Jackson, W. Turrentine. *Wagon Roads West*. New Haven, Conn., 1965.

Johnson, Clifton. *Highways and Byways of the Pacific Coast*. New York, 1908.

Kilgore, William H. *The Kilgore Journal of an Overland Journey to California in the Year 1850*. Ed. by Joyce Rockwood Muench. New York, 1949.

Laut, Agnes C. *The Overland Trail: The Epic Path of the Pioneers to Oregon*. New York, 1929.

Lavender, David. *Bent's Fort*. Garden City, N.Y., 1954.

Louisiana: A Guide to the State. Comp. by Workers of the Writers' Program of Works Project Administration in the State of Louisiana. New York, 1941.

Magoffin, Susan Shelby. *Down the Santa Fe Trail and into Mexico*. New Haven, Conn., 1962.

Marshall, James. *Santa Fe: The Railroad That Built an Empire*. New York, 1945.

McGlashan, C. F. *History of the Donner Party*. Stanford, Cal., 1947.

McIntyre, John T. *In Texas with Davy Crockett*. Philadelphia, 1914.

Meacham, A. L. *Barlow Road*. Oregon City, n.d.

Meacham, Walter. *Applegate Trail*. n.p., n.d.

Meeker, Ezra. *Personal Experiences on the Old Oregon Trail Sixty Years Ago.* Seattle, 1912.

Moody, Ralph. *The Old Trails West.* New York, 1963.

Moore, J. Bernard. *Skagway in Days Primeval.* New York, 1968.

Moorhead, Max L. *New Mexico's Royal Road.* Norman, Okla., 1958.

Morgan, Dale. *The Humboldt.* New York, 1943.

———. *Overland in 1846. Diaries and Letters of the California-Oregon Trail.* Vols. 1 and 2. Georgetown, Cal., 1963.

Morgan, Gene. *Westward the Course of Empire: Story of the Pony Express.* Chicago, 1945.

Morgan, Murray. *One Man's Gold Rush.* Seattle, 1967.

Nardini, Louis Raphael. *My Historic Natchitoches, Louisiana and its Environment.* Natchitoches, La., 1963.

O'Connor, Richard. *Wild Bill Hickok.* Garden City, N.Y., 1959.

Oklahoma: A Guide to the Sooner State. Norman, Okla., 1941.

Olmsted, Frederick Law. *Journey Through Texas.* Austin, 1962.

Paden, Irene D. *Prairie Schooner Detours.* New York, 1949.

———. *The Wake of the Prairie Schooner.* New York, 1944.

Pancoost, Charles Edward. *A Quaker Forty-Niner.* Philadelphia, 1930.

Parkman, Francis. *The Oregon Trail.* New York, 1950.

Parrish, Philip H. *Before the Covered Wagon.* Portland, Oreg., 1934.

Penfield, Thomas. *Dig Here.* San Antonio, 1966.

Peters, De Witt C. *Kit Carson's Life and Adventures, from Facts Narrated by Himself.* Cincinnati, 1874.

Phares, Ross. *A Cavalier in the Wilderness.* Baton Rouge, La., 1952.

Pourade, Richard F. *The Call to California.* San Diego, 1968.

Powers, Alfred. *Marooned in Crater Lake: Stories of the Skyline Trail, the Umpqua Trail, and the Old Oregon Trail.* Portland, Oreg., 1930.

Read, Georgia Willis, and Gaines, Ruth, eds. *Gold Rush: The Journals, Drawings, and Other Papers of J. Goldsborough Bruff, April 2, 1849–July 20, 1851.* New York, 1949.

Richardson, Albert D. *Beyond the Mississippi.* Hartford, Conn., 1867.

Riesenberg, Felix, Jr. *The Golden Road.* New York, 1962.

Rollins, P. A. *The Cowboy: His Characteristics, His Equipment, and His Part in the Development of the West.* New York, 1927.

Russell, Don. *The Lives and Legends of Buffalo Bill.* Norman, Okla., 1960.

Ryers, W. H. *The Second William Penn: A True Account of Incidents That Happened along the Old Santa Fe Trail in the Sixties.* Kansas City, 1913.

Salisbury, Albert and Jane. *Here Rolled the Covered Wagons.* Seattle, 1948.

Sandoz, Marie. *Old Jules.* Boston, 1935.

Sante Fe Trail, The, eds. of *Look.* New York, 1946.

Sauer, Carl O. *The Geography of the Ozark Highland of Missouri.* Chicago, 1920.

Bibliography

Scofield, W. M. *Oregon's Historical Markers*. Pleasant Hill, Oreg., 1966.

Simonsen, S. J. *Among the Sourdoughs*. New York, 1940.

Siringo, Charles A. *A Texas Cowboy*. With an Introduction by J. Frank Dobie. New York, 1950.

Sperry, Armstrong. *Wagons Westward: The Old Trail to Santa Fe*. Chicago, 1936.

Stone, Irving. *Men to Match My Mountains*. Garden City, N.Y., 1956.

Tevis, James H. *Arizona in the '50's*. Albuquerque, N.M., 1954.

Texas, A Guide to the Lone Star State. New York, 1940.

Transactions of the Thirty-Third Annual Reunion of the Oregon Pioneer Association, June 15, 1905. Portland, Oreg., 1906.

Twain, Mark. *Roughing It*. New York, 1899.

Twitchell, Ralph Emerson. *Old Santa Fe: The Story of New Mexico's Ancient Capital*. Chicago, 1963.

Upham, Charles. *Life, Explorations and Public Services of John Charles Fremont*. Boston, 1856.

Vestal, Stanley. *Kit Carson, the Happy Warrior of the Old West*. Boston, 1928.

Walsh, Richard J. *The Making of Buffalo Bill*. New York, 1928.

Warren, Sidney. *Farthest Frontier*. New York, 1949.

Waters, L. L. *Steel Trails to Santa Fe*. Lawrence, Kan., 1950.

Watts, John S. *Indian Depredations in New Mexico and Arizona*. Tucson, 1964.

Wellman, Paul I. *Glory, God and Gold*. Garden City, N.Y., 1954.

———. *The Trampling Herd*. Garden City, N.Y., 1951.

Wetmore, Helen Cody and Grey, Zane. *Last of the Great Scouts* [Buffalo Bill]. New York, 1899.

White, Owen P. *Them Was the Days*. New York, 1925.

Wilson, Neill C. *Treasure Express*. New York, 1936.

Wilstock, Frank J. *The Plainsman: Wild Bill Hickok*. New York, 1937.

Winther, Oscar Osburn. *The Old Oregon Country*. Stanford, Cal., 1950.

Index

317

320

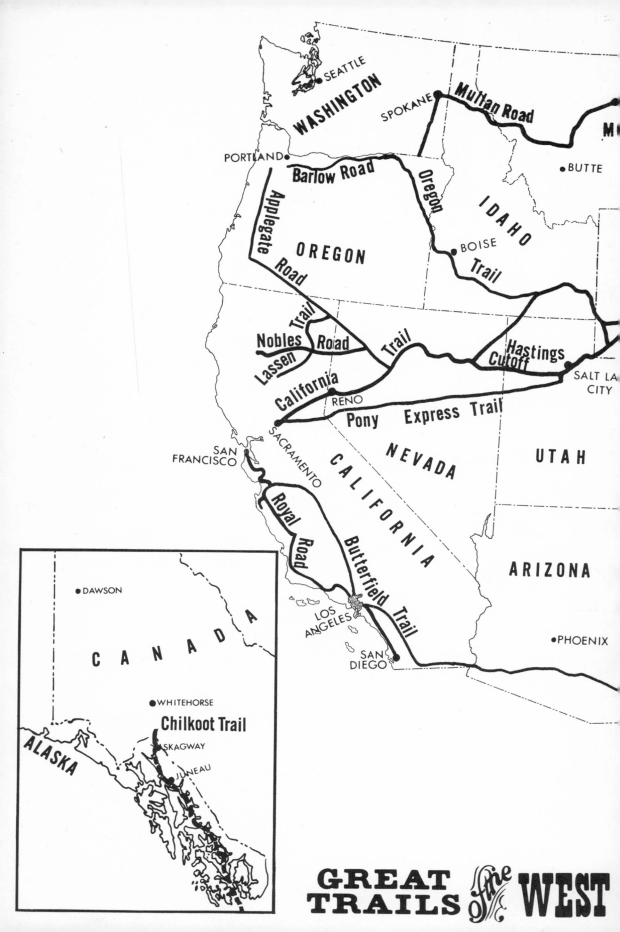

GREAT TRAILS *of the* WEST